Your Obt. Servt.
A. Lincoln

LINCOLN MEMORIAL.

THE

JOURNEYS

OF

ABRAHAM LINCOLN:

FROM SPRINGFIELD TO WASHINGTON, 1861,

AS PRESIDENT ELECT;

AND

FROM WASHINGTON TO SPRINGFIELD, 1865,

AS PRESIDENT MARTYRED;

COMPRISING AN ACCOUNT OF PUBLIC CEREMONIES ON THE ENTIRE ROUTE, AND FULL DETAILS OF BOTH JOURNEYS.

BY WILLIAM T. COGGESHALL.

PUBLISHED FOR THE BENEFIT OF THE OHIO SOLDIERS' MONUMENT FUND,

BY THE OHIO STATE JOURNAL, COLUMBUS.

1865.

PREFACE.

THIS book is published for the benefit of the fund devoted to the erection of monuments in Capitol Square, at Columbus, in memory of Abraham Lincoln, and of Ohio soldiers fallen in battle. The entire proceeds of its sale, after paying the expenses of publication, will be thus applied by the Publishers. The Editor has patiently endeavored to make a correct record of Mr. Lincoln's memorable journeys as President elect and President martyred; but cannot hope that he has entirely succeeded. He acknowledges himself indebted to the local press of the several cities through which the two processions passed, for reports of the ceremonies, only a portion of which, as condensed or abridged, are credited, in the pages to which they have been transferred. Paper-makers, printers and binders are entitled to honorable mention for liberal deductions from regular prices, on account of the object which this work is intended to promote.

That the period is not far distant when the Monument Committee can report that the funds received are ample for monuments worthy of the memories they will be designed to perpetuate, is the sincere trust of

THE PUBLISHERS.

CONTENTS.

ABRAHAM LINCOLN.

ABRAHAM LINCOLN, the sixteenth President of the United States, was born on the twelfth day of February, 1809, in that part of Hardin county, Kentucky, which is now known as Larue. His father, Thomas Lincoln, and his grandfather, Abraham, were natives of Rockingham county, Virginia, to which their ancestors emigrated from Berks county, Pennsylvania. In the year 1780 the grandfather removed his family to Kentucky, where, taking possession of a small tract of land in the wilderness, he erected a rude cabin, and proceeded to make his new home comfortable and his forest farm productive. His daily labors were attended with great personal danger. There was no other resident within two or three miles, and the country was infested with Indians, who allowed no opportunity of slaughtering the white settlers to pass unimproved. His gun was carried as regularly to his work as was any implement necessary to the successful clearing of the land, and at night the weapon was placed in a corner of his cabin, where it could be quickly grasped in the event of an attack from the savage enemy. Abraham Lincoln, for nearly four years, escaped their bloodthirsty cruelty; but then, while clearing a piece of land about four miles from home, was suddenly attacked and killed, and his scalped remains were found the next morning. The widow found herself without a neighbor in the wilderness, with three sons and two daughters. Poverty rendered it necessary that the family should separate; and all the children but Thomas bade adieu to their mother and left the county, the second son removing to Indiana, and the others to other counties of Kentucky.

Thomas also left home before he was twelve years old, but subsequently returned to Kentucky, and in the year 1806 married Nancy Hanks, who was a native of Virginia. Thomas Lincoln and his wife were conscientious members of the Baptist Church. Mrs. Lincoln could read but not write: her husband could do neither, except that he was able to write his own name. He respected, however, the superior learning of others; his kindness of heart was proverbial, and he was industrious and persevering. Mrs. Lincoln was a woman of excellent judgment and great piety, and a mother whose precepts and teachings exerted a happy influence in the formation of her children's characters. Thomas and Nancy Lincoln had three children—a daughter, a son who died in infancy, and Abraham. The sister attained the years of womanhood, and married, but died without issue.

When Abraham was seven years of age he was sent to school with an old copy of Deiworth's Spelling Book, one of the three books that formed the family library. His teacher had neither ambition nor ability to impart greater instruction than that which would enable his pupils to read and write. His term of schooling was of short duration.

Thomas Lincoln had witnessed the evils of the "peculiar institution," and longed to be free from the effects of a condition of society by which the laborer was degraded, and whose labors were controlled by an unprincipled and lazy master. In October, 1816, finding a purchaser for his farm, he made arrangements for removal. The price paid by the purchaser was ten barrels of whisky, of forty gallons each, valued at two hundred and eighty dollars, and twenty dollars in money. Such transactions in real estate were then common, and recognized as proper.

The farm was near Rolling Fork river. Mr. Lincoln, with such assistance as Abraham could give him, hewed out a flat-boat, loaded it with his household articles and tools and the whisky, and began a hazardous journey to Indiana, to select a new home. His journey down the Rolling Fork and into the Ohio river, was accomplished without accident, but soon afterwards his boat was upset, and its cargo thrown into the water. Some men standing on the bank witnessed the accident and saved the boat and its owner, but all the freight was lost except a few carpenter's tools, axes, three barrels of whisky and some minor articles. Again getting started, Mr. Lincoln proceeded to a well-known ferry on the river, from whence he was guided into the interior by an old settler, to whom he gave his boat in payment for his services. After several days of difficult traveling, much of the time being employed in cutting a road through the forest wide enough for a team, Spencer county, Indiana, was reached, at a point eighteen miles from the river. The site for his new home having been selected, Mr. Lincoln, returned to Kentucky on foot, and made preparations to remove his family.

Not many days were required for these preparations. The emigrant party left their old home in true backwoods style—Mrs. Lincoln and her daughter riding one horse, Abraham another, and the father a third. After seven days' journey through an uninhabited country, their resting-place at night being the ground, they arrived at the quarter section selected for their future residence. No delays were permitted to interfere with the immediate clearing of a site for a cabin. An axe was placed in Abraham's hands, and with the assistance of a neighbor, in a few days Mr. Lincoln had a neat log house about eighteen feet square. It had only one room, but slabs laid across logs overhead gave additional accommodations which were obtained by climbing a rough ladder in one corner. A bed, table and four stools were made by the new settlers, father and son. The loft was Abraham's bedroom, one coarse blanket his mattress and another being his covering. During the ensuing winter Abraham did not neglect his reading and spelling, and also practiced frequently with a rifle, becoming a skillful marksman, though taking part regularly with his father, in the severe toils which their forest life required.

About a year after the settlement in Spencer county Mrs. Lincoln died. Abraham was then ten years old. He was able to read the bible; his mother having patiently directed and instructed him. He could also write, and greatly astonished the neighbors by writing a letter inviting a minister to preach over his mother's grave. When he was eleven years old his father married Mrs. Sally Johnston, of Elizabethtown, Kentucky, a widow-lady with three children, and a superior woman, between whom and Abraham, a devoted attachment was cultivated, which was unbroken at the day of his death. When the young backwoodsman was about twelve years of age, a man named Crawford opened a school in Spencer county. Mr. Lincoln immediately sent Abraham. With buckskin clothes, a coonskin cap, and an old arithmetic which had been somewhere found for him, he commenced his studies in the "higher branches." His progress was rapid, and his perseverance and faithfulness won the interest and esteem of his teacher.

In that thinly-settled country a book was a great rarity, but whenever Mr. Lincoln heard of one he endeavored to procure it for Abraham's perusal. In this way he became acquainted with Bunyan's Pilgrim's Progress, Esop's Fables, a Life of Henry Clay, and Weem's Life of Washington. The "hatchet" story of Washington made a strong impression upon Abraham, and was one of those unseen, gentle influences, which helped to form his character for integrity and honesty. Its effect may be traced in the following story, which bids fair to become as never-failing an accompaniament to a Life of Lincoln as the hatchet incident to that of Washington:

Mr. Crawford had lent him a copy of Ramsay's Life of Washington. During a severe storm Abraham improved his leisure by reading his book. One night he had laid it down carefully, as he thought, and the next morning he found it soaked through! The wind had changed, the storm had beaten in through a crack in the logs, and the appearance of the book was ruined. How could he face the owner under such circumstances? He had no money to offer as a return, but he took the book, went directly to Mr. Crawford, showed him the irreparable injury, and frankly and honestly offered to work for him until he should be satisfied. Mr. Crawford accepted the offer and gave Abraham the book for his own, in return for three days steady labor in "pulling fodder." His manliness and straightforwardness won the esteem of all the neighborhood.

At nineteen years of age Abraham Lincoln made a trip to New Orleans, in company with a son of the owner of a flat-boat, who entrusted a valuable cargo to their care. On the way they were attacked by seven negroes, and their lives and property were in great danger, but owing to their good use of the muscular force they had acquired as backwoodsmen, they succeeded in driving off the invaders, and pushing their boat out into the stream in safety. The result of the voyage was satisfactory to the owner, and Abraham Lincoln gained, in addition to his ten dollars a month, a reputation as a youth of promising business talent.

In 1830 the family moved to the neighborhood of Decatur, Illinois, the journey occupying fifteen days. Abraham was now twenty-one, but did not commence his independent life until he had aided his father in settling his family, breaking the ground for corn, and making a rail fence around the farm. Those rails have passed into song and story, and gave Mr. Lincoln, during the Presidential campaign of 1860, the title of the "Great Rail Splitter." After the first winter in Illinois, which was of uncommon severity, and required more than his father's care to keep the family in food, which was mostly obtained by hunting, Abraham Lincoln began life for himself. Sometimes he hired himself out as a farm-hand, and sometimes his learning procured him a situation as clerk in a store. When the Black Hawk war broke out in 1832, he joined a volunteer company, and was made captain. He is said to have been an efficient, faithful officer, watchful of his men, and prompt in the discharge of duty, and his courage and patriotism shrank from no dangers or hardships.

After his military life was over he looked about for something to do. He ran for the Legislature, but was beaten; though his own precinct gave him 277 votes out of 284. This was the only time he was ever beaten before the people. He bought a store and stock of goods on credit, and was appointed postmaster. The store proved unprofitable, and he sold out. All this time he pursued his studies. He had already learned grammar, and he had now opportunities for more extensive reading. He wrote out the synopsis of every book he read, and thus fixed it in his memory.

About this time he met John Calhoun, since President of the Lecompton (Kansas) Constitutional Convention. He proposed to Lincoln to take up surveying, and himself aided in his studies. He had success as a surveyor, and won a good reputation in this new line of business. In 1834 he was sent to the Legislature, and the political life commenced which his countrymen's votes have ever since shown they fully appreciated. When the session of the Legislature was over he set himself to the study of law in good earnest. In 1836 he obtained a law license, and in April, 1837, he removed to Springfield and commenced the practice of the law in partnership with his friend and former colleague, Hon. T. Stuart.

An instance which occurred during Mr. Lincoln's early legal practice is worthy of extended publication. At a camp meeting held in Menard county a fight took place which ended in the murder of one of the participants in the quarrel. A young man named Armstrong, a son of an aged couple for whom many years before Abraham Lincoln had worked, was charged with the deed, arrested and examined, and a true bill found against him, and lodged in jail to await his trial. As soon as Mr. Lincoln received intelligence of the affair, he addressed a letter to Mrs. Armstrong, stating his anxiety that her son should have a fair trial, and offering in return for her kindness to him while in adverse circumstances some years before, his services gratuitously. Investigation convinced the volunteer attorney that the young man was the victim of a conspiracy, and he determined to postpone the case until the excitement had subsided. The day of trial finally arrived, and the accuser testified positively that he saw the accused plunge the knife into the heart of the murdered man. He remembered all the circumstances perfectly; the murder was committed about half-past nine o'clock at night, and the moon was shining brightly. Mr. Lincoln reviewed the testimony carefully, and then proved conclusively that the moon, which the accuser had sworn was shining brightly, did not rise until an hour or more after the murder was committed. Other discrepancies were exposed, and in thirty minutes after the jury retired they returned with a verdict of "Not Guilty."

In 1836, in 1838 and in 1840 Mr. Lincoln was chosen as a legislator by the people of Sangamon county.

On the third of March, 1837, a protest was presented to the House of Representatives of Illinois and signed by "Daniel Stone and Abraham Lincoln, Representatives from Sangamon county," which is the first record the world has of the sentiments of the great emancipator on the slavery question. It was in opposition to a series of resolutions which had been adopted, taking an extreme Southern view of slavery, for which Mr. Lincoln refused to vote.

After 1840 Mr. Lincoln remained six years in private life, devoting himself to the practice of the law, displaying remarkable ability, and gaining an enviable reputation. In every campaign, however, from 1836 to 1852, he was a Whig candidate for Presidential Elector, and in 1844 he stumped the entire State of Illinois for Henry Clay; and then crossing the line into Indiana, spoke daily at large meetings until the day of election. In 1846 Mr. Lincoln was elected to Congress from the Central District of Illinois, by a majority of over fifteen hundred votes, the largest ever given in that District to any candidate opposed to the Democratic party. Illinois elected seven Representatives that year; and all were Democrats but

Mr. Lincoln. He took his seat on the first Monday of December, 1847.

Although, like a majority of the Whig party opposed to the declaration of war with Mexico by the President, he never failed to vote for any resolution or bill which had for its object the sending of supplies to our troops who had been ordered to the seat of war.

He supported measures for the "improvement" of western rivers and harbors, and on several occasions voted for the reception of petitions and memorials in favor of the abolition of slavery in the District of Columbia; against the slave trade, and advocating the prohibition of slavery in the territory that might be acquired from Mexico.

On the seventeenth of February, 1848, Mr. Lincoln voted for a loan bill reported by the Committee of Ways and Means, authorizing the raising of sixteen millions of dollars to enable the Government to provide for its debts, principally incurred in Mexico.

On the nineteenth of June he first had an opportunity to record his views upon the tariff question, by voting in favor of a resolution instructing the Committee of Ways and Means to inquire into the expediency of reporting a bill increasing the duties on foreign luxuries of all kinds, and on "such foreign manufactures as are now coming into ruinous competition with American labor." He subsequently voted for a resolution instructing the Committee of Ways and Means to inquire into the expediency of reporting a tariff bill based upon the principles of the tariff of 1842.

On the 28th of July, 1848, the celebrated bill establishing territorial governments for Oregon, California and New Mexico, the peculiar feature of which was a provision prohibiting the Legislatures of California and New Mexico from passing laws in favor of or against slavery, and providing that the laws of the Legislatures should be subject to the sanction of Congress, was argued, and after an exciting debate, laid on the table, Mr. Lincoln voting with Mr. Webster, Mr. Corwin, and other illustrious colleagues for this disposition of the bill. He opposed the annexation of Texas, and vigorously urged and supported the "Wilmot Proviso."

In the Whig National Convention of 1848, Mr. Lincoln was an active delegate, and earnestly advocated the selection of General Zachary Taylor as the nominee for the Presidency, and during the canvass which followed, he traversed the States of Indiana and Illinois, speaking on behalf of the choice of his party.

In 1849 he was a candidate before the Legislature of Illinois for United States Senator, but his political opponents being in the majority, General Shields was chosen. From that time until 1854, he confined himself almost exclusively to the practice of his profession, but in that year he again entered the political arena, taking an earnest part in the campaign which resulted in victory for the first time to the opposition of the Democratic party in Illinois, and gave that State a Republican Legislature, and sent Lyman Trumbull to the United States Senate, During the canvass, Mr. Lincoln was frequently brought into controversy upon the stand with Stephen A. Douglas, with whom he had formed acquaintance while a member of the Legislature.

Mr. Lincoln was, the following year, offered the nomination for Governor of Illinois, but declined in favor of Mr. Bissell; was also presented, but ineffectually, at the first Republican Convention for Vice-President; and at the next Presidential election headed the Fremont electoral ticket, and labored industriously in support of that candidate.

On the 2d of June, 1858, the Republican State Convention met at Springfield, and nominated Mr. Lincoln as their candidate for the United States Senate.

The contest which followed was one of the most exciting and remarkable ever witnessed in this country. Stephen A. Douglas, his opponent, had few superiors as a political debater. He had made many enemies by his course upon the Nebraska bill, but his personal popularity had been greatly increased by his independence, and by the opposition manifested to him by the Administration of James Buchanan.

Illinois was stumped throughout its length and breadth by both candidates and their respective advocates, and the people of the entire country watched with interest the struggle. From county to county, township to township, and village to village, the two leaders traveled, frequently in the same car or carriage, and in the presence of immense crowds of men, women and children, and face to face, the opposing champions argued the important points of their political belief, and contended for the mastery.

The Republican vote in the State was largely augmented, but more Democrats than Republicans were chosen to the Legislature. The popular vote stood 126,084 for the Republican candidates, 121,940 for the Douglas Democrats, and 5,091 for the Lecompton candidates. Mr. Douglas was elected United States Senator because in the Legislature his supporters had a majority of eight on joint ballot.

The manner in which Mr. Lincoln had met Douglas on the stump, the skill and power with which he had presented and argued the principles and policies underlying the Nebraska bill and the doctrine of "Popular Sovereignty," gave him a national reputation as a political orator. Characteristics of his intellect and spirit now familiar to the people, were then approvingly dwelt upon by writers for the press, one of whom justly wrote as follows:

"In perhaps the severest test that could have been applied to any man's temper—his political contest with Senator Douglas in 1858—Mr. Lincoln not only proved himself an able speaker and a good tactician, but demonstrated that it is possible to carry on the fiercest political warfare without once descending to rude personality and coarse denunciation. We have it on the authority of a gentleman who followed Abraham Lincoln throughout the whole of that campaign, that, in spite of all the temptations to an opposite course to which he was continuously exposed, no personalities against his opponent, no vituperation or coarseness, ever defiled his lips. His kind and genial nature lifted him above a resort to any such weapons of political warfare, and it was the commonly expressed regret of fiercer natures that he treated his opponent too courteously and urbanely. Vulgar personalities and vituperation are the last thing that can be truthfully charged against Abraham Lincoln. His heart is too genial, his good sense too strong, and his innate self-respect too predominant to permit him to indulge in them. His nobility of nature—and we may use the term advisedly—has been as manifest throughout his whole career as his temperate habits, his self-reliance, and his mental and intellectual power."

The people of Illinois immediately brought forward Abraham Lincoln as a candidate for the Presidency of the United States. He was invited to speak in Ohio, in Indiana, in New York and in the New England States, and delivered a series of political addresses, which confirmed in the public mind the favorable impressions made by reports of his Illinois campaigns. At a meeting of the Illinois State Republican Convention in 1859, a veteran Democrat of Macon county presented to the Convention two old fence-rails, gayly decorated with flags and ribons, and upon which the following words were inscribed:

> ABRAHAM LINCOLN,
>
> THE RAIL CANDIDATE
>
> FOR PRESIDENT IN 1860.
>
> Two rails from a lot of 3,000 made in 1830, by Thos. Hanks and Abe Lincoln—whose father was the first pioneer of Macon county.

This "delegation" was received with enthusiastic ap plause, and Mr. Lincoln was sent for to acknowledge the rails, which he did, modestly but happily.

The Republican Convention, called to nominate candidates for President and Vice-President of the United States, met at Chicago, Illinois, on the 16th of May, 1860. Two days were occupied in organization, and in the discussion and adoption of a Platform. On the third day Abraham Lincoln was nominated, as the candidate for the Presidency. On the first ballot he received 102 votes, Mr. Seward receiving, on the same ballot, 173½ votes, the votes of the remainder of the delegates being divided between Salmon P. Chase, Simon Cameron, and other candidates. On the second ballot, the vote stood: Lincoln, 181; Seward, 184½; and on the third, Mr. Lincoln received 230½ votes, or within one and one-half of a nomination. One of the delegates then changed four votes of his State, giving them to Mr. Lincoln, thus nominating him. Amid a scene of the most intense excitement, vote after vote was changed to the successful candidate. The nomination was then made unanimous, with the most marked enthusiasm, on the motion of Mr. William Evarts of New York.

Mr. Lincoln was immediately officially, but informally, notified of his nomination; and in a few days the President of the Nominating Convention, Geo. Ashman of Massachusetts, in conjunction with a committee from different States, appointed for that purpose, addressed him a letter, to which he responded as follows:

"SPRINGFIELD, ILLINOIS, May 23d, 1860.

"*Hon. George Ashmun, President of the Republican National Convention:*

"SIR,—I accept the nomination tendered me by the Convention over which you presided, and of which I am formally apprised in the letter of yourself and others, acting as a committee of the Convention for that purpose.

"The declaration of principles and sentiments, which accompanies your letter, meets my approval; and it shall be my care not to violate, or disregard it, in any part.

"Imploring the assistance of Divine Providence, and with due regard to the views and feelings of all who were represented in the Convention; to the rights of all the States and Territories, and people of the nation; to the inviolability of the Constitution, and the perpetual union, harmony and prosperity of all, I am most happy to co-operate for the practical success of the principles declared by the Convention.

"Your obliged friend and fellow-citizen,

"ABRAHAM LINCOLN."

The canvass which succeeded the National Convention of 1860, was one of the most earnest and strenuous ever witnessed in our country.

On the sixth of November the election for President

took place, with the following result: Mr. Lincoln received 491,275 over Mr. Douglas; 1,018,499 over Mr. Breckenridge, and 1,275,821 over Mr. Bell; and the electoral vote was subsequently proclaimed by Congress to have been as follows:

For Abraham Lincoln, of Illinois	180
For John C. Breckenridge, of Kentucky	72
For John Bell, of Tennessee	39
For Stephen A. Douglas, of Illinois	12

SECESSION.

Immediately after it was known that Mr. Lincoln had been elected President, preparations were openly made for the dissolution of the American Union. South Carolina seceded, then Mississippi, then Alabama, then Florida, Georgia, Louisiana, and Texas. Custom-houses, arsenals and United States buildings were seized by "Confederate" troops, under authority of the "Confederate Government," organized at Montgomery, Alabama, on the 18th of February, 1861, by the inauguratian of Jefferson Davis as President, and Alexander H. Stephens as Vice-President. The people of the North were divided upon the "right of secession" and the power of the Government to "coerce States." James Buchanan, President of the United States, in his last annual message, Dec. 4, 1860, met the question of resistance, or submission to the progress of the work of secession and threats of armed rebellion, in the following words:

"The question, fairly stated, is, Has the Constitution delegated to Congress the power to coerce a State into submission which is attempting to withdraw, or has actually withdrawn, from the confederacy? If answered in the affirmative, it must be on the principle that the power has been conferred on Congress to make war on a State. After much serious reflection, I have arrived at the conclusion that no such power has been delegated to Congress, nor to any other department of the Federal Government."

Virginia, Tennessee, Kentucky, Missouri, and Arkansas were expected to join the "Confederacy," and a strong spirit of rebellion was manifest in Maryland. The public mind was occupied with one great thought—How far will the South go, and what can the North do to check Secession and crush Rebellion? In seeking a solution of this problem naturally public attention was turned to the President elect, and, under such circumstances, Mr. Lincoln was called upon to take leave of his neighbors and proceed to Washington, to assume the duties and responsibilities to which the people had called him.

THE JOURNEY TO WASHINGTON AS PRESIDENT ELECT.

FAREWELL TO HOME.

Mr. Lincoln left Springfield, Illinois, on the 11th of February, 1861. He was accompanied to the depot by a large concourse of friends and neighbors. A few minutes before the time appointed for the starting of the cars, Mr. Lincoln, who had personally bid farewell to nearly all present, appeared upon the platform of the car set apart for the use of himself, family and personal friends, and made the following farewell address:

"MY FRIENDS:—No one not in my position can appreciate the sadness I feel at this parting. To this people I owe all that I am. Here I have lived more than a quarter of a century; here my children were born, and here one of them lies buried. I know not how soon I shall see you again. A duty devolves upon me which is, perhaps, greater than that which has devolved upon any other man since the days of Washington. He never would have succeeded except for the aid of Divine Providence, upon which he at all times relied. I feel that I cannot succeed without the same Divine aid which sustained him, and on the same Almighty Being I place my reliance for support; and I hope you, my friends, will all pray that I may receive that Divine assistance, without which I cannot succeed, but with which success is certain. Again, I bid you all an affectionate farewell."

The persons accompanying Mr. Lincoln were Dr. W. M. Wallace, John G. Nicolay, John M. Hay, Hon. N. P. Judd, Hon. O. H. Browning, Hon. David Davis, Col. E. V. Sumner, Maj. D. Hunter, Capt. Geo. Hazzard, Col. E. E. Ellsworth, Col. Ward, H. Lamon, J. M. Burgess, Geo. C. Latham, W. S. Wood, Mrs. Lincoln, Robt. T. Lincoln, a nurse and two children.

FROM SPRINGFIELD TO INDIANAPOLIS.

Along the route several speeches were made by Mr. Lincoln, in response to the earnest solicitation of the people, who had gathered in crowds at the way stations. At the last point in the State of Illinois, in response to repeated calls, Mr. Lincoln presented himself to the people, and said:

"I am leaving you on an errand of national importance, attended, as you are aware, with considerable difficulties. Let us believe, as some poet has expressed it, 'Behind the cloud the sun is shining still.' I bid you an *affectionate farewell.*"

RECEPTION AT INDIANAPOLIS.

In this railroad city, business was temporarily suspended, and the visit of the President elect was the all-absorbing topic of conversation. The citizens had made preparation for giving Mr. Lincoln a reception, commensurate with the dignity of the position of the incoming of the Chief Magistrate. The principal buildings of the city were gaily decorated with flags. The Legislature was not in session during the forenoon, and adjourned shortly after convening in the afternoon. The special train, containing Mr. Lincoln and suite, which consisted, in addition to those previously mentioned, of N. Bateman, E. Peck, J. Grimshaw, W. R. Morrison, L. W. Ross, M. H. Cassell, O. M. Hatch, Wm. S. Underwood, W. M. Butler, Wm. H. Carlin, J. A. Hough, D. H. Gilmer, Gov. Yates, and Ex-Gov. Moore, arrived at five o'clock. As it approached the Union depot, a national salute of thirty-four guns was fired by the City Greys Artillery. On arriving at the depot, Gov. Morton welcomed the President in an earnest speech, in the course of which he said:

"In every free government there will be differences of opinion, and these differences result in the formation of parties; but when the voice of the people has been expressed through the forms of the Constitution, all patriots yield to its obedience. Submission to the popular will is the essential principle of republican government, and so vital is this principle that it admits of but one exception, which is revolution. To weaken it is anarchy; to destroy it is despotism. It recognizes no appeal beyond the ballot-box; and, while it is preserved, liberty may be wounded, but never slain. To this principle the people of Indiana—men of all parties—are loyal, and they here welcome you as the Chief Magistrate elect of the Republic.

"When our fathers framed the Constitution, they declared it was to form a more perfect Union; to establish justice, and to secure the blessings of liberty to themselves and their posterity; and for these considerations we proclaim our purpose to maintain that Constitution inviolate, as it came from their hands. This Union has been the idol of our hopes, the parent of our prosperity, our shield of protection abroad, and our title to the respect and consideration of the world. 'May it be preserved,' is the prayer of every patriotic heart in Indiana, and that it shall be is their determination."

The guests of the State were then escorted through the principal streets of the Capital by a procession composed of both Houses of the Legislature, the public officers, municipal authorities, military, and firemen. On reaching the Bates House, Mr. Lincoln was called for with great enthusiasm, and he addressed the people as follows:

"FELLOW-CITIZENS OF THE STATE OF INDIANA: I am here to thank you much for this magnificent welcome, and still more for the very generous support given by your State to that political cause, which I think is the true and just cause of the whole country and the whole world. Solomon says 'there is a time to keep silence;' and when men wrangle by the mouth, with no certainty that they mean the same thing while using the same words, it perhaps were as well if they would keep silence. The words 'coercion' and 'invasion' are much used in these days, and often with some temper and hot blood. Let us make sure, if we can, that we do not misunderstand the meaning of those who use them. Let us get the exact definitions of these words, not from dictionaries, but from the men themselves, who certainly deprecate the things they would represent by the use of the words. What, then, is 'coercion?' What is 'invasion?' Would the marching of an army into South Carolina, without the consent of her people, and with hostile intent towards them, be invasion? I certainly think it would, and it would be 'coercion' also if the South Carolinians were forced to submit. But if the United States should merely hold and retake its own forts and other property, and collect the duties on foreign importations, or even withhold the mails from places where they were habitually violated, would any or all of these things be 'invasion' or 'coercion?' Do our professed lovers of the Union, but who spitefully resolve that they will resist coercion and invasion, understand that such things as these, on the part of the United States, would be coercion or invasion of a State? If so, their idea of means to preserve the object of their great affection would seem to be exceedingly thin and airy. If sick, the little pills of the homœopathist would be much too large for it to swallow. In their view, the Union, as a family relation, would seem to be no regular marriage, but rather a sort of 'free-love' arrangement, to be maintained on passional attraction. By the way, in what consists the special sacredness of a State? I speak not of the position assigned to a State in the Union by the Constitution, for that is the bond we all recognize. That position, however, a State cannot carry out of the Union with it. I speak of that assumed primary right of a State to rule all which is less than itself, and to ruin all which is larger than itself. If a State and a County, in a given case, should be equal in extent of territory and equal in number of inhabitants, in what, as a matter of principle, is the State better than the County? Would an exchange of name be an exchange of rights? Upon what principle, upon what rightful principle, may a State, being no more than one-fiftieth part of the nation in soil and population, break up the nation, and then coerce a proportionably larger subdivision of itself in the most arbitrary way? What mysterious right to play tyrant is conferred on a district of country with its people, by merely calling it a State? Fellow-citizens, I am not asserting any thing. I am merely asking questions for you to consider. And now allow me to bid you farewell."

FROM INDIANAPOLIS TO CINCINNATI.

At eleven o'clock on the 12th, the special train provided for the accommodation of the President elect and suite, started from the Union Depot at Indianapolis, amid the shouts and cheers of five thousand ardent patriots. The train consisted of four passenger cars and a baggage car. The third and fourth cars were occupied by the Cincinnati Reception Committee, Mr. Lincoln and his suite, and the representatives of the press; the other two by excursionists—ladies and gentlemen. On boarding the cars Mr. Lincoln was welcomed to Cincinnati by Judge Este, on behalf of the citizens, and by Major Dennis J. Yoohey, on behalf of the Board of Common Council. Mr. Lincoln replied in a brief and timely speech, acknowledging his gratitude to the citizens of Cincinnati for such marked respect and esteem. The first stop was made at Shelbyville, lasting but two minutes. Mr. Lincoln merely appeared on the rear platform and courteously bowed in response to the cheering of the enthusiastic multitude. At Greensburgh a similar stop was made. Mr. Lincoln briefly returned his thanks to the crowd for the compliment they paid him in assembling in such numbers to honor his visit to the Hoosier State. A rapid rate of speed was kept up on the entire route; the trip, includding "rests," being made in five hours and fifteen minutes.

At Lawrenceburgh, Mr. Lincoln delivered a short speech.

He hoped those whom he addressed were Union men. (A voice: "Indeed we are.") "The answer shows that you are right," responded Mr. Lincoln. "You ask only what is right for either side of this river, and I say to you that the power intrusted to me shall be exercised as perfectly to protect the rights of your neighbors across the river, as to protect yours on this side. I know no difference in the protection of constitutional rights on either side of the river. (A voice: 'May the public men be as right as the people are.') Yes, that is the thing precisely. And let me tell you, that if the people remain right, your public men can never betray you. If, in my brief term of public office, I shall be wicked or foolish, if you remain right, and true, and honest, you cannot be betrayed. My power is temporary and fleeting—yours is as eternal as the principle of liberty. Cultivate and protect that sentiment, and your ambitious leaders will be reduced to the position of servants instead of masters."

Nothing else worthy of notice occurred during the trip, except that the family of General Harrison were assembled around his grave, to whom Mr. Lincoln bowed his respects to the memory of that patriot.

RECEPTION AT CINCINNATI.

A more beautiful day seldom graced the month of February. The sun shone brilliantly. The heavens were not darkened by a cloud during the day. As the hour approached for the arrival of the train, every avenue leading in the direction of the Indianapolis and Cincinnati railroad depot was thronged with citizens, hurrying thither in order to obtain as convenient a position as possible. The numbers increased as the time grew less, until the space in front of and below and above the depot was crowded with a mass of human beings. The windows and the roofs of the neighboring houses were occupied and the board and coal piles were covered with the expectant people. The bridge leading over the canal at the foot of Wood-street was so densely packed that its sudden fall was looked for by many, who advised those upon it to station themselves elsewhere. This advice was unheeded; but, fortunately, no accident happened. About half-past two o'clock the municipal and special police arrived, in command of Capt. Lewis Wilson. After clearing the depot and a carriage way in the street, they took position on Front-street, west of the depot. The military arrived soon after, and took the position assigned them. This set the spectators on the *qui vive*, and they indulged in frequent shouts as some mischievous urchin would start the report that the train was coming. But people on such occasions are always doomed to disappointment; their impatience makes the time seem doubly long. Finally the boom of the cannon on the bank of the river announced the approach of the train. As it neared the depot the crowd gave a loud and prolonged cheer, which was again renewed when Mr. Lincoln was seen stepping from a car with Mayor R. M. Bishop, followed by his suite and the various committees. After a number of provoking delays, they reach the carriages, when the rowd became perfectly wild with enthusiasm. Cheer after cheer rent the air; shouts after shouts for the "President" and the "Union;" and amid the exciting scene, Mr. Lincoln rose in the carriage, uncovered his head, and acknowledged the greeting with repeated bows. The procession soon after started, but it was with much difficulty that Mr. Lincoln's carriage was driven through the mass of the people that blocked up the way from the depot to Freeman-street.

THE PROCESSION.

The procession moved in the following order:

Miles Greenwood, Grand Marshal, and Aids, mounted.
Major-General Lytle and Staff, mounted.
Brigadier-General Bates and Staff.
Steuben Artillery, Captain Ammis.
First Cincinnati Battalion, in command of Major Kennett, composed of the following companies:
Lafayette, Guards, Capt. Miller.
German Yagers, Capt. Sommer.
Rover Guards, Lieut. Hubbell, commanding.
Cincinnati Zouaves, Lieut. Anderson, commanding.
First Company Second Cincinnati Battalion, Capt. Pendrey.
Continental Battalion, in command of Colonel Jones, as follows:
Company A, Capt. Jackson.
Company B. Capt. Whitcom.
Independent Guthrie Greys Battalion—two companies, in command of Major Bosley.
Detachment of Washington Dragoons, acting as special guard to the carriage, Capt. Pfau.
ABRAHAM LINCOLN, President elect, in carriage, drawn by six white horses.
Second Detachment of Washington Dragoons, Capt. Pfau.
Carriages with the suite of President elect.
Committees, in carriages.
Citizens, on horseback.
Citizens, in carriages.

The carriage in which Mr. Lincoln rode was an open one and was drawn by six white horses, which were beautifully caparisoned with the national colors. Mayor Bishop occupied a seat by the side of the guest. Ex-Mayor Foley, of Covington, and Mayor Hawkins, of Newport, occupied the remaining seats in the carriages.

The carriage was accompanied by Major Burke and Capt. Cloon, two of Maj. Gen. Lytle's staff, whom he detailed especially for this service. A detachment of police marched in such a manner as to surround the carriage so as to prevent serious delays from the pressure of the crowd.

ROUTE AND DECORATIONS.

The route lay on Front and Freeman streets from the depot to Sixth street, up Sixth to Mound street, out Mound to Eighth, on Eighth street to Elm, up Elm to Fifteenth, out Fifteenth to Vine, down Vine to the Burnet House.

A large number of residences along the route were decorated with national flags and various patriotic devices. Some of them were more marked than others, and are worthy of special mention. The yard and residence of R. M. Corwine, Esq., on Sixth street, attracted much attention. Beside the other decorations on the west side of the house, was a large flag, bearing these expressive words: "*Welcome to the President of Thirty-four States.*" Mayor Bishop's house, corner of Eighth and Mound, was very neatly and very patriotically decorated. The house of Mr. Stratton had in large white letters on a blue ground, this one word, dear to every patriot, "*Union.*" Elm street to the intersection of Fifteenth was decorated in an attractive manner, but Vine street to the canal presented the most attractive and patriotic appearance. There was hardly a residence or a public building that did not have every window decorated with flags. Banners were stretched across the streets, and there were portraits of Washington and of Lincoln surrounded with wreaths of evergreen. The city in other parts was profusely decorated. The Court House, City Buildings, Custom House, all of the Engine Houses, and Times, Commercial and Gazette offices, had the stars and stripes flung to the breeze, and the business houses generally had very handsome flags extended from their establishments. The Catholic Institute exhibited the most beautiful and costly flag. The decorations of the Gibson House, drew forth the heartiest praises of any in the city. An immense transparency, sixty feet in length and twenty in breadth, made of red, white and blue muslin, was elevated on the lower balcony of the hotel. At one end it contained a portrait of Lincoln, at the other a portrait of Hamlin, and in the center a portrait of Washington above the federal coat of arms. The intervening spaces were filled with the following mottoes: "The people will sustain the people's choice." "Honor to a President, not to a Partisan." "A union of hearts, a union of hands." "A union that nothing can sever." "A union of States, a union of lands." "The American Union, forever." "The Union must and shall be preserved." "Protection to the Rights of all Sections." "Maintenance of the Letter and Spirit of the Constitution and Preservation of the Union at all hazards." "The time has come when Demagogues must go Under." "The security of a Republic is in the maintenance of the Laws." Beneath all this, on a pink ground work, were the names of the thirty-four States, each encircled with evergreens. Under those which seceded were the words: "*Out on paper.*" The whole was exceedingly patriotic and apropos. The transparency, with the entire hotel front, was brilliantly illuminated in the evening. At the Banner Ward House on Vine street, there was displayed a rich silk banner which was intended to be presented to Mr. Lincoln. In the centre, on one side, were the initial letters "A. L." encircled by a wreath of evergreens. Around this were the words; "*Protect this banner against any insult, whatsoever.*" On the reverse side were the words "Our Constitution," encircled by evergreen, and above this sentence: "Be firm, and the hopes of freeman are fulfilled."

At the Orphan Asylum all of the children were assembled, and on the approach of Mr. Lincoln's carriage they sang a patriotic song to the tune of "Hail Columbia," waving at the same time flags which they held in their hands. On Vine street, at the Banner Ward House, there were a dozen or more tables on the line of the street, upon which stood twenty or thirty little girls dressed in white. Mr. Lincoln's carraige was stopped while they sang the "Star Spangled Banner." One of the little girls was taken in the arms of a brawny German and carried to the carriage, when she modestly handed Mr. Lincoln a single flower, and he in return stooped and kissed the child. The incident, so touching and beautiful, filled many eyes with tears, and the effect was not lost on the hearts of any. Further on Vine, a large German sitting on a huge beer barrel, with a glass of lager in his hand, thus addressed the President elect: "*God be with you. Enforce the laws and save our country. Here's your health.*" From the canal to the Burnet House the streets were lined with thousands of people. From Fifth to Third one mass of human beings thronged the way, and it was with the greatest difficulty that the carriage moved at all. From every window and housetop handkerchiefs waved, and from the people in the streets the most enthusiastic cheers rent the air. Mr. Lincoln stood up in the carriage and bowed acknowledgment to either side. The Post Office steps and the intersections of Fourth and Vine and

Third and Vine presented the most magnificent spectacles ever witnessed in Cincinnati. A large portion of the immense gathering was composed of ladies, who vied with each other in waving, with handkerchiefs, a welcome to the President elect.

The Burnet House was reached at five o'clock, but it was half an hour later before Mr. Lincoln appeared upon the balcony. He was introduced to the people by Mayor Bishop, in the following words:

"HONORED SIR: In the name of the people of all classes of my fellow-citizens, I extend to you a cordial welcome, and in their behalf I have the honor of offering you the hospitalities of Cincinnati. Our city needs no eulogy from me. Her well known character for enterprise, liberality and hospitality, is not more distinguished than is her undying devotion to the Union of these States, and a warm, filial and affectionate regard for that glorious ensign which has

'Braved the battle and the breeze,'

upon land and sea so many years. The people under the solemn and dignified forms of the Constitution have chosen you as President of the United States, and as such I greet you. And you will believe me, when I say, that it is the earnest and united desire of our citizens that your Administration of the General Government may be marked by wisdom, patriotism and justice, to all sections of the country, from the Atlantic to the Pacific oceans, from the northern boundary of Maine to the Gulf of Mexico. So that when you retire from office your fellow-citizens may greet you everywhere with the cheering words, 'Well done thou good and faithful servant.'

"But, sir, I see in this great and anxious concourse not only the citizens of Ohio, but also many from our sister state, Kentucky—the land of Clay, the former home of your parents and mine, and the place of your birth. These, too, greet you, for they, like us, are, and ever will be, loyal to the Constitution and the Union. I again welcome you to our noble city, and trust that your short stay with us may be an agreeable one, and that your journey to our Federal Capital may be pleasant and safe."

The President elect responded as follows:

"MR. MAYOR, LADIES AND GENTLEMEN: Twenty-four hours ago, at the Capital of Indiana, I said to myself, I have never seen so many people assembled together in winter weather. I am no longer able to say that. But it is what might reasonably have been expected—that this great city of Cincinnati would thus acquit herself on such an occasion. My friends, I am entirely overwhelmed by the magnificence of the reception which has been given, I will not say to me, but to the President elect of the United States of America. Most heartily do I thank you one and all for it. I am reminded by the address of your worthy Mayor, that this reception is given, not by one political party, and even if I had not been so reminded by His Honor, I could not have failed to know the fact by the extent of the multitude I see before me now. I could not look upon this vast assemblage without being made aware that all parties were united in this reception. This is as it should be. It is as it should have been if Senator Douglas had been elected; it is as it should have been if Mr. Bell had been elected; as it should have been if Mr. Breckinridge had been elected; as it should ever be when any citizen of the United States is constitutionally elected President of the United States. Allow me to say that I think what has occurred here to-day could not have occurred in any other country on the face of the globe, without the influence of the free institutions which we have unceasingly enjoyed for three-quarters of a century. There is no country where the people can turn out and enjoy this day precisely as they please, save under the benign influence of the free institutions of our land. I hope that, although we have some threatening national difficulties now, while these free institutions shall continue to be in the enjoyment of millions of free people of the United States, we will see repeated every four years what we now witness. In a few short years I and every other individual man who is now living will pass away. I hope that our national difficulties will also pass away, and I hope we shall see in the streets of Cincinnati—good old Cincinnati—for centuries to come, once every four years, the people give such a reception as this to the constitutionally elected President of the whole United States. I hope you shall all join in that reception, and that you shall also welcome your brethren across the river to participate in it. We will welcome them in every State in the Union, no matter where they are from. From away South, we shall extend to them a cordial good will, when our present differences shall have been forgotten and blown to the winds forever.

"I have spoken but once before this in Cincinnati. That was a year previous to the late Presidential election. On that occasion, in a playful manner but with sincere words, I addressed much of what I said to the Kentuckians. I gave my opinion that we as Republicans would ultimately beat them as Democrats, but that they could postpone that result longer by nominating Senator Douglas for the Presidency than they could in any other way. They did not in the true sense of the word nominate Douglas, and the result has come certainly as soon as I expected. I also told them how I expected they would be treated after they should have been beaten; and I now wish to call or recall their attention to what I then said upon that subject. I then said: 'When we do, as we say, beat you, you perhaps will want to know what we will do with you. We mean to treat you as near as we possibly can as Washington, Jefferson and Madison treated you. We mean to leave you alone and in no way to interfere with your institutions, to abide by all and every compromise of the Constitution; and, in a word, coming back to the original proposition to treat you as far as degenerate men, if we have degenerated, may according to the examples of those noble fathers Washington, Jefferson and Madison. We mean to remember that you are as good as we—that there is no difference between us—other than the difference of circumstances. We mean to recognize and bear in mind always that you have as good hearts in your bosoms as other people, or as good as we claim to have and treat you accordingly.'

"Fellow-citizens of Kentucky, friends, brethren: May I call you such? In my new position I see no occasion and feel no inclination to retract a word of this. If it shall not be made good be assured that the fault shall not be mine."

Prolonged cheers signified general approval of this speech.

About half-past eight o'clock near two thousand of the Germans, Free Workingmen of the city, marched in procession to the Burnet House, many of them bearing torches, and called upon the President elect. Mr. Lincoln was escorted to the balcony, and was greeted on behalf of the workingmen by Mr. Fred. Oberkleine, to whom he replied:

MR. CHAIRMAN: I thank you and those you represent for the compliment paid me by the tender of this address. In so far as there is an allusion to our present national difficulties, and the suggestion of the views of the gentlemen who present this address, I beg you will excuse me from entering particularly upon it. I deem it due to myself and the whole country, in the present extraordinary condition of the country, and of public opinion, that I should wait and see the last development of public opinion before I give my views or express myself at the time of the inauguration. I hope at that time to be false to nothing you have been taught to expect of me.

I agree with you Mr. Chairman, and the address of your constituents in the declaration, that workingmen are the basis of all government. That remark is due to them more than to any other class, for the reason that there are more of them than of any other class. And as your address is presented to me not only on behalf of the workingmen, but especially of Germans, I may say a word as to classes. I hold the value of life is to improve one's condition. Whatever is calculated to advance the condition of the honest struggling laboring man, so far as my judgment will enable me to judge of a correct thing, I am for that thing. An allusion has been made to the Homestead Law. I think it worthy of consideration, and that the wilds of the country should be distributed so that every man should have the means and opportunity of benefitting his condition. I have said I do not desire to enter into details, nor will I.

In regard to Germans and foreigners. I esteem foreigners no better than other people, nor any worse. [Laughter and cheers.] They are all of the great family of men, and if there is one shackle upon any of them it would be far better to lift the load from them than to pile additional loads upon them. And inasmuch as the continent of America is comparatively a new country, and the other countries of the world are old countries, there is more room here comparatively speaking than there is there; and if they can better their condition by leaving their old homes, there is nothing in my heart to forbid them coming; and I bid them all God speed. [Cheers.] Again, gentlemen, thanking you for your address I bid you good night."

FROM CINCINNATI TO COLUMBUS.

The President elect and suite, to which Captain John Pope had been added, left Cincinnati on the morning of the 13th for the Capital of Ohio, upon a special train of cars provided by the Little Miami Railway. At most of the stations *en route* large numbers of people had assembled to welcome Mr. Lincoln, but no incidents worthy of special notice occurred.

RECEPTION AT THE CAPITAL OF OHIO.

On the 31st of January, 1860, the General Assembly of Ohio passed a resolution inviting Mr. Lincoln to visit the Capital on his way to Washington, and the following members were appointed a committee to extend the invitation and superintend the necessary preparations for the visit: *On the part of the House*—S. E. Brown, of Miami; J. Scott, of Warren; W. G. Flagg, of Hamilton; John Welsh, of Athens; G. W. Andrews, of Auglaize; E. Parrott, of Montgomery; Jesse Baldwin, of Cuyahoga. *On the part of the Senate*—James Monroe, of Lorain; F. P. Cuppy, of Montgomery, and G. W. Holmes, of Hamilton.

The committee invited the co-operation of the city authorities of Columbus, and at a special meeting of Council it was determined, on motion of C. P. L. Butler, cordially to co-operate, and the following named gentlemen were designated as a committee of Invitation: Mayor, L. English, President of Council, L. Donaldson,

Theo. Comstock, C. P. L. Butler, and J. H. Stauring. Committee of Arrangements: A. L. Buttles, Joseph H. Riley, and S. E. Ogden.

The invitation to visit the Capital was extended to Mr. Lincoln by the State and city committees at Indianapolis, and was promptly accepted. Preparations for the reception were immediately begun upon a scale befitting the importance and interest attaching to the visit; and on the morning of the 13th of February the several committees and the Adjutant General of the State issued the following:

PROGRAMME.—The President elect and suite, accompanied by the committees appointed on the part of the General Assembly and the Executive, will reach Columbus about 2 o'clock P. M. to-day, and will proceed at once to the State Capitol in carriages, under escort of the 1st Battalion, 2d Regiment, Lieut. Col. Mills commanding. The Governor will receive the President elect at the Executive Rooms; thence, accompanied by the committee of Escort, they will proceed to the Hall of Representatives, when the Governor will present the President elect to the General Assembly, through Lieut. Gov. Kirk, its presiding officer; after which the President elect will proceed to the rotunda of the Capitol, where he will receive the citizens until 5 o'clock P. M. From 8½ o'clock to 10 P. M. there will be a levee at the House of Representatives for ladies and their escorts. This levee, and all ceremonies, will close at 10 o'clock precisely. The President elect will be the guest of the Governor during his stay in the city, and with his suite, accompanied by the Governor's aids and the proper committees, will leave for Pittsburg by special train at 8 o'clock A. M. on Thursday. The execution of this programme will be intrusted to Brig. Gen. Lucian Buttles, who is appointed Marshal of the day. Proper salutes will be fired on the arrival and departure of the President elect.

JOINT COMMITTEES OF ARRANGEMENT.

Senate Committee—James Monroe, F. P. Cuppy, Geo. W. Holmes.

House Committee—Samuel Brown, G. W. Andrews, E. Parrott, J. Scott, Wm. J. Flagg, Isaac Welsh, Jesse Baldwin.

Committee of City Council—A. B. Buttles, J. H. Riley, S. E. Ogden.

General Headquarters, Adjt. Gen.'s Office,
Columbus, O., February 9, 1861.

Special Order, No. 45.

Quartermaster General D. L. Wood will make proper provision for the salutes, and Lieut. Col. Mills will furnish the infantry escort contemplated in the official programme for the reception of the President elect of the United States at the Capitol of Ohio, February 13, 1861, announced by the joint committee of the General Assembly of this day.

By order. H. B. CARRINGTON,
Adjutant General.

On the 13th, propitious weather and enthusiasm drew thousands of people together to pay their respects to the President elect. At an early hour High street was swarming with excited humanity. The people continued to arrive till noon, when not less than five thousand strangers were in the city. At about one o'clock the military of the city, headed by Goodman's band, formed and marched to the depot. Here the crowd was immense. Every eligible spot in the vicinity of the depot buildings was black with men, women and youths, who were painfully anxious to get a glimpse of the distinguished guest whom they had assembled to honor. As the time for the arrival of the special train drew near, the excitement grew intense; it could be felt rather than observed through the ordinary channels; and when the train was signalled from the first bridge, and the first of the thirty-four gun salute fired, this excitement found vent in a vigorous huzza. The train drove slowly up, and was at once besieged by hundreds of men wild with enthusiasm, who demanded that the President elect should show himself. A minute or two only elapsed after the train came to a halt, when Mr. Lincoln appeared on the rear platform of the train, and with head uncovered and a pleasant smile, bowed acknowledgment of the manifestations of consideration and respect which met him on all hands. The air was rent with deafening shouts, as the President elect passed from the train to the open carriage in waiting. Then commenced the triumphal march to the State House. First in order were the military escort and band, then the President elect, followed by his suite and reception committee. This cavalcade was flanked by great crowds of the excited populace, while the more staid, in buggies, with foot passengers who could not find room on the flanks, brought up the rear. The band discoursed the national airs with great vigor, the crowd huzzahed their irrepressible enthusiasm, and the ladies and children waved their respect from the sidewalks and windows with handkerchiefs and miniature flags. The western steps and portico of the State House were densely packed with an expectant throng, while the broad walks leading from the western entrance of the yard to the building, and the space immediately in front, were jammed. Through this dense mass of humanity the President elect, escorted by the reception committee, directed his way, preceded by the military, who opened up a path to the vestibule of the Capitol. Cheer upon cheer, hearty and deafening, followed the distinguished guest as he passed into the State House to receive the respects of the Governor and Legislature. The crowd—a very good natured one, indeed—remained stationary, making the most of their uncomfortable position (being packed together as closely as pickles in a jar), until they should be favored with a speech and a levee from the President elect, which they knew were in store for them. Many pleasantries, suggested by the occasion and circumstances, were perpetrated, producing much good feeling.

While the crowd was thus held in suspense, waiting for the conclusion of the in-door proceedings, but one incident worthy of record occurred. The stars and stripes were elevated above the State House, and as they danced gaily in the breeze, three loud cheers were given with a will.

The fortunate people who had passes—and these, beside the legislators, were very few—began to crowd the Hall of the House, directly after the doors were opened. Lovely women, with the promptness of the sex on public occasions, took possession of the galleries; and when (as the reporter of the Ohio State Journal described the scene) "these were inundated with successive waves of crinoline, the rules were suspended and the ladies admitted to the floor of the House." The Senators had taken seats with the Representatives. A tumult near the door of the hall announced the arrival of the President. Mr. Lincoln entered the room, attended by Governor Dennison and the legislative committees, and advanced to the Clerk's desk, the members of the two Houses rising to receive him. Governor Dennison introduced him to the Legislature, and the President of the Senate responded in the following speech of welcome:

"SIR: On this day, and probably this very hour, the Congress of the United States will declare the verdict of the people, making you their President. It is my pleasurable duty, in behalf of the people of Ohio, speaking through this General Assembly, to welcome you to their Capital. Never in the history of this Government has such fearful responsibility rested upon the Chief Executive of the nation as will now devolve upon you. Never since the memorable time our patriotic fathers gave existence to the American Republic, have the people looked with such intensity of feeling to the inauguration and future policy of a President, as they do to yours. I need not assure you that the people of Ohio have full confidence in your ability and patriotism, and will respond to you in their loyalty to the Union and the Constitution. It would seem, sir, that the great problem of self-government is to be solved under your administration. All nations are deeply interested in its solution, and they wait with breathless anxiety to know whether this form of government, which has been the admiration of the world, is to be a failure or not. It is the earnest and united prayer of our people, that the same kind Providence which protected us in our colonial struggles, and has attended us thus far in our prosperity and greatness, will so imbue your mind with wisdom, that you may dispel the dark clouds that hang over our political horizon, and thereby secure the return of harmony and fraternal feeling to our now distracted and unhappy country. Again I bid you a cordial welcome to our Capital."

Mr. Lincoln responded in these words:

"GENTLEMEN OF THE SENATE, AND CITIZENS OF OHIO: It is true, as has been said by the President of the Senate, that very great responsibility rests upon me in the position to which the votes of the American people have called me. I am deeply sensible of that weighty responsibility. I cannot but know, what you all know, that without a name—perhaps without a reason why I should have a name—there has fallen upon me a task such as did not rest upon the Father of his Country. And so feeling, I cannot but turn and look for the support without which it will be impossible for me to perform that great task. I turn, then, and look to the American people, and to that God who has never forsaken them.

"Allusion has been made to the interest felt in relation to the policy of the new administration. In this I have received from some a degree of credit for having kept silence, from others some depreciation. I still think I was right. In the varying and repeatedly shifting scenes of the present, without a precedent which could enable me to judge for the past, it has seemed fitting that before speaking upon the difficulties of the country I should have gained a view of the whole field. To be sure, after all, I would be at liberty to modify and change the course of policy as future events might make a change necessary.

"I have not maintained silence from any want of real anxiety. It is a good thing that there is no more than anxiety, for there is nothing going wrong. It is a consoling circumstance that when we look out there is nothing that really hurts anybody. We entertain different views upon political questions, but nobody is suffering anything. This is a most consoling circumstance, and from it I judge that all we want is time and patience, and a reliance on that God who has never forsaken this people."

The speeches were listened to with attention, and rereceived with deep feeling. At the conclusion of Mr. Lincoln's remarks the applause was quick and hearty. The reporter for the Ohio State Journal, describing the incidents of the day, said:

"The impression which the appearance of the President elect created was most agreeable. His great height was conspicuous even in that crowd of goodly men, and lifted him fully in view as he walked up the aisle. When he took the Speaker's stand, a better opportunity was afforded to look at the man upon whom more hopes hang than upon any other living. At first the kindness and amiability of his face strikes you; but as he speaks, the greatness and determination of his nature are apparent. Something in his manner, even more than in his words, told how deeply he was affected by the enthusiasm of the people; and when he appealed to them for encouragement and support, every heart responded with mute assurance of both. There was the simplicity of greatness in his unassuming and confiding manner, that won its way to instant admiration. He looked somewhat worn with travel and the fatigues of popularity, but warmed to the cordiality of his reception."

After the ceremonies in the Hall, the Presidential party went to the western steps of the Capitol, where Mr. Lincoln addressed a vast concourse of people. He said:

"LADIES AND GENTLEMEN: I appear before you only to address you very briefly. I shall do little else than to thank you for this very kind reception; to greet you and bid you farewell. I should not find strength, if I were otherwise inclined, to repeat speeches of very great length, upon every occasion similar to this—although few so large—which will occur on my way to the Federal Capital. The General Assembly of the great State of Ohio has just done me the honor to receive me, and to hear a few broken remarks from myself. Judging from what I see, I infer that the reception was one without party distinction, and one of entire kindness—one that had nothing in it beyond a feeling of the citizenship of the United States of America. Knowing, as I do, that any crowd, drawn together as this has been, is made up of the citizens near about, and that in this county of Franklin there is great difference of political sentiment, and those agreeing with me having a little the shortest row; from this and the circumstances I have mentioned, I infer that you do me the honor to meet me here without distinction of party. I think this is as it should be.

Many of you who were not favorable to the election of myself to the Presidency, were favorable to the election of the distinguished Senator from the State in which I reside. If Senator Douglas had been elected to the Presidency in the late contest, I think my friends would have joined heartily in meeting and greeting him on his passage through your Capital, as you have me to-day. If any of the other candidates had been elected, I think it would have been altogether becoming and proper for all to have joined in showing honor quite as well to the office and the country as to the man. The people are themselves honored by such a concentration. I am doubly thankful that you have appeared here to give me this greeting. It is not much to me, for I shall very soon pass away from you; but we have a large country and a large future before us, and the manifestations of good will towards the Government, and affection for the Union, which you may exhibit, are of immense value to you and your posterity forever. In this point of view it is that I thank you most heartily for the exhibition you have given me; and with this, allow me to bid you an affectionate farewell."

The speaking concluded, hand-shaking commenced. Mr. Lincoln took his position in the rotunda near the stairway leading to the Library, and the people admitted at the south door, passed through and out at the north door. Almost immediately the vast rotunda was crowded with eager, turbulent, pushing, crowding, jostling sovereigns, frantic to wrench the hand of the President elect. An attempt was made to preserve a lane through which the hand-shakers might pass to Mr. Lincoln, and furious and heroic were the struggles to keep this avenue open. With a sublime devotion, which demands highest praise, a few spartans held back the crowd, which heaved and surged to and fro. For a while the President greeted the people with his right hand only, but as the officers gave way before the irresistible crowd, he shook hands right and left, with astonishing rapidity. The physical exertion must have been tremendous. People plunged at his arms with frantic enthusiasm, and all the infinite variety of shakes, from the wild and irrepressible pump-handle movement to the dead grip, was executed upon the devoted sinister and dexter of the President. Some glanced into his face as they grasped his hand; others invoked the blessings of heaven upon him; others affectionately gave him their last gasping assurance of devotion; others, bewildered and furious, with hats crushed over their eyes, seized his hand in a convulsive grasp, and passed on as if they had not the remotest idea who, what, or where they were, nor what anything was at all about. But at last the performance became intolerable to the President, who retired to the stair-case in exhaustion, and contented himself with looking at the crowd as it swept before him. It was a very good-natured crowd, nothing occurred to mar the harmony of the occasion, and the utmost enthusiasm prevailed. The President remained in the Capitol until half-past four, and then withdrew to the Governor's residence.

In the evening the State officers, members of the Legislature, City Council, and others paid their respects to the President elect, at the residence of Governor Dennison, where a collation was served. At half-past eight o'clock Mr. Lincoln repaired to the State House, where he held a brief levee, meeting many prominent citizens, and exchanging pleasant salutations.

FROM COLUMBUS TO PITTSBURG.

The President elect and party left Columbus at eight o'clock on the morning of the 14th. The morning was wet, but, in spite of the rain, numbers had collected in the depot, who bid Mr. Lincoln adieu. At Newark, Frazeesburg, Dresden, Coshocton, Newcomerstown and Urichsville large crowds of ladies and gentlemen had collected, notwithstanding a pelting rain. The train stopped at Cadiz Junction, where an elegant dinner was prepared by Mrs. T. L. Jewett, wife of the President of the Steubenville and Indiana Railroad. Mrs. Jewett was invited and accompanied the train; also the Steubenville committee. When the cars reached Steubenville the rain had ceased, and there was a demonstration of about five thousand people at the depot. Amid the firing of the cannon, Mr. Lincoln ascended the stage and was welcomed by Judge Loyd. Mr. Lincoln responded briefly. He said:

"I fear that great confidence in my abilities is unfounded. The place I am about to assume is encompassed by vast difficulties. As I am, nothing shall be wanting on my part; unless sustained by the American people and God, I cannot hope to be successful. I believe the devotion to the Constitution is equally great on both sides of the river; it is only the different understandings of it. The only dispute is, what are their rights? If the majority should not rule, who should be the judge? When such a judge is found we must be all bound by his decision. That judge is the majority of the American people; if not, then the minority must control. Would that be right, just or generous? Assuredly not. He reiterated that the majority should rule. If he adopted a wrong policy, the opportunity to condemn it would occur in four years; then I can be turned out, and a better man, with better views, put in my place." The time being up, the speech was cut short.

Mr. McCullough, President of the Cleveland and Pittsburg road, got on the train to accompany the party to Cleveland; also the committee to invite Mr. Lincoln to the reception at Alleghany City. At Wellsville the Cleveland committee joined the party.

RECEPTION AT PITTSBURG.

A pelting rain prevented the intended demonstration to some extent. The party proceeded in carriages to the Monongahela House, Pittsburg, where Mr. Lincoln addressed an immense crowd. He said he would not give them a speech, as he thought it more rare, if not more wise, for a public man. He expressed his gratification and surprise at seeing so great a crowd and such boundless enthusiasm manifested in the night time, and under such untoward circumstances, to greet so unworthy an individual as himself. This was undoubtedly attributable to the position to which, more by accident than by merit, he had attained. He remarked, further, that if all these energetic, whole-souled people whom he saw before him were for the preservation of the Union, he did not see how it could be in danger. [Cheering—cries of Union and no compromise.] He had intended to say a few words to the people of Pittsburg, the greatest manufacturing city in the United States, upon such matters as he believed they desired to hear; but as he had adopted the plan of holding his tongue for the most part during the last canvass, and since his election, he had, perhaps, better now hold his tongue. [Cries of "Go on."] Well, I am reminded that there is an Alleghany City as well as an Alleghany county; the former the banner town and the latter the banner county, perhaps, of the world. I am glad to see both of them and the good people of both. That I may not disappoint these, I will say a few words to-morrow as to the peculiar interests of Alleghany county." As he closed some one proposed three cheers for "The Union as it is," which were given with a will.

It was announced that Mr. Lincoln would speak in the morning at eight o'clock, and then be escorted by the military through both cities, and would then leave at eleven o'clock for Cleveland. Had it not been for the pelting storm, the display would have been fine.

On the morning of the 15th Mr. Lincoln made the following address to the people of Pittsburg:

"In every short address I have made to the people, and in every crowd through which I have passed of late, some allusion has been made to the present distracted condition of the country. It is naturally expected that I should say something on this subject, but to touch upon it at all would involve an elaborate discussion of a great many questions and circumstances, would require more time than I can at present command, and would perhaps unnecessarily commit me upon matters which have not yet fully developed themselves.

"The condition of the country, fellow-citizens, is an extraordinary one, and fills the mind of every patriot with anxiety and solicitude. My intention is to give this subject all the consideration which I possibly can before I speak fully and definitely in regard to it, so that, when I do speak, I may be as nearly right as possible. And when I do speak, fellow-citizens, I hope to say nothing in opposition to the spirit of the Constitution, contrary to the integrity of the Union, or which will in any way prove inimical to the liberties of the people or to the peace of the whole country. And, furthermore, when the time arrives for me to speak on this great subject, I hope to say nothing which will disappoint the reasonable expectations of any man, or disappoint the people generally throughout the country, especially if their expectations have been based upon anything which I may have heretofore said.

"Notwithstanding the troubles across the river, [the speaker, smiling, pointed southwardly to the Monongahela river,] there is really no crisis springing from anything in the Government itself. In plain words, there is really no crisis except an artificial one. What is there now to warrant the condition of affairs presented by our friends 'over the river?' Take even their own view of the questions involved, and there is nothing to justify the course which they are pursuing. I repeat it, then, there is no crisis, except such a one as may be gotten up at any time by turbulent men, aided by designing politicians. My advice, then, under such circumstances, is to keep cool. If the great American people will only keep their temper on both sides of the line, the trouble will come to an end, and the question which now distracts the country will be settled just as surely as all other difficulties of like character which have originated in this Government have been adjusted. Let the people on both sides keep their self-possession, and just as other clouds have cleared away in due time, so will this, and this great nation shall continue to prosper as heretofore."

He then referred to the subject of the tariff, and said:

"According to my political education, I am inclined to believe that the people in the various portions of the country should have their own views carried out through their representatives in Congress; that consideration of the tariff bill should not be postponed until the next session of the National Legislature. No subject should engage your representatives more closely than that of the tariff. If I have any recommendation to make, it will be that every man who is called upon to serve the people, in a representative capacity, should study the whole subject thoroughly, as I intend to do myself, looking to all the varied interests of the common country, so that, when the time for action arrives, adequate protection shall be extended to the coal and iron of Pennsylvania and the corn of Illinois. Permit me to express the hope that this important subject may receive such consideration at the hands of your representatives that the interests of no part of the country may be overlooked, but that all sections may share in the common benefits of a just and equitable tariff."

FROM PITTSBURG TO CLEVELAND.

Mr. Lincoln and party left Pittsburg in a smart shower, amid enthusiastic plaudits. At Bayard a large crowd had assembled, notwithstanding the mud and rain. Mr. Lincoln bowed in response. At Alliance an elegant dinner was given by Mr. McCullough, President of the road. Salutes were fired, smashing windows, including the one at which Mrs. Lincoln sat during dinner. An elegant company of Zouaves stood guard, the band playing national airs. The train also stopped at Ravenna and Hudson for a few minutes, which places were alive with people.

RECEPTION AT CLEVELAND.

On the fifth of February, resolutions were adopted by the council of the city of Cleveland, inviting Mr. Lincoln to accept its hospitalities; and a committee of arrangements was appointed, which consisted of the Mayor, G. B Senter; the President of Council, I. U. Masters, and the following named members of the Council: C. L. Russell, W. H. Haywood, and O. M. Oviatt. A citizens' committee, to co-operate with that of the Council, was subsequently appointed, S. J. Andrews being the chairman, and Merrill Barlow secretary. Under the direction of these committees, admirable preparations were made for the reception.

From various public buildings were suspended national flags. The Weddell, Johnson, and other public houses, showed their colors. The City Hall building was decorated with a number of flags, and on a rope between Hoffman's Block and the U. S. Post Office buildings were several. From the Herald building to the Weddell House a rope was extended and supported seven flags.

The railroads from the south and west brought large numbers of visitors to the city. The exceedingly bad condition of the roads prevented the arrival of so large a number from the country, in wagons, as would otherwise have been present. There was, however, a good attendance of strangers. The buildings, affording a view of the route of the procession, were crowded by spectators, and immense numbers thronged the streets.

Everything being in readiness, the escort proceeded to the Euclid Street Station of the C. & P. R. R., to await the arrival of the President's train. The following was the order of the procession fixed upon by the Marshal:

Cleveland Regiment Light Artillery, Colonel James Barnett, consisting of the following companies: Company A, Capt. Simmons; Company B, Capt. Mack; Company D, Capt. Rice; Company E, Capt. Hechman.

Cleveland Light Dragoons, Capt. Holtnorth.

Cleveland Greys, Capt. Paddock.

City Council, in carriages.

The President elect in an open barouche.

The President's suite in carriages.

Citizens' Committee in carriages.

Firemen—Phœnix No. 4 and Firemen's Board.

Citizens in carriages, manufacturing establishments, and various representations of the business interests of the city.

In the latter division of the procession was a full rigged ship, decorated with national flags, and manned by stalwart tars, the representatives of the lake shipping interest. This was arranged by the Council committee.

Two large omnibusses were filled with workmen from the Cuyahoga Steam Furnace Works, and joined in the escort.

The members of Phœnix Fire Company No. 4, accompanied by representatives of the Firemen's General Board, were also in the line as representatives of the Fire Department, their machine being decorated with national colors.

In the procession of citizens were men of all shades of political feeling, uniting cordially in this spontaneous manifestation of respect for the President elect and the high office to which he had been called. The line was very long, and contained every ordinary manner of conveyance.

The crowd at the station was immense, and it was with difficulty that the police of Marshal Craw could restrain the surging populace. The Greys occupied the east platform, and the artillery, firemen, carriages, etc., were arranged on the west side. At 4 o'clock the approach of the train was announced by the guns of the artillery, in accordance with telegraphic advices. Mr. Lincoln was quickly passed to a carriage drawn by four white horses, driven by Mr. H. Nottingham. The crowd cheered and shouted in the wildest enthusiasm, and the procession started. In spite of the inclement weather, Euclid street from end to end was crowded. The people along the line were wild, and rushed recklessly to and fro in endeavors to obtain a glimpse of the President. The reception was at the Weddell House. The balcony was hung with colored lanterns. It was half past five o'clock when Mr. Lincoln was brought out to face the dense crowd that filled the street. Mr. I. U. Masters, President of the Council, welcomed the President elect:

"HONORED SIR:—The pleasant duty devolves upon me to extend to you, in behalf of the citizens of Cleveland, through their municipal representatives, a cordial welcome to this city and community. In extending this welcome, I am but speaking the voice of our men of business; our mechanics, whose representatives are around me; of farmers, who have largely gathered here; of men of all trades, avocations, professions and parties, who merge all distinction in that name common to them all, of highest distinction to them all, and best beloved by them all—American citizens. They bid me welcome you as the official representative of their country, chosen in accordance with the Constitution which they venerate with love. They bid me express to you their unconditional loyalty to the Constitution and country, which their fathers transmitted to them, and which they fervently hope may, by the blessing of God, be transmitted unimpaired to their children and their children's children. Again I bid you a hearty welcome."

Hon. Sherlock J. Andrews then, on behalf of the Citizens' Committee, spoke as follows:

"MR. LINCOLN—*Sir:* I have the honor, on behalf of the citizens of Cleveland, to repeat the welcome you have already received through the official organ of the city, and to express the great satisfaction that we all derive from this personal interview. We come to-day, sir, forgetful of party distinctions, and as citizens of a common country, to tender you the homage of our sincere respect, both for your personal character and for the high station to which you have been called by the popular will; and, though unexampled difficulties and embarrassments stand upon the threshold of your administration, we still cherish the hope that, by the blessing of Divine Providence, you may be enabled so to execute the great trust confided to you as to allay excitement, correct misapprehension, restore harmony, and reinstate this glorious Union of ours in the affections and confidence of the whole people. It is true, indeed, that in the late peaceful contest for the Chief Magistracy, we have acted under various political organizations, and have differed as to men and measures. Yet, sir, in every enlightened effort to support the prerogatives and honor of the General Government, in every determination to uphold the supremacy of law, in every measure wisely designed to maintain unimpaired the constitutional rights of all the States or of any of the States, and every concession consistent with truth and justice, that looks to the promotion of peace and concord, there is not a man in the vast multitude here assembled to do you honor, who will not give you his cordial and earnest support. Such, I am persuaded, sir, are the views of those I represent, and to whom, for any further expression of their sentiments, I shall now refer you.

"Fellow citizens, I have the honor of introducing to you the Hon. Abraham Lincoln, the President elect of the United States."

In response, Mr. Lincoln said:

"MR. CHAIRMAN AND FELLOW CITIZENS OF CLEVELAND AND OHIO:—We have had a very inclement afternoon. We have been marching in procession for about two miles through snow, rain and deep mud. The large numbers that have turned out under these circumstances testify that you are in earnest about something or other. But do I think so meanly of you as to suppose that earnestness is about me personally? I should be doing you injustice to suppose you did. [A voice, "We all love you."] You have assembled to testify your respect to the Union, the Constitution and the Laws. And here let me say that it is with you, the people, to advocate the great cause of the Union and the Constitution, and not with any one man. I repeat, it rests with you alone. This fact is strongly impressed on my mind at present. In a community like this, whose appearance—as I may say whose very clothes—whose well built houses, whose numerous schools, and all other evidences before me, testify to their intelligence, I am convinced that the cause of Liberty and the Union can never be in danger.

"Frequent allusion is made to the excitement at present existing in our national politics. It is well that I should also allude to it here. I think there is no occasion for any excitement. The crisis, as it is called, is altogether an artificial crisis. In all parts of the nation there are differences of opinion on politics. There are differences of opinion even here. You did not all vote for the person who now addresses you. A large number of you did—enough for all practical purposes—but not all of you. Farther away there were fewer who voted for me, and their numbers decreased as they got farther away. What is happening now will not hurt those who are farther away from here. Have they not all the rights now that they ever had? Do they not have their fugitive slaves returned as ever? Have they not the same Constitution that they have lived under for the last seventy odd years? Have they not a position as citizens of this common country, and have we any power to change that position? What, then, is the matter with them?

Why all this excitement? Why all these complaints? As I said before, this crisis is all artificial. It has no foundation in facts. It was not argued up, as the saying is, and cannot therefore be argued down. Let it alone, and it will go down of itself.

"Mr. Lincoln said they must be content with but a few words from him. He was very much fatigued, and had spoken so frequently that he was already hoarse. He thanked them for the cordial, the magnificent reception they had given him. Not less did he thank them for the votes they gave him last fall. And quite as much he thanked them for the efficient aid they had given the cause which he represented--a cause which, he would say, was a good one. He had one word more to say. He was given to understand that this reception was tendered not only by his own party supporters, but by men of all parties. This is as it should be. If Judge Douglas had been elected, and had been here on his way to Washington, as I am to-night, the Republicans should have joined his supporters in welcoming him, just as his friends have joined with mine to-night. If all don't join now to save the good old ship of the Union this voyage, nobody will have a chance to pilot her on another voyage."

He concluded by thanking all present for the devotion they had shown to the cause of the Union. A number of boquets and wreaths were given to Mr. Lincoln at the close of his speech.

In the evening there was a general reception at the Weddell House, which was crowded to excess. Mr. Lincoln stood at the head of the stairs, and greeted the visitors as they passed by him. This ceremony soon became too fatiguing, however, and Mr. Lincoln was removed to a parlor in the front of the house where he joined Mrs. Lincoln, and where for an hour or more they received their friends. Hon. John Crowell, who was in Congress with Mr. Lincoln, and Col. Mygatt, aid to Gov. Dennison, introduced the visitors. Many ladies patiently endured the crushing pressure of the dense crowd. After the general reception a number of soldiers of the war of 1812 waited upon Mr. Lincoln, and were cordially received. Col. Sturgis' staff and the officers of the Cleveland Wide Awake regiment were afterward presented. The Cleveland Greys, who were on duty in the house during the evening, were introduced, and also the officers of the Light Artillery regiment. The President elect was now very much fatigued, and retired to his room for the night.

Large numbers of people were early astir the following morning, to obtain a parting glimpse of the President and party. This was all that could be afforded, the early departure of the train precluding anything like a demon stration. The escort from the hotel to the station consisted of Col. James Barnett and staff and the Cleveland Greys. The President was conducted to his carriage amid the cheers of the people, and the procession commenced its march. The route was down Superior street, Union lane and River street to the depot. Here the Greys were drawn up on the platform to keep a space clear for the Presidential party. Mr. Lincoln occupied the rear car, upon which was a national flag. The engine selected for the special train was the "William Case." It was decorated with flags, and superintendent Nottingham took charge of the train as conductor. The reception committee from Erie and Buffalo were on the train, and occupied one of the three cars. Various representatives of the press and invited guests filled the third car.

As the train moved out of the depot, Mr. Lincoln came upon the platform of the rear car bowing his acknowledgments to the people, as cheer after cheer went up from the enthusiastic multitude. Several men clung to the end of the car where Mr. Lincoln stood, following it as long as the increasing speed of the train would permit, and stretching up their hands to the President elect. Mr. Lincoln reached out his hand to take that of one of these followers on foot, when it was seized by three or four and shaken with at least hearty good will. After that the crowd was forced to be content with farewell bows.

In concluding an account of the reception at Cleveland, the editor of the Herald said—

"Among the escorting party from Columbus were Cols. Geo. S. Mygatt and Geo. F. O'Hara, aids to Gov. Dennison, the Governor having deputed these gentlemen to accompany Mr. Lincoln, charging them with the duty of attending him through Ohio. This action of the Governor was an appropriate hospitality to the distinguished visitor, and his aids handsomely executed their duty."

BUFFALO.

On Saturday Mr. Lincoln was escorted to Buffalo. At various places along the line of the railroad, both in Ohio and in New York, enthusiastic welcomes were given him, but no addresses were made, nor did any incidents transpire which are entitled to special report. The train arrived at Buffalo late in the afternoon, and was met by an immense concourse of citizens, headed by ex-President Fillmore.

Arriving at the hotel, Mr. Lincoln was welcomed in a brief speech by the acting chief magistrate, to which he made reply as follows:

"MR. MAYOR AND FELLOW-CITIZENS:—I am here to thank you briefly for this grand reception given to me, not personally, but as the representative of our great and beloved country. Your worthy mayor has been pleased to mention in his address to me, the fortunate and agreeable journey which I have had from home—only it is rather a circuitous route to the Federal Capital. I am very happy that he was enabled, in truth, to congratulate myself and company on that fact. It is true, we have had nothing thus far to mar the pleasure of the trip. We have not been met alone by those who assisted in giving the election to me; I say not alone, but by the whole population of the country through which we have passed. This is as it should be. Had the election fallen to any other of the distinguished candidates instead of myself, under the peculiar circumstances, to say the least, it would have been proper for all citizens to have greeted him as you now greet me. It is an evidence of the devotion of the whole people to the Constitution, the Union, and the perpetuity of the liberties of this country. I am unwilling, on any occasion, that I should be so meanly thought of as to have it supposed for a moment that these demonstrations are tendered to me personally. They are tendered to the country, to the institutions of the country, and to the perpetuity of the liberties of the country for which these institutions were made and created. Your worthy mayor has thought fit to express the hope that I may be able to relieve the country from the present, or I should say, the threatened difficulties. I am sure I bring a heart true to the work. For the ability to perform it, I trust in that Supreme Being who has never forsaken this favored land, through the instrumentality of this great and intelligent people. Without that assistance I should surely fail; with it I cannot fail. When we speak of the threatened difficulties to the country, it is natural that it should be expected that something should be said by myself with regard to particular measures. Upon more mature reflection, however—and others will agree with me—that when it is considered that these difficulties are without precedent, and never have been acted upon by any individual situated as I am, it is most proper I should wait and see the developments, and get all the light possible, so that when I do speak authoritatively, I may be as near right as possible. When I shall speak authoritatively, I hope to say nothing inconsistent with the Constitution, the Union, the rights of all the States, of each State, and of each section of the country, and not to disappoint the reasonable expectations of those who have confided to me their votes. In this connection allow me to say that you, as a portion of the great American people, need only to maintain your composure, stand up to your sober convictions of right, to your obligations to the Constitution, and act in accordance with those sober convictions, and the clouds which now arise in the horizon will be dispelled, and we shall have a bright and glorious future; and when this generation shall have passed away, tens of thousands shall inhabit this country where only thousands inhabit it now. I do not propose to address you at length. I have no voice for it. Allow me again to thank you for this magnificent reception, and bid you farewell."

ALBANY.

Mr. Lincoln proceeded from Buffalo to Albany, various demonstrations of welcome being given him on the way. At Albany he was met by the Mayor, the City Councils, and Legislative Committees, and was conducted to the Capitol, where he was welcomed by Governor Morgan, and responded as follows:

"GOVERNOR MORGAN:—I was pleased to receive an invitation to visit the capital of the great Empire State of this nation, while on my way to the Federal capital. I now thank you, and through you, the people of the capital of the State of New York, for this most hearty and magnificent welcome. If I am not at fault, the great Empire State at this time contains a larger population than did the whole of the United States of America at the time they achieved their national independence; and I was proud to be invited to visit its capital, to meet its citizens as I now have the honor to do. I am notified by your governor that this reception is tendered by citizens without distinction of party. Because of this, I accept it the more gladly. In this country, and in any country where freedom of thought is tolerated, citizens attach themselves to political parties. It is but an ordinary degree of charity to attribute this act to the supposition that, in thus attaching themselves to the various parties, each man, in his own judgment, supposes he thereby best advances the interests of the whole country. And when an election is passed, it is altogether befitting a free people that, until the next election, they should be one people. The reception you have extended to me to-day is not given to me personally. It should not be so, but as the representative, for the time being, of the majority of the nation. If the election had fallen to any of the more distinguished citizens, who received the support of the people, this same honor should have greeted him that greets me this day, in testimony of the unanimous devotion of the whole people to the Constitution, the Union, and to the perpetual liberties of succeeding generations in this country. I have neither the voice nor the strength to address you at any greater length. I beg you will, therefore, accept my most grateful thanks for this manifest devotion—not to me but to the institutions of this great and glorious country."

The President elect was then conducted to the Legislative halls, where, in reply to an address of welcome, he again adverted to the troubles of the country in the following terms:

"MR. PRESIDENT AND GENTLEMEN OF THE LEGISLATURE OF THE STATE OF NEW YORK:—It is with feelings of great diffidence, and, I may say, feelings even of awe, perhaps greater than I have recently experienced, that I meet you here in this place. The history of this great State, the renown of its great men, who have stood in this chamber, and have spoken their thoughts, all crowd around my fancy, and incline me to shrink from an attempt to address you. Yet I have some confidence given me by the generous manner in which you have invited me, and the still more generous manner in which you have received me. You have invited me and received me without distinction of party. I could not for a moment suppose that this has been done in any considerable degree with any reference to my personal self. It is very much more grateful to me that this reception and the invitation preceding it were given to me as the representative of a free people than it could possibly have been were they but the evidence of devotion to me or to any one man. It is true that, while I hold myself, without mock-modesty, the humblest of all the individuals who have ever been elected President of the United States, I yet have a more difficult task to perform than any one of them has ever encountered. You have here generously tendered me the support, the united support, of the great Empire State. For this, in behalf of the nation—in behalf of the present and of the future of the nation—in behalf of the cause of civil liberty in all time to come—I most gratefully thank you. I do not propose now to enter upon any expressions as to the particular line of policy to be adopted with reference to the difficulties that stand before us in the opening of the incoming Administration. I deem that it is just to the country, to myself, to you, that I should see everything, hear everything, and have every light that can possibly be brought within my reach to aid me before I shall speak officially, in order that, when I do speak, I may have the best possible means of taking correct and true grounds. For this reason, I do not now announce anything in the way of policy for the new Administration. When the time comes, according to the custom of the government, I shall speak, and speak as well as I am able for the good of the present and of the future of this country—for the good of the North and of the South—for the good of one and of the other, and of all sections of it. In the meantime, if we have patience, if we maintain our equanimity, though some may allow themselves to run off in a burst of passion, I still have confidence that the Almighty Ruler of the Universe, through the instrumentality of this great and intelligent people, can and will bring us through this difficulty, as he has heretofore brought us through all preceding difficulties of the country. Relying upon this, and again thanking you, as I forever shall, in my heart, for this generous reception you have given me, I bid you farewell."

ALBANY TO NEW YORK.

At Albany, Mr. Lincoln was met by a delegation from the city authorities of New York, and on the 19th started for that city. At Poughkeepsie, he was welcomed by the Mayor of the city. Mr. Lincoln, in reply, said:

"I am grateful for this cordial welcome, and I am

gratified that this immense multitude has come together, not to meet the individual man, but the man who, for the time being, will humbly but earnestly represent the majesty of the nation. These receptions have been given me at other places, and, as here, by men of different parties, and not by one party alone. It shows an earnest effort on the part of all to save, not the country, for the country can save itself, but to save the institutions of the country—those institutions under which, for at least three-quarters of a century, we have become the greatest, the most intelligent, and the happiest people in the world. These manifestations show that we all make common cause for these objects; that if some of us are successful in an election, and others are beaten, those who are beaten are not in favor of sinking the ship in consequence of defeat, but are earnest in their purpose to sail it safely through the voyage in hand, and, in so far as they may think there has been any mistake in the election, satisfying themselves to take their chance at setting the matter right the next time. That course is entirely right. I am not sure—I do not pretend to be sure—that in the selection of the individual who has been elected this term, the wisest choice has been made. I fear it has not. In the purposes and in the principles that have been sustained, I have been the instrument selected to carry forward the affairs of this Government. I can rely upon you, and upon the people of the country; and with their sustaining hand, I think that even I shall not fail in carrying the Ship of State through the storm."

NEW YORK CITY.

The reception of Mr. Lincoln in New York city was a most imposing demonstration. Places of business were generally closed, and hundreds of thousands were in the streets. On the next day he was welcomed to the city by Mayor F. Wood, and replied as follows:

"MR. MAYOR:—It is with feelings of deep gratitude that I make my acknowledgments for the reception given me in the great commercial city of New York. I cannot but remember that this is done by a people who do not, by a majority, agree with me in political sentiment. It is the more grateful, because in this I see that, for the great principles of our Government, the people are almost unanimous. In regard to the difficulties that confront us at this time, and of which your Honor has thought fit to speak so becomingly and so justly, as I suppose, I can only say that I agree in the sentiments expressed. In my devotion to the Union, I hope I am behind no man in the nation. In the wisdom with which to conduct the affairs tending to the preservation of the Union, I fear that too great confidence may have been reposed in me; but I am sure that I bring a heart devoted to the work. There is nothing that could ever bring me to willingly consent to the destruction of this Union, under which not only the great commercial city of New York, but the whole country, acquired its greatness, except it be the purpose for which the Union itself was formed. I understand the ship to be made for the carrying and the preservation of the cargo, and so long as the ship can be saved with the cargo, it should never be abandoned, unless there appears no possibility of its preservation, and it must cease to exist, except at the risk of throwing overboard both freight and passengers. So long, then, as it is possible that the prosperity and the liberties of the people be preserved in this Union, it shall be my purpose at all times to use all my powers to aid in its perpetuation. Again thanking you for the reception given me, allow me to come to a close."

TRENTON.

On the following day, Mr. Lincoln left for Philadelphia. At Trenton he remained a few hours, and visited both Houses of the New Jersey Legislature. On being received in the Senate, he thus addressed that body:

"MR. PRESIDENT, AND GENTLEMEN OF THE SENATE OF THE STATE OF NEW JERSEY:—I am very grateful to you for the honorable reception of which I have been the object. I cannot but remember the place that New Jersey holds in our early history. In the early Revolutionary struggle, few of the States among the old Thirteen had more of the battle-fields of the country within its limits than old New Jersey. May I be pardoned, if, upon this occasion, I mention, that away back in my childhood, the earliest days of my being able to read, I got hold of a small book, such a one as few of the younger members have ever seen, 'Weems' Life of Washington.' I remember all the accounts there given of the battle-fields and struggles for the liberties of the country, and none fixed themselves upon my imagination so deeply as the struggle here at Trenton, New Jersey. The crossing of the river—the contest with the Hessians—the great hardships endured at that time—all fixed themselves on my memory more than any single revolutionary event; and you all know, for you have all been boys, how these early impressions last longer than any others. I recollect thinking then, boy even though I was, that there must have been something more than common that those men struggled for. I am exceedingly anxious that that thing which they struggled for—that something even more than National Independence—that something that held out a great promise to all the people of the world to all time to come—I am exceedingly anxious that this Union, the Constitution, and the liberties of the people, shall be perpetuated in accordance with the original idea for which that struggle was made, and I shall be most happy indeed if I shall be an humble instrument in the hands of the Almighty, and of this, His almost chosen people, for perpetuating the object of that great struggle. You give me this reception, as I understand, without distinction of party. I learn that this body is composed of a majority of gentlemen who, in the exercise of their best judgment in the choice of a Chief Magistrate, did not think I was the man. I understand, nevertheless, that they come forward here to greet me as the constitutional President of the United States—as citizens of the United States, to meet the man who, for the time being, is the representative man of the nation, united by a purpose to perpetuate the Union and liberties of the people. As such, I accept this reception more gratefully than I could do did I believe it was tendered to me as an individual."

Mr. Lincoln then passed into the Chamber of the Assembly, and upon being introduced by the Speaker, addressed that body as follows:

"MR. SPEAKER AND GENTLEMEN:—I have just enjoyed the honor of a reception by the other branch of this Legislature, and I return to you and them my thanks for the reception which the people of New Jersey have given, through their chosen representatives, to me, as the representative for the time being, of the majesty of the people of the United States. I appropriate to myself very little of the demonstrations of respect with which I have been greeted. I think little should be given to any man, but that it should be a manifestation of adherence to the Union and the Constitution. I understand myself to be received here by the representatives of the people of New Jersey, a majority of whom differ in opinion from those with whom I have acted. This manifestation is therefore to be regarded by me as expressing their devotion to the Union, the Constitution, and the liberties of the people. You, Mr. Speaker, have well said, that this is a time when the bravest and wisest look with doubt and awe upon the aspect presented by our national affairs. Under these circumstances, you will readily see why I should not speak in detail of the course I shall deem it best to pursue. It is proper that I should avail myself of all the information and all the time at my command, in order that when the time arrives in which I must speak officially, I shall be able to take the ground which I deem the best and safest, and from which I may have no occasion to swerve. I shall endeavor to take the ground I deem most just to the North, the East, the West, the South, and the whole country. I take it, I hope, in good temper—certainly with no malice towards any section. I shall do all that may be in my power to promote a peaceful settlement of all our difficulties. The man does not live who is more devoted to peace than I am—none who would do more to preserve it. But it may be necessary to put the foot down firmly. And if I do my duty, and do right, you will sustain me, will you not? Received, as I am, by the members of a Legislature, the majority of whom do not agree with me in political sentiments, I trust that I may have their assistance in piloting the Ship of State through this voyage, surounded by perils as it is; for if it should suffer shipwreck now, there will be no pilot ever needed for another voyage."

PHILADELPHIA.

On arriving in Philadelphia, Mr. Lincoln was received with great enthusiasm, and the Mayor greeted him with a cordial welcome, to which Mr. Lincoln replied:

"MR. MAYOR AND FELLOW-CITIZENS OF PHILADELPHIA:—I appear before you to make no lengthy speech but to thank you for this reception. The reception you have given me to-night is not to me, the man, the individual, but to the man who temporarily represents, or should represent, the majesty of the nation. It is true, as your worthy Mayor has said, that there is anxiety among the citizens of the United States at this time. I deem it a happy circumstance that the dissatisfied portion of our fellow-citizens do not point us to any thing in which they are being injured, or are about to be injured; for which reason I have felt all the while justified in concluding that the crisis, the panic, the anxiety of the country at this time, is artificial. If there be those who differ with me upon this subject, they have not pointed out the substantial difficulty that exists. I do not mean to say that an artificial panic may not do considerable harm; that it has done such I do not deny. The hope that has been expressed by your Mayor, that I may be able to restore peace, harmony, and prosperity to the country, is most worthy of him; and happy indeed will I be if I shall be able to verify and fulfill that hope. I promise you, in all sincerity, that I bring to the work a sincere heart. Whether I will bring a head equal to that heart, will be for future times to determine. It were useless for me to speak of details of plans now; I shall speak officially next Monday week, if ever. If I should not speak then, it were useless for me to do so now. If I do speak then, it is useles for me to do so now. When I do speak, I shall take such ground as I deem best calculated to restore peace, harmony, and prosperity to the country, and tend to the perpetuity of the nation, and the liberty of these States and these people. Your worthy Mayor has expressed the wish, in which I join with him, that it were convenient for me to remain with your city long enough to consult your merchants and manufacturers; or, as it were, to listen to those breathings rising within the consecrated walls wherein the Constitution of the United States, and, I will add, the Declaration of Independence, were originally framed and adopted. I assure you and your Mayor, that I had hoped on this occasion, and upon all occasions during my life, that I shall do nothing inconsistent with the teachings of these holy and most sacred walls. I never asked any thing that does not breathe from those walls. All my political warfare has been in favor of the teachings that come forth from these sacred walls. May my right hand forget its cunning, and my tongue cleave to the roof of my mouth, if ever I prove false to those teachings. Fellow-citizens, now allow me to bid you good-night."

On the next morning, Mr. Lincoln visited the old "Independence Hall," for the purpose of raising the national flag over it. There he was received with a warm welcome, and made the following address:

"I am filled with deep emotion at finding myself standing here, in this place, where were collected the wisdom, the patriotism, the devotion to principle, from which sprang the institutions under which we live. You have kindly suggested to me that in my hands is the task of restoring peace to the present distracted condition of the country. I can say in return, sir, that all the political sentiments I entertain have been drawn, so far as I have been able to draw them, from the sentiments which originated and were given to the world from this hall. I have never had a feeling, politically, that did not spring from the sentiments embodied in the Declaration of Independence. I have often pondered over the dangers which were incurred by the men who assembled here, and framed and adopted that Declaration of Independence. I have pondered over the toils that were endured by the officers and soldiers of the army who achieved that independence. I have often inquired of myself what great principle or idea it was that kept this Confederacy so long together. It was not the mere matter of the separation of the colonies from the mother-land, but that sentiment in the Declaration of Independence which gave liberty, not alone to the people of this country, but, I hope, to the world for all future time. It was that which gave promise that in due time the weight would be lifted from the shoulders of all men. This is a sentiment embodied in the Declaration of Independence. Now, my friends, can this country be saved upon this basis? If it can, I will consider myself one of the happiest men in the world if I can help to save it. If it cannot be saved upon that principle, it will be truly awful. But if this country cannot be saved without giving up that principle, I was about to say I would rather be assassinated on this spot than surrender it. Now, in my view of the present aspect of affairs, there need be no bloodshed or war. There is no necessity for it. I am not in favor of such a course; and I may say, in advance, that there will be no bloodshed unless it be forced upon the Government, and then it will be compelled to act in self-defense.

"My friends, this is wholly an unexpected speech, and I did not expect to be called upon to say a word when I came here. I supposed it was merely to do something towards raising the flag. I may, therefore, have said something indiscreet. I have said nothing but what I am willing to live by, and, if it be the pleasure of Almighty God, to die by."

The President elect and suite and the several reception committees then proceeded to a platform erected in front of the State House, and Mr. Benton of the Select Council, invited Mr. Lincoln to raise the flag. He responded in a brief speech, stating his cheerful compliance with the request, and alluded to the original flag of thirteen stars, saying that the number had increased as time rolled on, and we became a happy and a powerful people, each star adding to its prosperity. "The future," he added, is in the hands of the people. It is on such an occasion as this that we can reason together, reaffirm our devotion to the country and the principles of the Declaration of Independence. Let us make up our mind, that when we do put a new star upon our banner, it shall be a fixed one, never to be dimmed by the horrors of war, but brightened by the contentment and prosperity of peace. Let us go on to extend the area of our usefulness, add star upon star, until their light shall shine upon five hundred millions of a free and happy people."

The President elect then raised the flag to the top of the staff.

HARRISBURG.

At half past nine o'clock, on the 22d of February, Mr. Lincoln left Philadelphia for Harrisburg. Both Houses of the Legislature were visited by Mr. Lincoln, and to an address of welcome, the President elect thus replied:

"I appear before you only for a very few brief remarks, in response to what has been said to me. I thank you most sincerely for this reception, and the generous words in which support has been promised me upon this occasion. I thank your great commonwealth for the overwhelming support it recently gave, not to me personally, but the cause, which I think a just one, in the late election. Allusion has been made to the fact—the interesting fact, perhaps we should say—that I, for the first time, appear at the Capital of the great Commonwealth of Pennsylvania upon the birthday of the Father of his Country, in connection with that beloved anniversary connected with the history of this country. I have already gone through one exceedingly interesting scene this morning in the ceremonies at Philadelphia. Under the high conduct ot gentlemen there, I was, for the first time, allowed the privilege of standing in Old Independence Hall, to have a few words addressed to me there, and opening up an opportunity of expressing, with much regret, that I had not more time to express something of my own feelings, excited by the occasion, somewhat to harmonize and give shape to the feelings that had been really the feelings of my whole life. Besides this, our friends there had provided a magnificent flag of the country. They had arranged it so that I was given the honor of raising it to the head of its staff. And when it went up I was pleased that it went to its place by the strength of my own feeble arm; when, according to the arrangement, the cord was pulled, and it flaunted gloriously to the wind without an accident, in the bright glowing sunshine of the morning, I could not help hoping that there was in the entire success of that beautiful ceremony at least something of an omen of what is to come. Nor could I help feeling then, as I often have felt, in the whole of that proceeding, I was a very humble instrument. I had not provided the flag; I had not made the arrangements for elevating it to its place. I had applied but a very small portion of my feeble strength in raising it. In the whole transaction I was in the hands of the people who had arranged it, and if I can have the same generous co-operation of the people of the nation, I think the flag of our country may yet be kept flaunting gloriously. I recur for a moment but to repeat some words uttered at the hotel in regard to what has been said about the military support which the General Government may expect from the commonwealth of Pennsylvania in a proper emergency. To guard against any possible mistake do I recur to this. It is not with any pleasure that I contemplate the possibility that a necessity may arise in this country for the use of the military arm. While I am exceedingly gratified to see the manifestation upon your streets of your military force here, and exceedingly gratified at your promise here to use that force upon a proper emergency— while I make these acknowledgments, I desire to repeat, in order to preclude any possible misconstruction, that I do most sincerely hope that we shall have no use for them; that it will never become their duty to shed blood, and most especially never to shed fraternal blood. I promise that, so far as I may have wisdom to direct, if so painful a result shall in any wise be brought about, it shall be through no fault of mine. Allusion has also been made by one of your honored speakers to some remark recently made by myself at Pittsburg, in regard to what is supposed to be the especial interests of this great commonwealth of Pennsylvania. I now wish only to say, in regard to that matter, that the few remarks which I uttered on that occasion were rather carefully worded. I took pains that they should be so. I have seen no occasion since to add to them or substract from them. I leave them precisely as they stand, adding only now, that I am pleased to have an expression from you, gentlemen of Pennsylvania, significant that they are satisfactory to you. And now, gentlemen of the General Assembly of the Commonwealth of Pennsylvania, allow me to return you again my most sincere thanks."

FROM HARRISBURG TO WASHINGTON.

At Harrisburg information, from friends at Washington, was communicated to Mr. Lincoln that a plot to assassinate him had been discovered at Baltimore, and therefore that it would not be wise to follow out the programme which had been announced for his journey on the 23d, by way of the Northern Central Railway to that city. Consequently the President elect, with a confidential friend, took a special train from Harrisburg to Philadelphia, and early on the morning of the 23d of February, reached Washington.

RECEPTION AT WASHINGTON.

Very decided surprise was manifested at Washington when it became known that the President elect had reached the Capital in advance of his escort. The manner of his coming was severely denounced by both friends and foes, but subsequent developments established the fact of an organized movement to prevent Mr. Lincoln's inauguration by assassination at Baltimore, and the wisdom of the manner in which it was defeated was vindicated. In a day or two after his arrival, the President elect was waited upon by the Mayor and other municipal authorities, who welcomed him to the city, and to whom he made the following reply:

"MR. MAYOR:—I thank you, and through you the municipal authorities of this city who accompany you, for this welcome. And as it is the first time in my life since the present phase of politics has presented itself in this country, that I have said anything publicly within a region of country where the institution of slavery exists, I will take this occasion to say that I think very much of the ill-feeling that has existed, and still exists, between the people in the sections from whence I came and the people here, is dependent upon a misunderstanding of one another. I therefore avail myself of this opportunity to assure you, Mr. Mayor, and all the gentlemen present, that I have not now, and never have had, any other than as kindly feelings towards you as the people of my own section. I have not now, and never have had, any disposition to treat you in any respect otherwise than as my own neighbors. I have not now any purpose to withhold from you any of the benefits of the Constitution, under any circumstances, that I would not feel myself constrained to withhold from my neighbors; and I hope, in a word, that, when we shall become better acquainted, and I say it with great confidence, we shall like each other the more. I thank you for the kindness of this reception."

On the second evening of his residence in Washington the Republican Association tendered Mr. Lincoln a serenade, which attracted a large crowd of friends and curious inquirers, to whom he made the following remarks:

"My friends, I suppose that I may take this as a compliment paid to me, and as such please accept my thanks for it. I have reached this city of Washington under circumstances considerably differing from those under which any other man has ever reached it. I am here for the purpose of taking an official position amongst the people, almost all of whom were politically opposed to me, and are yet opposed to me as I suppose. I propose no lengthy address to you. I only propose to say, as I did on yesterday, when your worthy Mayor and Board of Aldermen called upon me, that I thought much of the ill-feeling that has existed between you and the people of your surroundings and that people from amongst whom

I came, has depended, and now depends, upon a misunderstanding.

"I hope that, if things shall go along as prosperously as I believe we all desire they may, I may have it in my power to remove something of this misunderstanding; that I may be enabled to convince you, and the people of your section of the country, that we regard you as in all things our equals, and in all things entitled to the same respect and the same treatment that we claim for ourselves; that we are in nowise disposed, if it were in our power, to oppress you, to deprive you of any of your rights under the Constitution of the United States, or even narrowly to split hairs with you in regard to those rights, but are determined to give you, as far as lies in our hands, all your rights under the Constitution—not grudgingly, but fully and fairly. I hope that, by thus dealing with you, we will become better acquainted, and be better friends. And now, my friends, with these few remarks, and again returning my thanks for this compliment, and expressing my desire to hear a little more of your good music, I bid you good-night."

Well-grounded fears were entertained at Washington that demonstrations of violence, to prevent Mr. Lincoln's inauguration, would be made on the fourth of March, by emissaries of the rebel confederacy. Ample preparations to crush such demonstrations by military power, were made by Lieut.-General Scott, yet apprehensions of assassination were widely entertained by prominent supporters of the Government, and these apprehensions were shared in by the great mass of the people of the loyal States. The interest, therefore, centering at the Capitol on the Fourth of March, 1861, was greater than it had ever been in the history of that city. The ceremonies were imposing, a large number of troops participating in the procession. The secessionists were overawed. From a platform on the east front of the Capitol, Mr. Lincoln delivered to a very large assemblage of the people from all parts of the country, the following

INAUGURAL ADDRESS.

"FELLOW-CITIZENS OF THE UNITED STATES: In compliance with a custom as old as the Government itself, I appear before you to address you briefly, and to take, in your presence, the oath prescribed by the Constitution of the United States to be taken by the President, before he enters on the execution of his office.

"I do not consider it necessary, at present, for me to discuss those matters of administration about which there is no special anxiety or excitement. Apprehension seems to exist among the people of the Southern States, that, by the accession of a Republican Administration, their property and their peace and personal security are to be endangered. There has never been any reasonable cause for such apprehension. Indeed, the most ample evidence to the contrary has all the while existed, and been open to their inspection. It is found in nearly all the published speeches of him who now addresses you. I do but quote from one of those speeches, when I declare that 'I have no purpose, directly or indirectly, to interfere with the institution of slavery in the States where it exists.' I believe I have no lawful right to do so; and I have no inclination to do so. Those who nominated and elected me, did so with the full knowledge that I had made this, and made many similar declarations, and had never recanted them. And more than this, they placed in the platform, for my acceptance, and as a law to themselves and to me, the clear and emphatic resolution which I now read:

"'*Resolved*, That the maintenance inviolate of the rights of the States, and especially the right of each State to order and control its own domestic institutions according to its own judgment exclusively, is essential to that balance of power on which the perfection and endurance of our political fabric depend; and we denounce the lawless invasion by armed force of the soil of any State or Territory, no matter under what pretext, as among the gravest of crimes.'

"I now reiterate these sentiments; and in doing so I only press upon the public attention the most conclusive evidence of which the case is susceptible, that the property, peace, and security of no section are to be in anywise endangered by the now incoming Administration.

"I add, too, that all the protection which, consistently with the Constitution and the laws, can be given, will be cheerfully given to all the States when lawfully demanded, for whatever cause, as cheerfully to one section as to another.

"There is much controversy about the delivering up of fugitives from service or labor. The clause I now read is as plainly written in the Constitution as any other of its provisions:

"'No person held to service or labor in one State under the laws thereof, escaping into another, shall, in consequence of any law or regulation therein, be discharged from such service or labor, but shall be delivered up on claim of the party to whom such service or labor may be due.'

"It is scarcely questioned that this provision was intended by those who made it for the reclaiming of what we call fugitive slaves; and the intention of the lawgiver the law.

"All members of Congress swear their support to the whole Constitution—to this provision as well as any other. To the proposition, then, that slaves whose cases come within the terms of this clause 'shall be delivered up,' their oaths are unanimous. Now, if they would make the effort in good temper, could they not, with nearly equal unanimity, frame and pass a law by means of which to keep good that unanimous oath?

"There is some difference of opinion whether this clause should be enforced by national or by State authority; but surely that difference is not a very material one. If the slave is to be surrendered, it can be of but little consequence t› him or to others by which authority it is done; and should any one, in any case, be content that this oath shall go unkept on a merely unsubstantial controversy as to how it shall be kept?

"Again, in any law upon this subject, ought not all the safeguards of liberty known in the civilized and humane jurisprudence to be introduced, so that a free man be not, in any case, surrendered as a slave? And might it not be well at the same time to provide by law for the enforcement of that clause in the Constitution which guarantees that 'the citizens of each State shall be entitled to all the provileges and immunities of citizens in the several States?'

"I take the official oath to-day with no mental reservations, and with no purpose to construe the Constitution or laws by any hypercritical rules; and while I do not choose now to specify particular acts of Congress as proper to be enforced, I do suggest that it will be much safer for all, both in official and private stations, to conform to and abide by all those acts which stand unrepealed, than to violate any of them, trusting to find impunity in having them held to be unconstitutional.

"It is seventy-two years since the first inauguration of a President under our national Constitution. During that period fifteen different and very distinguished citizens have in succession administered the executive branch of the government. They have conducted it through many perils, and generally with great success. Yet, with all this scope for precedent, I now enter upon the same task, for the brief constitutional term of four years, under great and peculiar difficulties.

"A disruption of the Federal Union, heretofore only menaced, is now formidably attempted. I hold that in the contemplation of universal law and of the Constitution, the Union of these States is perpetual. Perpetuity is implied, if not expressed, in the fundamental law of all national governments. It is safe to assert that no government proper ever had a provision in its organic law for its own termination. Continue to execute all the express provisions of our national Constitution, and the Union will endure forever, it being impossible to destroy it except by some action not provided for in the instrument itself.

"Again, if the United States be not a government proper, but an association of States in the nature of a contract merely, can it, as a contract, be peaceably unmade by less than all the parties who made it? One party to a contract may violate it—break it, so to speak; but does it not require all to lawfully rescind it? Descending from these general principles, we find the proposition that in legal contemplation the Union is perpetual, confirmed by the history of the Union itself.

"The Union is much older than the Constitution. It was formed, in fact, by the Articles of Association in

1774. It was matured and continued in the Declaration of Independence in 1776. It was further matured, and the faith of all the then thirteen States expressly plighted and engaged that it should be perpetual, by the Articles of Confederation, in 1778; and, finally, in 1787, one of the declared objects for ordaining and establishing the Constitution was to form a more perfect Union. But if the destruction of the Union by one or by a part only of the States be lawfully possible, the Union is less than before, the Constitution having lost the vital element of perpetuity.

"It follows from these views that no State, upon its own mere motion, can lawfully get out of the Union; that resolves and ordinances to that effect are legally void; and that acts of violence within any State or States against the authority of the United States are insurrectionary or revolutionary, according to circumstances.

"I therefore consider that, in view of the Constitution and the laws, the Union is unbroken, and, to the extent of my ability, I shall take care, as the Constitution itself expressly enjoins upon me, that the laws of the Union shall be faithfully executed in all the States. Doing this, which I deem to be only a simple duty on my part, I shall perfectly perform it, so far as is practicable, unless my rightful masters, the American people, shall withhold the requisition, or, in some authoritative manner, direct the contrary.

"I trust this will not be regarded as a menace, but only as the declared purpose of the Union that it will constitutionally defend and maintain itself.

"In doing this there need be no bloodshed or violence, and there shall be none unless it is forced upon the national authority.

"The power confided to me *will be used to hold, occupy,*

and possess the property and places belonging to the government, and collect the duties and imposts; but beyond what may be necessary for these objects there will be no invasion, no using of force against or among the people anywhere.

"Where hostility to the United States shall be so great and so universal as to prevent competent resident citizens from holding the Federal offices, there will be no attempt to force obnoxious strangers among the people that object. While strict legal right may exist of the government to enforce the exercise of these offices, the attempt to do so would be so irritating, and so nearly impracticable withal, that I deem it better to forego for the time the uses of such offices.

"The mails, unless repelled, will continue to be furnished to all parts of the Union.

"So far as possible, the people everywhere shall have that sense of perfect security which is most favorable to calm thought and reflection.

"The course here indicated will be followed, unless current events and experience shall show a modification or change to be proper; and in every case and exigency my best discretion will be exercised according to the circumstances actually existing, and with a view and hope of a peaceful solution of the national troubles, and the restoration of fraternal sympathies and affections.

"That there are persons, in one section or another, who seek to destroy the Union at all events, and are glad of any pretext to do it, I will neither affirm nor deny. But if there be such, I need address no word to them.

"To those, however, who really love the Union, may I not speak, before entering upon so grave a matter as the destruction of our national fabric, with all its benefits, its memories, and its hopes? Would it not be well to ascertain why we do it? Will you hazard so desperate a step, while any portion of the ills you fly from have no real existence? Will you, while the certain ills you fly to, are greater than all the real ones you fly from? Will you risk the commission of so fearful a mistake? All profess to be content in the Union if all constitutional rights can be maintained. Is it true, then, that any right, plainly written in the Constitution, has been denied? I think not. Happily the human mind is so constituted, that no party can reach to the audacity of doing this.

"Think, if you can, of a single instance in which a plainly written provision of the Constitution has ever been denied. If, by the mere force of numbers, a majority should deprive a minority of any clearly written constitutional right, it might, in a moral point of view, justify revolution; it certainly would, if such right were a vital one. But such is not our case.

"All the vital rights of minorities and of individuals are so plainly assured to them by affirmations and negations, guarantees and prohibitions in the Constitution, that controversies never rise concerning them. But no organic law can ever be framed with a provision specifically applicable to every question which may occur in practical administration. No foresight can anticipate, nor any document of reasonable length contain, express provisions for all possible questions. Shall fugitives from labor be surrendered by national or by State authorities? The Constitution does not expressly say. Must Congress protect slavery in the territories? The Constitution does not expressly say. From questions of this class spring all our constitutional controversies, and we divide upon them into majorities and minorities.

"If the minority will not acquiesce, the majority must,

or the government must cease. There is no alternative for continuing the government but acquiescence on the one side or the other. If a minority in such a case will secede rather than acquiesce, they make a precedent which in turn will ruin and divide them, for a minority of their own will secede from them whenever a majority refuses to be controlled by such a minority. For instance, why not any portion of a new confederacy, a year or two hence, arbitrarily secede again, precisely as portions of the present Union now claim to secede from it? All who cherish disunion sentiments are now being educated to the exact temper of doing this. Is there such perfect identity of interests among the States to compose a new Union as to produce harmony only, and prevent renewed secession? Plainly, the central idea of secession is the essence of anarchy.

"A majority held in restraint by constitutional checks and limitations, and always changing easily with deliberate changes of popular opinions and sentiments, is the only true sovereign of a free people. Whoever reject it, does, of necessity, fly to anarchy or to despotism. Unanimity is impossible; the rule of a majority, as a permanent arrangement, is wholly inadmissible. So that, rejecting the majority principle, anarchy or despotism in some form is all that is left.

"I do not forget the position assumed by some that constitutional questions are to be decided by the Supreme Court, nor do I deny that such decisions must be binding in any case apon the parties to a suit, as to the object of that suit, while they are also entitled to very high respect and consideration in all parallel cases by all other departments of the government; and while it is obviously possible that such decision may be erroneous in any given case, still the evil effect following it, being limited to that particular case, with the chance that it may be overruled and never become a precedent for other cases, can better be borne than could the evils of a different practice.

"At the same time, the candid citizen must confess that, if the policy of the government upon the vital questions affecting the whole people is to be irrevocably fixed by the decisions of the Supreme Court, the instant they are made, as in ordinary litigation between parties in personal actions, the people will have ceased to be their own masters, unless having to that extent practically resigned their government into the hands of that eminent tribunal.

"Nor is there in this view any assault upon the court or the judges. It is a duty from which they may not shrink, to decide cases properly brought before them; and it is no fault of theirs if others seek to turn their decisions to political purposes. One section of our country believes slavery is right, and ought to be extended, while the other believes it is wrong, and ought not to be extended; and this is the only substantial dispute; and the fugitive slave clause of the Constitution, and the law for the suppression of the foreign slave trade, are each as well enforced, perhaps, as any law can ever be in a community where the moral sense of the people imperfectly supports the law itself. The great body of the people abide by the dry legal obligation in both cases, and a few break over in each. This, I think, cannot be perfectly cured, and it would be worse, in both cases, after the separation of the sections, than before. The foreign slave trade, now imperfectly suppressed, would be ultimately revived, without restriction, in one section; while fugitive slaves, now only partially surrendered, would not be surrendered at all by the other.

"Physically speaking, we cannot separate—we cannot remove our respective sections from each other, nor build an impassible wall between them. A husband and wife may be divorced, and go out of the presence and beyond the reach of the other; but the different parts of our country cannot do that. They cannot but remain face to face; and intercourse, either amicable or hostile, must continue between them. Is it possible, then, to make that intercourse more advantageous or more satisfactory after separation than before? Can aliens make treaties easier than friends can make laws? Can treaties be more faithfully enforced between aliens than laws can among friends? Suppose you go to war, you cannot fight always; and when, after much loss on both sides, and no gain on either, you cease fighting, the identical questions as to terms of intercourse are again upon you.

"This country, with its institutions, belongs to the people who inhabit it. Whenever they shall grow weary of the existing government, they can exercise their constitutional right of amending, or their revolutionary right to dismember or overthrow it. I cannot be ignorant of the fact that many worthy and patriotic citizens are desirous of having the national Constitution amended. While I make no recommendation of amendment, I fully recognize the full authority of the people over the whole subject, to be exercised in either of the modes prescribed in the instrument itself, and I should, under existing circumstances, favor, rather than oppose, a fair opportunity being afforded the people to act upon it.

"I will venture to add that to me the convention mode seems preferable, in that it allows amendments to originate with the people themselves, instead of only permitting them to take or reject propositions originated by others not especially chosen for the purpose, and which might not be precisely such as they would wish either to accept or refuse. I understand that a proposed amendment to the Constitution (which amendment, however, I have not seen), has passed Congress, to the effect that the Federal Government shall never interfere with the domestic institutions of States, including that of persons held to service. To avoid misconstruction of what I have said, I depart from my purpose not to speak of particular amendments, so far as to say that, holding such a provision to now be implied constitutional law, I have no objection to its being made express and irrevocable.

"The chief magistrate derives all his authority from the people, and they have conferred none upon him to fix the terms for the separation of the States. The people themselves, also, can do this if they choose, but the Executive, as such, has nothing to do with it. His duty is to administer the present government as it came to his hands, and to transmit it, unimpaired by him, to his successor. Why should there not be a patient confidence in the ultimate justice of the people? Is there any better or equal hope in the world? In our present differences, is either party without faith of being in the right? If the Almighty Ruler of Nations, with His eternal truth and justice, be on your side of the North, or on yours of the South, that truth and that justice will surely prevail by the judgment of this great tribunal, the American people. By the frame of the government under which we live, this same people have wisely given their public servants but little power for mischief, and have, with equal wisdom, provided for the return of that little to their own hands at very short intervals. While the people retain their virtue and vigilance, no administration, by any extreme wickedness or folly, can very seriously injure the government in the short space of four years.

"My countrymen, one and all, think calmly and well upon this whole subject. Nothing valuable can be lost by taking time.

"If there be an object to hurry any of you, in hot haste, to a step which you would never take deliberately, that object will be frustrated by taking time; but no good object can be frustrated by it.

"Such of you as are now dissatisfied still have the old Constitution unimpaired, and, on the sensitive point, the laws of your own framing under it; while the new administration will have no immediate power, if it would, to change either.

"If it were admitted that you who are dissatisfied hold the right side in the dispute, there is still no single reason for precipitate action. Intelligence, patriotism, Christianity, and a firm reliance on Him who has never yet forsaken this favored land, are still competent to adjust, in the best way, all our present difficulties.

"In your hands, my dissatisfied fellow-countrymen, and not in mine, is the momentous issue of civil war. The government will not assail you.

"You can have no conflict without being yourselves the aggressors. You have no oath registered in heaven to destroy the government; while I shall have the most solemn one to 'preserve, protect, and defend it.'

"I am loth to close. We are not enemies, but friends. We must not be enemies. Though passion may have strained, it must not break our bonds of affection.

"The mystic cords of memory, stretching from every battlefield and patriot grave to every living heart and hearthstone all over this broad land, will yet swell the chorus of the Union, when again touched, as surely as they will be, by the better angels of our nature."

Chief Justice Taney then administered the oath of office, and President Lincoln left the Capitol for the White House, where he held a public reception.

MR. LINCOLN'S ADMINISTRATION.

It is not within the purpose of this work to record the acts or sketch the characteristics of Mr. Lincoln's administration, nor to give a history of the events which succeeded his inauguration. War against the United States was declared by the rebel confederacy by firing upon the Star of the West, a vessel sent with provisions to the garrison in Fort Moultrie, in Charleston harbor; and, under orders of General Beauregard, Fort Sumter was bombarded on the 12th of April, 1861, and on the 15th, Major Anderson and his command of seventy men were compelled to evacuate. From that day war to crush the rebellion was prosecuted, with varying fortunes, until April 9th, 1865, when Gen. Robert E. Lee, Commander-in-Chief of the forces of the Confederacy, surrendered the army of Northern Virginia to Lieut.-General Grant, of the United States army. Richmond, the capital of the Confederacy, had previously been occupied, and on the 14th of April, 1865, the anniversary of the removal of the American flag from Fort Sumter—and the day appointed for the replanting of the national colors upon its battered walls—on that day, celebrated by the loyal people of the nation as the crowning hour of national victory—a Good Friday of loyal congratulations—Abraham Lincoln, who had been unanimously renominated by the Union Convention, which met at Baltimore, June 7th, 1864, and had been re-elected by a majority on the popular vote of 411,281 ballots over his competitor, Gen. Geo.

B. McClellan, was assassinated at Ford's Theatre, in the city of Washington.

Frequent threats of assassination had been reported after the discovery of the plot at Baltimore, in 1861, and some apprehensions were entertained on the day of Mr. Lincoln's re-inauguration, March 4th, 1865, but no demonstrations other than of the most enthusiastic and cordial approval were witnessed, and the President announced to a very large assemblage of the people the general policy of his second term of service, in the following remarkable

INAUGURAL ADDRESS.

"FELLOW COUNTRYMEN:—At this second appearing to take the oath of the Presidential office, there is less occasion for an extended address than there was at the first. Then a statement somewhat in detail of a course to be pursued seemed very fitting and proper. Now, at the expiration of four years, during which public declarations have constantly been called forth on every point and phase of the great contest which still absorbs the attention and engrosses the energies of the nation, little that is new could be presented.

"The progress of our arms, upon which all else chiefly depends, is as well known to the public as to myself, and it is, I trust, reasonably satisfactory and encouraging to all. With high hope for the future, no prediction in regard to it is ventured. On the occasion corresponding to this four years ago all thoughts were anxiously directed to an impending civil war. All dreaded it; all sought to avoid it. While the inaugural address was being delivered from this place, devoted to saving the Union without war, insurgent agents were in the city seeking to destroy it with war; seeking to dissolve the Union and divide the effects by negotiation.

"Both parties deprecated war, but one of them would make war rather than let the nation survive, and the other would accept war rather than let it perish, and the war came.

"One-eighth of the whole population were colored slaves, not distributed generally over the Union, but located in the southern part of it. These slaves constituted a peculiar and powerful interest. All knew that this interest was somehow the cause of this war. To strengthen, perpetuate, and extend this interest was the object for which the insurgents would rend the Union by war, while the Government claimed no right to do more than restrict the territorial enlargement of it. Neither party expected the magnitude or the duration which it has already attained. Neither anticipated that the cause of the conflict might cease even before the conflict itself should cease. Each looked for an easier triumph and a result less fundamental and astounding. Both read the same Bible and pray to the same God, and each invokes his aid against the other. It may seem strange that any man should dare to ask a just God's assistance in wringing his bread from the sweat of other men's faces. But let us judge not, that we be not judged.

"The prayer of both could not be answered. That of neither has been fully answered. The Almighty has his own purposes. 'Woe unto the world because of offences, for it must needs be that offences come, but woe to that man by whom the offence cometh.' If we shall suppose that American slavery is one of the offences, which, in the providence of God must needs come, but which, having through His appointed time, He now wills to remove, and that he gives to both North and South this terrible war as the woe due to those by whom the offence came, shall we discern therein any departure from those Divine attributes which the believer in a God always ascribe to him?

"Fondly do we hope, fervently do we pray that this mighty scourge of war may speedily pass away. Yet, if God wills that it continue until all the wealth piled by the bondsman's two hundred and fifty years of unrequited toil shall be sunk, and until every drop of blood drawn by the lash shall be paid by another drawn by the sword, as was said three thousand years ago, so still it must be said, that the judgments of the Lord are true and righteous altogether.

"With malice toward none, with charity for all, with firmness in the right, as God gives us to see the right, let us strive on to finish the work we are in, to bind up the nation's wounds, to care for him who shall have borne the battle, and for his widow and his orphans, to do all which may achieve and cherish a just and lasting peace among ourselves and with all nations."

THE ASSASSINATION.

On the evening of the Fourteenth of April, when every loyal American heart was full of joy over a great victory which promised the immediate re-establishment of peace and good order in all the insurgent States—when illuminations and processions and music, and shouts and speeches and good cheer made gay and glad all the cities and towns and villages of the loyal States, a plot to assassinate the President and his Cabinet, long premeditated and deliberately planned, culminated in the shooting of Mr. Lincoln, and in a desperate attempt to destroy the life of the Secretary of State, Mr. Seward.

It had been announced that Mr. Lincoln, Gen. Grant and a party of friends would visit Ford's Theatre, for the purpose of witnessing the performance of "Our American Cousin," by Laura Keene's dramatic company. Gen. Grant was unexpectedly called to New Jersey, and left Washington on the evening train. Mr. Lincoln went to the theatre with reluctance, explaining that he did not wish the audience to be disappointed, which, Gen. Grant having left the city, it would be if he did not go. He was accompanied by Mrs. Lincoln, Miss Clara Harris, and Maj. H. B. Rathbone. The box set apart for the President and friends was in the second tier, to the right of the audience. The assassin chose for the moment of the attack a period in the third act of the play, when there was a temporary pause in the action. The entrance from the President's box was by a door from the adjoining gallery. Having entered by deceiving the guard, the assassin found himself in a dark corridor, of which the wall made an acute angle with the door. He had previously gouged a channel from the plaster and placed near by a stout piece of board, which he now inserted between the wall and the panel of the door. Ingress then became impossible. He next turned toward the entrances to the box: these were two, as the box by a sliding partition was convertible into two when desired. The door at the bottom of the passage was open; that nearer the murderer was closed. Both had spring-locks, but their screws had been carefully loosened so as to yield to a slight pressure if necessary. In the hither door a small hole had been bored, through which to survey the interior of the box. To this the assassin resorted, after fastening the door first described, and discovered that the occupants had taken seats in an order favorable to his purpose: the President in an armed-chair nearest the audience, Mrs. Lincoln next, then, after a considerable space, Miss Clara Harris in the corner nearest the stage, and Maj. H.

R. Rathbone on a lounge along the further wall. The report of a pistol first announced the presence of an assassin, who uttered the word "Freedom," and advanced toward the front. Maj. Rathbone discerned him through the smoke, and grappled with him. The murderer dropped his pistol and aimed a violent blow with a knife at the breast of his antagonist, who caught the blow in the upper part of his left arm, but was unable to detain the desperado, though immediately seizing him again and tearing his clothes as he vaulted ten or twelve feet down upon the open stage, tangling his spur in the draped flag below the box and stumbling in his fall. Recovering himself immediately, he flourished his dagger, shouted "*Sic semper tyrannis!*" and "The South is avenged!" and retreated successfully through the familiar labyrinth of the theatre. Between the deed and the escape there was not the lapse of a minute. The hour was about half-past ten. There was only one pursuer—Col. Stuart, of Washington—from the audience, but he was outstripped.

The screams of Mrs. Lincoln first disclosed to the audience the fact that the President had been shot, when all present rose to their feet, rushing toward the stage, many exclaiming, "Hang him, hang him!" The excitement was of the wildest possible description, and of course there was an abrupt termination to the theatrical performance.

There was a rush toward the President's box, when cries were heard: "Stand back and give him air." "Has any one stimulants?" On immediate examination, it was found that Mr. Lincoln was shot in the back of the head, behind the left ear, the ball traversing an oblique line to the right ear. He was rendered instantaneously unconscious, and never knew friends or pain again. He was conveyed as soon as possible to the house of Mr. Peterson, opposite the theatre, and there expired next morning at twenty-two minutes past seven o'clock, attended by the principal members of his Cabinet, Senator Sumner, Major Hay, his Assistant Secretary, General Halleck, General Meigs, Rev. Dr. Gurley, and several surgeons. Mrs. Lincoln and her son Robert were in an adjoining apartment—the former bowed down with anguish, the latter strong enough to sustain and console her. Soon after nine o'clock the body was removed to the White House under military escort.

When the excitement in the streets of Washington created by the assassination of Mr. Lincoln and the wild rumors associated with the horrible crime, was at a fearful pitch, augmented intensity was given it by a report that Secretary Seward had also been murdered. The facts were that about ten o'clock a man on horseback rode to the Secretary's house, rang the bell, and told the servant attending upon the door that he had a prescription from Dr. Verdi, Mr. Seward's attending physician, which he must deliver to the Secretary in person, Mr. Seward being confined to his room by injuries received a few days previous, having been thrown from a carriage. The servant took him up stairs and ushered him into Mr. Frederick Seward's room, where he delivered the same message, but was assured by Mr. Seward that he could not see his father. He then started to retire, when he turned with an inaudible mutter and leveled a blow at Frederick with a slung shot. A scuffle ensued, in which the assassin used a knife, and very seriously wounded the Assistant Secretary, then rushing by him he passed through the door into the father's room. He found the Secretary in charge of his male nurse, and with a violent rush drew his knife and struck the Secretary several times. The nurse (Mr. Robinson) grappled him. Disen-

gaging himself by the use of his knife he darted out, when he encountered Major Clarence Seward, who seized him and endeavored to detain him, without knowing the horrid tragedy he had enacted. He again used his knife, but was most eager to escape, and as soon as he had cut himself loose fled to the outer door, mounted his horse, and was off before the inmates of the house could give general alarm. A surgeon was promptly called, who discovered that in haste and eagerness the assassin had missed his mark and had only inflicted a slight wound upon the Secretary's face, but had severely if not mortally wounded Frederick Seward, his skull being fractured.

The assassin at the Seward mansion was unrecognized, but the wretch who fired the shot which made the President a martyr was distinctly identified by several actors and attendants at the theater as John Wilkes Booth, an actor of some reputation, and a son of the distinguished tragedian, Junius Brutus Booth. His hat, which he left in the President's box, and a spur, which fell as he sprang upon the stage, were identified as his property.

The police force of Washington was promptly aroused and put actively at work, and every road leading out of the city was immediately picketed, but the only tidings gained of the assassin were that Booth had escaped upon a horse which was held in waiting for him by a boy in an alley near the theater.

The following day arrests were made of several persons in Washington upon suspicion of complicity with the assassination, and liberal rewards were advertised for the capture of Booth.

THE ARREST.

A large detective force, together with numerous deachments of cavalry and infantry, were, on Saturday, the 15th, quietly but industriously employed. For a few days the information seemed doubtful and conflicting, and the different heads of the respective forces were divided in opinion as to the direction of Booth's escape. Evidence began to multiply, however, that Booth, in company with some accomplice, had passed over what is known as the Navy Yard Bridge across the eastern branch of the Potomac, in the southeastern section of the city, before it was guarded by the troops after the alarm had been given of the assassination.

Parties familiar with the counties of Prince George, Charles, and St. Mary's, gave information to the proper authorities to the effect that Booth had spent much time in Charles county; that he had been in correspondence with people residing there; that it was known that nearly all of them were avowed opponents of the Government, and sympathizers with rebellion.

Col. C. L. Baker's detectives and others, and the cavalry, therefore directed their attention to the section named, and soon secured a clue of the way Booth was trying to escape. On Saturday morning, April 15, after riding hard all night, to about thirty or thirty-five miles from Washington, near Bogantown, Charles county, Maryland, Booth, accompanied by David C. Harrold, a young man of Washington, who had been a familiar associate, was taken to Dr. Mudd, living in that vicinity, to have one of his legs attended, which they represented had either been badly fractured or bruised by being thrown or having fallen from a horse. He remained several hours, his leg swelling so that he could not wear a boot, but manifesting a great desire to push on toward the Potomac. It afterward appeared that this fracture of his leg was caused by the jump from the box to the stage, after firing the fatal shot.

The detectives and cavalry hearing that two strangers had visited Dr. Mudd's house early on that morning, proceeded there two or three days after, and took the Doctor and all his family into custody. In the house was found the boot left there by Booth, and inside of the boot leg was the name of Booth, written in ink by the maker.

From there Col. Baker and Marshal Maroy, detectives, tracked Booth and Harrold toward the Potomac. They made arrests at certain places of people where the two villains were harbored from day to day and night. At some portions of the chase the officers were not more than an hour or two behind them. The assassins were aided in their escape in various ways by the rebel sympathizers, so numerous in lower Maryland. The officers were confident that Booth and Harrold could not get across the Potomac. The gunboats patroled it in the day time within sight of each other, and at night used great Drummond lights to render the surface of the river almost as bright as day. Besides all of these precautions, it was known that the Potomac flotilla had destroyed all the small boats on both shores of the Potomac, so as to prevent spies, deserters, and blockade runners from crossing either way. Now and then some man managed to hide a boat, but he was soon detected and the boat destroyed, and the owner generally arrested.

In addition, however, to all these precautions, Col. Baker had cavalry detailed on the Virginia side. They were landed at Belle Plain, at the mouth of Potomac creek, near Fredericksburg, Virginia, with instructions to look out for any suspicious persons on that side of the Potomac river.

In the meantime Booth and Harrold were making their way toward the Potomac. Either from the vigilance of the officers, or because of Booth's fractured leg, and

probably from both causes, their progress was slow after they left Mudd's house at Bogantown. They were one week crossing the tributaries of the Great Wycomico river to the place called Swan Point. While near Swan Point the detectives were very close on the heels of the fleeing men. Had they been familiar with the roads and swamps, or had they received aid from the inhabitants, it is not believed that the fugitives could have reached the Potomac river. It is supposed that on Sunday, the 23d, during the night, they crossed the Potomac in a canoe, for which they paid a very large sum to its owner to ferry them across.

Meanwhile the pursuing forces on the Virginia side of the Potomac were watchful. They consisted of a detachment of twenty-six men of Company D, 16th New York Cavalry, commanded by Lieut. Dougherty, accompanied by two of Col. Baker's experienced detectives. The cavalry landed at Belle Plain in the night and immediately started out in pursuit of Booth and his associate, having previously ascertained from a colored man that they had crossed the river into Virginia at Swan Point. The cavalry crossed the Rappahannock at Fredericksburg, and moved down the Bowling Green road, and then over to Port Royal. There they obtained news of Booth from an old colored man, who said that four men, in company with a rebel Captain, had crossed the Rappahannock a short time previous, going in the direction of Bowling Green, and added that the Captain would probably be found at that place, as he was courting a young lady there. The Captain was found at the hotel in Bowling Green and taken in custody. From him it was ascertained that Booth and Harrold were at the house of John and William Garratt, three miles back toward Port Royal, and about a quarter of a mile from the road passed by the cavalry. Returning, they arrived at Garratt's house about three o'clock on the morning of the 26th. The cavalrymen were posted around it by Lieut. Baker, a brother of Col. L. C. Baker, and Lieut. Conger, of Col. Baker's force. The two detectives accompanying the cavalry went to Garratt's house and obtained from one of the Garratt's a reluctant confession that the criminals were in the barn. Going to the barn, Baker knocked on the door with the butt of his revolver, at the same time saying, "Booth, we want you."

"Here I am," replied Booth; "who are you, Confederate or Yankee?"

Lieutenant Baker informed him who he was, and demanded his surrender, but met with a flat refusal. Quite a parley ensued, Harrold at one time expressing a desire to surrender, but Booth told him that he was a coward. Booth could see the party outside through the cracks of the barn. They could see nothing of him. He swore not to be taken alive, and declared that he could kill five men and then kill himself should they attempt to break into the barn.

Lieutenant Baker, fearing that guerrillas and paroled soldiers, with whom the country swarmed, might come to the rescue, posted cavalrymen at the end of the barn, which was filled with hay, a portion of which was pulled through a crack and lighted. The flames ran up the crack to the top of the hay-mow, over which they spread. When Booth saw the fire, he climbed up on the mow, and vainly attempted to extinguish it. He then returned to his position on the floor, between two barn doors, with his back against the hay-mow, and with two revolvers in his hands.

Meanwhile the soldiers approached the barn, and Harrold started with his pistol to surrender. Booth, with terrible oaths, denounced his cowardice. Harrold, in return, implored Booth to give up, dropped his arms and rushed out of the barn. Booth then proposed to fight each man singly, at thirty paces, and declared that the first man who came near he would shoot.

At this moment—fifteen minutes past 4 o'clock—Sergeant Boston Corbett, Company I, 16th New York Cavalry, had a sight of him through a crack, and drawing his cavalry six-shooter, fired, and Booth fell over, holding in each hand a six-barreled revolver. Detectives Conger and Baker, and Lieutenant Dougherty and Sergeant Corbett rushed into the barn and brought Booth out. The ball had entered the back part of his neck and passed entirely through his head.

He was still conscious. Detective Baker laid Booth on the ground and held his head in his lap. "It's all up now, I am gone," he pensively articulated. Booth did not deny killing the President, but showed no signs of repentance or humility. To Lieutenant Dougherty he said, "Tell my mother I died in defense of my country."

His death was not easy; at three minutes past 7 o'clock, April 26, the assassin of Abraham Lincoln breathed his last in a country barn-yard. The body was taken to Washington, identified, and secretly buried. Harrold was lodged in old Capitol Prison.

THE NATION IN MOURNING.

When on the morning of April 15th, by telegrams to the newspapers, and by official dispatches from the Secretary of War, the news, that the President had been murdered, and that a plot to murder other prominent Government officers had been frustrated only by accident, was communicated to the people, the nation's joy was turned to mourning. Flags which had been hung out as tokens of rejoicing were draped in mourning—business was suspended—emblems of sorrow were displayed on nearly every dwelling-house in the loyal States, and public meetings—spontaneous gatherings of the people—expressive of unfeigned regret and intense indignation, were held in a large majority of their cities, towns and villages. A meeting of Congressmen and others was convened at the Capitol on Monday, April 17, 1865, at noon. The Hon. Lafayette S. Foster, of Connecticut, President pro tem. of the Senate, was called to the Chair, and Hon. Schuyler Colfax was chosen Secretary.

On motion of Senator Sumner, of Massachusetts, a Committee of five members from each house was ordered to report at four o'clock in the afternoon, what action was fitting for a meeting relative to arrangements for the funeral of the deceased President.

The Chairman appointed Senators Sumner, Harris, Johnson, Ramsey and Conness, and Representatives Washburn, Smith, Schenck, Pike and Coffroth; and, on motion of Mr. Schenck, the Chairman and Secretary of the meeting were added to the Committee.

The meeting then adjourned until 4 P. M.

The meeting again convened, pursuant to adjournment. Mr. Sumner, from the Committee heretofore appointed, reported that they had selected as pall-bearers, on the part of the Senate, Messrs. Foster, Morgan, Johnson, Yates, Wade and Conness; on the part of the House, Messrs. Dawes, Coffroth, Smith, Colfax, Worthington, and Washburne.

They recommended the appointment of one member of Congress, from each State and Territory, to act as Congressional Committee, to accompany the remains of the late President to Illinois; and presented the following names as the Committee, the Chairman of the meeting to have authority to appoint, hereafter, for States and Territories, not represented to-day, from which members may be present at the Capitol by the day of the funeral:

Maine, Mr. Pike; New Hampshire, Mr. Rollins; Massachusetts, Mr. Sumner; Vermont, Mr. Foote; Rhode Island, Mr. Anthony; Connecticut, Mr. Dixon; New York, Mr. Harris; Pennsylvania, Mr. Cowan; Ohio, Mr. Schenck; Kentucky, Mr. Smith; Indiana, Mr. Julian; Illinois, Delegation; Michigan, Mr. Chandler; Wisconsin, ——; California, Mr. Shannon; Minnesota, Mr. Ramsey; Oregon, Mr. Williams; Kansas, Mr. Clarke; West Virginia, Mr. Willey; Nevada, Mr. Nye; Nebraska, Mr. Hitchcock; Colorado, Mr. Bradford; Dakota, Mr. Tweed; Idaho, Mr. Wallace.

The Committee recommended that the following resolution be adopted:

Resolved, That the Sergeants-at-Arms of the Senate and House, with their respective assistants, be requested to attend the Committee accompanying the remains of our late President, and make all necessary arrangements.

All of which was concurred in unanimously.

Mr. Sumner, from the Committee, also reported the following, which was agreed to:

The members of the Senate and House now assembled in Washington, humbly confessing their dependence upon Almighty God, who rules all that is done for human good, make haste, at this informal meeting, to express the emotions with which they have been filled by the appalling tragedy, which has deprived the nation of its head, and covered the land with mourning; and in further declaration of their sentiments, unanimously

Resolved, That in testimony of their veneration and affection for the illustrious dead, who has been permitted, under Providence, to do so much for his country and for liberty, they will attend his funeral services, and by an appropriate committee will accompany his remains to their place of burial, in the State for which he was taken for national service.

THE BODY IN STATE AT THE WHITE HOUSE.

On the 18th of April arrangements were completed which permitted the people of the District of Columbia to pay their last personal tokens of respect and affection to the martyred President. The body, which had been embalmed, lay then in state at the White House. It had been publicly announced that the doors would not be opened till 10 o'clock that morning, but the crowd began to gather at the gates by 8:30, and by 9:30 the line, four and six persons deep, was nearly a quarter of a mile long. The arrangements at the house for entrance and exit were: entrance at the main door, thence to the Green Room, thence to the East Room, and out at the window by the customary steps. It was estimated that 25,000 persons passed through the rooms, and that half as many more, seeing the immense throng, left without trying to get in. The approaches were guarded by a battalion of Veteran Reserves. The East Room, in which the remains were laid, was decorated in mourning, under the supervision of Mr. John Alexander. The windows at either end of the room were draped with black barege, the frames of the mirrors between the windows, as well as those over the marble mantles, being heavily draped with the same material. The heavy gildings of the frames were entirely enshrouded, while the plates of the mirrors were covered with white crape. The chandeliers at the western and southern ends of the room were also draped with mourning—the central chandelier having been removed to make room for the catafalque. This was very handsome; the dais or platform, on which the coffin rested, was raised three feet from the floor, and covered with evergreens and japonicas.

The corpse was in charge of army and navy officers. A limited number of persons were admitted to the house at a time, and these were required to pass through as rapidly as was consistent with decency and propriety. The expressions and appearance of the people, as they looked for the last time on the face of the honored dead, were conclusive, as a reporter for the *New York Times* declared that the great majority regarded the President's death as a personal and individual loss, as well as a national calamity. Hundreds addressed words of farewell to the cold and inanimate body; and thousands passed from the platform with weeping eyes. Every class, race and condition of society was represented in the throng of mourners, and the sad tears and farewells of whites and blacks were mingled by the coffin of him to whom humanity was everywhere the same. The most touching exhibitions of sorrow were made by many whose dress marked them as of the poorer classes of society. "He was the poor man's friend," was a very common remark.

The vast throng outside, as well as inside, was quiet, orderly and reverent, all day, though two to three hours was the average period of waiting for admission, and many waited even five and six hours.

The clerks of each of the public departments were marshalled at 11 o'clock, under their respective heads of bureaus, and marched in grand and solemn procession into the White House and past the body in the east room.

The features of Mr. Lincoln retained their sweet, placid, natural expression, and the discoloration caused by the wound was so slight as not to amount to a disfigurement.

A silver plate upon the coffin over the breast bore the following inscription:

ABRAHAM LINCOLN,
SIXTEENTH PRESIDENT OF THE UNITED STATES,
Born July 12, 1809,
Died April 15, 1865.

PREPARATIONS FOR THE FUNERAL.

Upon consultation between the President, members of the Cabinet and of Congress, it was determined that the funeral obsequies at the Capital should be observed on the 19th of April. The acting Secretary of State accordingly issued the following address:

"*To the People of the United States*:

"The undersigned is directed to announce that the funeral ceremonies of the lamented Chief Magistrate will take place at the Executive Mansion, in this city, at 12 o'clock noon on Wednesday, the 19th instant.

"The various religious denominations throughout the country are invited to meet in their respective places of worship at that hour for the purpose of solemnizing the occasion with appropriate ceremonies.

"(Signed) W. HUNTER,
"Acting Secretary of State.

"DEPARTMENT OF STATE, WASHINGTON, April 17, 1865."

The general arrangements for the exercises were committed to Assistant Secretary Harrington, of the Treasury Department, assisted by Maj. B. B. French, Commissioner of Public Buildings, Gen. Augur having command of the military escort.

Orders were issued by the heads of the various departments respecting the observance of the solemn occasion.

That the Navy Department be closed and work suspended in all navy-yards and naval stations, and on all vessels of the United States. The flags of all vessels and at all the navy-yards and stations and marine barracks, to be kept at half-mast during the day; and at 12 o'clock M., twenty-one minute guns to be fired by the senior officer of each squadron and the commandants of each of the navy-yards and stations. Vice-Admiral D. G. Farragut and Rear-Admiral Wm. B. Shubrick were designated to make the necessary arrangements on the part of the navy and marine corps for attending the funeral.

That the State Department be closed, and Acting Secretary Hunter directed that all persons subject to the orders of the department wear crape for six months upon the left arm.

The Postmaster-General directed that all the post-offices in the United States be closed from 11 till 3, and that all work therein be suspended.

Secretary Usher directed that the Interior Department be closed; and sent orders to the various Indian agencies, land offices, pension agencies, etc., in connection with his department, for a proper observance of the day by a suspension of all business.

The Treasury Department was ordered to be closed, and Secretary McCulloch communicated to the various sub-treasuries his patriotic wishes and desires.

The Secretary of War and Lieut.-Gen. Grant directed that the headquarters of every department, post, station, fort and arsenal be draped in mourning for thirty days, and appropriate funeral honors be paid by every army in every department, and at every military post, and at the Military Academy at West Point, to the memory of the late illustrious Chief Magistrate of the nation, and Commander-in-Chief of its armies; and that the officers of the armies of the United States wear the badge of mourning on their left arm, and on their swords, and the colors of their commands and regiments to be put in mourning for the peried of six months; and further, that on Wednesday, the 19th, the national flag be everywhere displayed at half-mast, and at dawn thirteen guns be fired at every fort, arsenal and station, and at West Point, and afterwards at intervals of thirty minutes, between the rising and setting of the sun, a single gun, and at the close of the day a national salute of thirty-six guns.

The order of the funeral ceremonies was decided upon as follows:

Reading a portion of the Scriptures, by Rev. Dr. Hall.
Opening prayer, by Bishop Simpson.
Funeral address, by Rev. Dr. Gurley.
Closing prayer, by Rev. Dr. Gray.

The corpse to be conveyed to the Capitol, where Dr. Gurley would repeat the service and pronounce the benediction.

OFFICIAL PROGRAMME.

Arrangements at Washington for the funeral solemnities of the late Abraham Lincoln, President of the United States, who died at the seat of government, on Saturday, the 15th day of April, 1865:

WAR DEPARTMENT,
ADJUTANT-GENERAL'S OFFICE,
WASHINGTON, April 17, 1865.

The following order of arrangements is directed:

ORDER OF THE PROCESSION.

Funeral Escort in Column of March.
One Regiment of Cavalry.
Two Batteries of Artillery.
Battalion of Marines.
Two Regiments of Infantry.

Commander of the Escort and Staff.
Dismounted Officers of the Marine Corps.
Navy and Army in the order named.
Mounted Officers of the Marine Corps.
Navy and Army in the order named.
All Military Officers to be in uniform, with side arms.

CIVIC PROCESSION.

Marshal.
Clergy in attendance.
Surgeon General of the United States and Physicians to the deceased.
Pall Bearers on the part of the Senate:
Mr. Foster, of Connecticut.
Mr. Morgan, of New York.
Mr. Johnson, of Maryland.
Mr. Yates, of Illinois.
Mr. Wade, of Ohio.
Mr. Conness, of California.
The Hearse.
Pall Bearers on the part of the House of Representatives:
Mr. Davis, of Massachusetts; Mr. Coffroth, of Pennsylvania; Mr. Smith, of Kentucky; Mr. Colfax, of Indiana; Mr. Worthington, of Navada; Mr. Washburne, of Illinois.
Army.
Lieutenant General U. S. Grant, Major General H. W. Halleck, Brigadier General W. A. Nichols.
Navy.
Vice Admiral D. G. Farragut, Rear Admiral W. B. Shubrick, Colonel Jacob Zeiler, of the Marine Corps.
Civilians.
O. H. Browning, George Ashmun, Thomas Corwin, Simon Cameron.
Family.
Relatives.
The delegations of the States of Illinois and Kentucky as mourners.
The President.
The Cabinet Ministers.
The Diplomatic Corps.
Ex-Presidents.
The Chief Justice and Associate Justices of the Supreme Court.

The Senate of the United States, preceded by its officers.
The House of Representatives of the United States, preceded by its officers.
Governors of the several States and Territories.
Legislatures of the several States and Territories.
The Federal Judiciary and the Judiciary of the several States and Territories.
The Assistant Secretary of State, Treasury, War and Navy, and the Assistant Postmasters General, and the Assistant Attorney General.
Officers of the Smithsonian Institution.
The Members and Officers of the Sanitary and Christian Commissions.
Corporate Authorities of Washington and other cities.
Delegations of the several States.
The Reverend the Clergy of the various denominations.
The Clerks and Employees of the several Departments and Bureaus, preceded by the Bands of such Bureaus and their respective Chief Clerks.
Such societies as may wish to join the procession.
Citizens and strangers.

The troops designated to form the escort will assemble in the avenue north of the President's House, and form in line precisely at eleven o'clock A. M. on Wednesday, the 19th instant, with the left resting on Fifteenth street.

The procession will move precisely at two o'clock, on the conclusion of the religious services at the Executive Mansion, appointed to commence at twelve o'clock, noon, when minute guns will be fired by detachments of artillery stationed near St. John's Church, the City Hall, and at the Capitol. At the same hour the bells of the several churches in Washington, Georgetown and Alexandria will be tolled.

At sunrise on Wednesday, the 19th instant, a federal salute will be fired from the military stations in the vicinity of Washington, minute guns between the hours of twelve and three o'clock, and a national salute at the setting of the sun.

The usual badge of mourning will be worn on the left arm and on the hilt of the sword.

By order of the Secretary of War.

W. A. NICHOLS,
Assistant Adjutant General.

THE FUNERAL AT THE CAPITAL.

As early as 8 o'clock on the morning of the 19th of April, people began to throng the avenue, and by 11 o'clock many thousands were assembled in the vicinity of the departments and the Executive mansion. The avenue, between Fifteenth and Seventeenth streets, was kept clear by a strong guard of cavalry, for the purpose of forming the procession, though many of the societies had to wait on the side streets for hours. The arrangements made by the committee were carried out with accuracy. No one was allowed to enter the grounds of the Executive mansion save such as had been provided with tickets, which included enough, however, to fill the great east room, where the body lay in state. It was intended that the attendance upon the funeral services should be of a highly representative character, and the intention was carried out with great success.

At about 11 o'clock the various distinguished bodies and committees began to arrive, and to be ushered into their appropriate positions in the east room. Several tiers of low seats, or standing places, elevated one above another, just sufficient to give all a good view, had been erected on the east side and both ends of the room, and all covered with black muslin. On the west side of the room, against the door leading to the main corridor, were placed fifteen chairs, all draped, which were especially reserved by the arrangement committee for the use of the press. This grand east room was hung with black everywhere. All glitter and gay color, save in the carpet, had been covered with the emblem of grief. The only relief from the mournful shade which met the eye were the white silk sashes of the marshals and committees, the rich silver ornamentation of the coffin, and the white japonicas, roses and green leaves, which shed their perfume as incense over the dead.

The first to enter were the officiating clergymen, Rev. Dr. Hall, Rector of the Epiphany, Bishop Simpson, of the Methodist Episcopal Church, Rev. P. D. Gurley, of the New York Avenue Presbyterian Church, the President's Pastor, and Rev. E. H. Gray, Chaplain of the Senate and Pastor of the E street Baptist Church. Soon after came the merchants' committee of New York, followed by the committee of the Union League. They took position on the platform at the north end of the room. At 11:25 the Mayor of Washington and the Common Council entered, escorting the committee of the New York Common Council; also, Mayor Lincoln and a committee from Boston, and a like committee from Philadelphia. Then came the officers of the Senate and House of Representatives, who took appropriate positions; the officers and members of the Christian and Sanitary Commissions; the Assistant Secretaries; the delegations from Kentucky and Illinois, the States of the President's birth and residence, who were designated as mourners; Gov. Fenton of New York, Andrew of Massachusetts, Parker of New Jersey, Brough of Ohio, Oglesby of Illinois, Buckingham of Connecticut, and their staffs; the diplomatic corps in full court dress; the members of the Senate and House of Representatives; Admirals Gregory, Porter, Shubrick, and Goldsborough; the Supreme Court in the persons of Chief Justice Chase, Nelson, Davis, and Swayne; ex-Vice-President Hamlin; the pall-bearers, twenty-two in number, then Grant and Farragut, arm in arm, Burnside and Hunter, Gen. Dyer of the Ordnance Department, six lady mourners, the only ladies present, save one or two of the nurses of the household, Mrs. Stanton, Mrs. Usher, Mrs. Welles, Mrs. Dennison, Mrs. Sprague, and Miss Nettie Chase.

At 12 o'clock President Johnson, escorted by the venerable Preston King and the members of the Cabinet, entered and took their places on the right of the coffin. Private Secretaries Nicolay and Hay, and Capt. Robert Lincoln, the President's oldest son, and only member of the family present, then Gen. Todd, of Dakotah, and relatives of the family, who were seated near the foot of the catafalque.

The room was now full. The attendants upon the ceremonies had all arrived, and the scene was of a very imposing character.

At ten minutes past 12, Rev. Mr. Hall opened the services by reading from the Episcopal burial service as follows:

"'I am the resurrection and the life, saith the Lord; he that believeth in me, though he were dead, yet shall he live; and whosoever liveth and believeth in me shall never die.'—John xi., 25, 26.

"'I know that my Redeemer liveth, and that He shall stand at the latter day upon the earth, and though after my skin worms destroy this body, yet in my flesh shall I see God, whom I shall see for myself, and mine eyes shall behold, and not another.'—Job. xix., 25, 26, 27.

"We brought nothing into this world, and it is certain we can carry nothing out. 'The Lord gave and the Lord hath taken away. Blessed be the name of the Lord.'—I. Tim. vi., 6; Job. i., 21.

"Lord, let me know my end and the number of my days, that I may be certified how long I have to live. Behold Thou hast made my days as it were but a span long, and mine age is even as nothing in respect of Thee.

And verily every man living is altogether vanity; for man walketh in a vain shadow, and disquieteth himself in vain. He heapeth up riches, and cannot tell who shall gather them. And now, Lord, what is my hope? Truly my hope is ever in Thee; deliver me from all my offences, and make me not a rebuke unto the foolish. When Thou, with rebukes, doth chasten man for sin, Thou makest his beauty to consume away, like as it were a moth fretting a garment. Every man is, therefore, but vanity. Hear my prayer, O Lord, and with Thine ears consider my calling. Hold not Thy peace at my tears, for I am a stranger with Thee, and a sojourner, as all my fathers were. O, spare me a little, that I may recover my strength before I go hence and be no more seen. Lord, Thou hast been our refuge from one generation to another. Before the mountains were brought forth or even the earth and the world were made, thou art God from ever lasting and world without end. Thou turnest man to destruction; again thou sayest, come again, ye children of men, for a thousand years in thy sight are but as yesterday, seeing that it is past as a watch in the night. As soon as thou scatterest them, they are even as sheep and fade away suddenly like the grass. In the morning it is green and groweth up, but in the evening it is cut down, dried up and withered. For we consume away in Thy displeasure, and are afraid at Thy wrathful indignation. Thou hast set our misdeeds before Thee, and our secret sins in the light of Thy countenance; for when Thou art angry all our days are gone. We bring our years to an end as it were a tale that is told. The days of our age are threescore years and ten, and though men be so strong that they come to fourscore years, yet is their strength then but labor and sorrow, so soon passeth it away, and we are gone. So teach us to number our days that we may apply our hearts unto wisdom. Glory be to the Father and to the Son and to the Holy Ghost; as it was in the beginning, is now, and ever shall be, world without end. Amen."

Then was read the lesson from the 15th chapter of St. Paul to the Corinthians, beginning with the 20th verse.

Right Rev. Bishop Simpson, of the Methodist Episcopal Church, then offered an affecting prayer, after which Rev. Dr. Gurley, of the New York Avenue Presbyterian Church, in which the deceased President had worshipped, delivered the following funeral sermon:

DR. GURLEY'S SERMON.

"As we stand here to-day, mourners around this coffin and around the lifeless remains of our beloved Chief Magistrate, we recognize and we adore the sovereignty of God. His throne is in the heavens, and His kingdom ruleth over all. He hath done and He hath permitted to be done whatsoever He pleased. Clouds and darkness are round about Him; righteousness and judgment are the habitation of His throne. His way is in the sea, and His path in the great waters, and His footsteps are not known. Canst thou by searching find out God? Canst thou find out the Almighty unto perfection? It is as high as Heaven—what canst thou do? Deeper than Hell—what canst thou know? The measure thereof is longer than the earth and broader than the sea. If He cut off and shut up, or gather together, then who can hinder Him—for He knoweth vain men, He seeth wickedness: also will He not then consider it! We bow before His Infinite Majesty—we bow, we weep, we worship. There reason fails with all her powers—there faith prevails and love adores. It was a cruel, cruel hand, that dark hand of the assassin, which smote our honored wise, and noble President, and filled the land with sorrow. But above and beyond that hand, there is another, which we must see and acknowledge. It is the chastening hand of a wise and faithful Father. He gives us this bitter cup, and the cup that our Father has given us shall we not drink it?

God of the just, Thou givest us the cup,
We yield to Thy behest, and drink it up.

"'Whom the Lord loveth, he chasteneth.' Oh, how these blessed words have cheered and strengthened and sustained us through all these long and weary years of civil strife, while our friends and brothers on so many ensanguined fields were falling and dying for the cause of Liberty and Union. Let them cheer and strengthen and sustain us to-day. True, this new sorrow and chastening has come in such an hour and in such a way as we thought not, and it bears the impress of a rod that is very heavy, of mystery that is very deep, that such a life should be sacrificed at such a time, by such a foul and diabolical agency; that the man at the head of the nation, whom the people had learned to trust with a confiding and loving confidence, and upon whom more than upon any other were centered, under God, our best hopes for the true and speedy pacification of the country, the restoration of the Union, and the return of harmony and love—that he should be taken from among us, and taken just as the prospect of peace was brightly opening upon our torn and bleeding country, and just as he was beginning to be animated and gladdened with the hope of ere long enjoying with the people the blessed fruit and reward of his and their toils, care and patience, and self-sacrificing devotion to the interests of Liberty and the Union. Oh, it is a mysterious and a most afflicting visitation. But it is our Father in Heaven, the God of our fathers and our God, who permits us to be so suddenly and sorely smitten, and we know that His judgments are right, and that in faithfulness He has afflicted us in the midst of our rejoicings. We needed this stroke, this dealing, this discipline, and therefore He has sent it. Let us remember, our affliction has not come forth of the dust, and our trouble has not sprung out of the ground. Through and beyond all second causes, let us see the sovereign permissive agency of the great first cause. It is his prerogative to bring light out of darkness, and good out of evil. Surely the wrath of man shall praise Him, and the remainder of wrath He will restrain. In the light of a clearer day, we may yet see that the wrath which planned and perpetrated the death of the President was overruled by Him whose judgments are unsearchable, and his ways past finding out, for the highest welfare of all those interests which are so dear to the Christian patriot and philanthropist, and for which a loyal people have made such an unexampled sacrifice of treasure and of blood. Let us not be faithless, but believing. 'Blind unbelief is prone to err and scan His works in vain. God is His own interpreter, and he will make it plain.' We will wait for His interpretation; and we will wait in faith, nothing doubting. He who has led us so well, and defended and prospered us so wonderfully during the last four years of toil and struggle and sorrow, will not forsake us now. He may chasten, but He will not destroy. He may purify more and more in the furnace of trial, but He will not consume us. No, no. He has chosen us, as He did his people of old, in the furnace of affliction, and He has said of us, as He said of them, this people have reformed. For myself they shall show forth my praise. Let our principal anxiety now be that this new sorrow may be a sanctified sorrow, that it may lead us to deeper repentance, to a more humbling sense of our dependence upon God, and to the more unreserved consecration of ourselves and all that we have to the cause of truth and justice, of law and order, of liberty and good government, of pure and undefiled religion. Then, though weeping may endure for a night, joy will come in the morning. Blessed be God. Despite of the great, and sudden, and temporary darkness, the morning has begun to dawn, the morning of a bright and glorious day, such as our country has never seen. That day will come, and not tarry, and the death of a hundred Presidents and their Cabinets can never, never prevent it. While we are thus hopeful, however, let us also be humble. The occasion calls us to prayerful and tearful humiliation. It demands of us that we lie low, very low, before Him who has smitten us for our sins.

"O! that all our rulers, and all our people, may bow in the dust to-day beneath the chastening hand of God, and may their voices go up to Him as one voice, and their hearts go up to Him as one heart, pleading with Him for mercy, for grace to sanctify our great and sore bereavement, and for wisdom to guide us in this our time of need. Such a united cry and pleading will not be in vain. It will enter into the ear and heart of Him who sits upon the throne, and He will say to us, as to His ancients, 'In a little wrath, I hid my face from thee for a moment, but with everlasting kindness will I have mercy upon thee, saith the Lord, thy Redeemer.' I have said that the people confided in the late lamented President with a full and a loving confidence. Probably no man since the days of WASHINGTON was ever so deeply and firmly imbedded and enshrined in the very hearts of the people as ABRAHAM LINCOLN. Nor was it a mistaken confidence and love. He deserved it; deserved it well; deserved it all. He merited it by his character, by his acts, and by the tenor and tone and spirit of his life. He was simple and sincere, plain and honest, truthful and just, benevolent and kind. His perceptions were quick and clear, his judgments were calm and accurate, and his purposes were good and pure beyond a question, always and everywhere. He aimed and endeavored to be right and to do right. His integrity was thorough, all-pervading, all controlling and incorruptible. It was the same in every place and relation, in the consideration and control of matters great or small, the same firm and steady principle of power and beauty, that shed a clear and crowning lustre upon all his other excellencies of mind and heart, and recommended him to his fellow-citizens as the man who, in a time of unexampled peril, when the very life of the nation was at stake, should be chosen to occupy in the country, and for the country, its highest post of power and responsibility. How wisely and well, how purely and faithfully, how firmly and steadily, how justly and successfully, he did occupy that post and meet its grave demands, in cirsumstances of surpassing trial and difficulty, is known to you all—known to the country and the world; he comprehended from the first the perils to which treason had exposed the freest and best government on the earth—the vast interests of liberty and humanity that were to be saved or lost forever in the urgent impending conflict. He rose to the dignity and momentousness of the occasion, saw his duty as the Chief Magistrate of a great and imperiled people, and he determined to do his duty, and his whole duty, seeking the guidance and leaning upon the arm of Him of whom it is written—He giveth power to the faint, and to them that have no might. He increaseth the strength. Yes, he leaned upon His arm. He recognized and received the truth that the kingdom is the Lord's, and He is the governor among the nations. He remembered that God is in history, and he felt that nowhere had His hand and his mercy been so marvelously conspicuous as in the history of this nation. He hoped and he prayed that that same hand would continue to guide us, and that same mercy continue to abound to us in the time of our greatest need. I speak what I know and testify what I have often heard him say, when I affirm that guidance and mercy were the props on which he humbly and habitually leaned. That they were the best hope he had for himself and for his country. Hence when he was leaving home in Illinois, and coming to this city to take his seat in the Executive Chair of a disturbed and troubled nation, he said to the old and tried friends who gathered tearfully around him, and bade him farewell. I leave you with this request—pray for me. They did pray for him, and millions of others prayed for him. Nor did they pray in vain. Their prayers were heard, and the answer appears in all his subsequent history. It shines forth with a heavenly radiance in the whole course and tenor of his administration from its commencement to its close. God raised him up for a great and glorious mission, furnished him for his work, and aided him in its accomplishment. Nor was it merely by strength of mind and honesty of heart and purity and pertinacity of purpose, that He furnished him. In addition to these things He gave him a calm and abiding confidence in the overruling providence of God, and in the ultimate triumph of truth and righteousness through the power and the blessing of God. This confidence strengthened him in all his hours of anxiety and toil, and inspired him with calm and cheering hope when others were inclined to despondency and gloom.

"Never shall I forget the emotion with which he said in this very room to a company of clergymen and others who called to pay him their respects in the darkest day of our civil conflict: 'Gentlemen, my hope of success in this great and terrible struggle rests on that immutable foundation, the justice and goodness of God, and when events are very threatening and prospects very dark, I still hope that in some way which man cannot see, all will be well in the end, because our cause is just and God is on our side.' Such was his sublime and holy faith, and it was an anchor to his soul both sure and steadfast. It made him firm and strong. It emboldened him in the pathway of duty, however rugged and perilous it might be. It made him valiant for the right, for the cause of God and humanity, and it held him in steady, patient and unswerving adherence to a policy of administration which he thought, and which we all now think, both God and humanity required him to adopt. We admired and loved him on many accounts, for strong and various reasons. We admired his child-like simplicity; his freedom from guile and deceit; his staunch and sterling integrity; his kind and forgiving temper; his industry and patience; his persistent, self-sacrificing devotion to all the duties of his eminent position, from the least to the greatest; his readiness to hear and consider the cause of the poor and humble, suffering and oppressed; his charity; his inflexible purpose, that what freedom had gained in our terrible civil strife should never be lost, and that the end of the war should be the end of slavery, and as a consequence of rebellion; his readiness to spend and be spent for the attainment of such a triumph—a triumph, the blessed fruits of which should be as wide-spreading as the earth, and as enduring as the sun. All these things commanded and fixed our admiration, and the admiration of the world, and stamped upon his character and life the unmistakable impress of greatness. But more sublime than any and all of these, more holy and influential, more beautiful and strong and sustaining was his abiding confidence in God, and in the final triumph of truth and righteousness through Him and for His sake. This was his noblest virtue, his grandest principle, the secret alike of his strength, his patience and his success. This, it seems to me, after being near him steadily and with him often for more than four years, is the principle by which more than by any other, he being dead, yet speaketh. Yes, by his steady, enduring confidence in God, and in the complete ultimate success of the cause of God, which is the cause of humanity, more than in any other way, does he now speak to us and to the nation he loved and served so well. By this he speaks to his successor in office, and charges him to have faith in God. By this he speaks to the members of his Cabinet, the men with whom he counseled so often and associated with so long, and he charges them to have faith in God. By this he speaks to all who occupy positions of influence and authority in these sad and tumultuous times, and he charges them all to have faith in God. By this he speaks to this great people as they sit in sackcloth to-day, and weep for him with a bitter wailing, and refuse to be comforted, and he charges them to have faith in God; and by this he will speak through the ages, and to all rulers and people in every land, and His message to them will be, Cling to liberty and right, battle for them, bleed for them, die for them if need be, and have confidence in God. O, that the voice of this testimony may sink down into our hearts to-day and every day, and into the hearts of the nation, and exert appropriate influence upon our feelings, our faith, our patience and our devotion to the cause, now dearer to us than ever before, because consecrated by the blood of its conspicuous defender, its truest and most fondly-trusted friend.

"He is dead! But the God in whom he trusted lives, and He can guide and strengthen his successor as He guided and strengthened him. He is dead! But the memory of his virtues; of his wise and patriotic counsels and labors; of his calm and steady faith in God, lives as precious, and will be a power for good in the country quite down to the end of time. He is dead! But the cause he so ardently loved; so ably, patiently, toward those who questioned the correctness of his opinions and the wisdom of his policy; his wonderful skill in reconciling differences among the friends of the Union, leading them away from abstractions and inducing them to work together, and harmoniously, for the common weal; his true and enlarged philanthropy, that knew no distinction of color or race, but regarded all men as brethren, and endowed alike by their creator with certain inalienable rights, amongst which are life, liberty, and the pursuit of happiness; faithfully represented and defended, not for himself only, not for us only, but for all people in all their coming generations till time shall be no more. That cause survives his fall and will survive it. The light of its brightening prospects flashes cheeringly to-day athwart the gloom occasioned by his death, and the language of God's united providences is telling us that, though the friends of liberty die, liberty itself is immortal. There is no assassin strong enough and no weapon deadly enough to quench its inexhaustible life, or arrest its onward march to the conquest and empire of the world. This is our confidence and this is our consolation, as we weep and mourn to-day; though our beloved President is slain, our beloved country is saved; and so we sing of mercy as well as of judgment. Tears of gratitude mingle with those of sorrow, while there is also the dawning of a brighter, happier day upon our stricken and weary land.

"God be praised that our fallen chief lived long enough to see the day dawn, and the day-star of joy and peace arise upon the nation. He saw it and was glad. Alas! alas! He only saw the dawn when the sun has risen, full-orbed and glorious, and a happy, reunited people are rejoicing in its light. It will shine upon his grave, but that grave will be a precious and a consecrated spot. The friends of Liberty and of the Union will repair to it in years and ages to come, to pronounce the memory of its occupant blessed, and, gathering from his very ashes, and from the rehearsal of his deeds and virtues, fresh incentives to patriotism, they will there renew their vows of fidelity to their country and their God.

"And now I know not that I can more appropriately conclude this discourse, which is but a sincere and simple utterance of the heart, than by addressing to our departed President, with some slight modification, the language which Tacitus, in his life of Agricola, addresses to his venerable and departed father-in-law: 'With you we may now congratulate. You are blessed not only because your life was a career of glory, but because you were released when your country was safe, it was happiness to die. We have lost a parent, and in our distress it is now an addition to our heartfelt sorrow that we had it not in our power to commune with you on the bed of languishing and receive your lasting embrace. Your dying words would have been ever dear to us. Your commands we should have treasured up, and graven them on our hearts. This sad comfort we have lost, and the wound, for that reason, pierces deeper. From the world of spirits behold your disconsolate family and people. Exalt our minds from fond regret and unavailing grief to the contemplation of your virtues. Those we must not lament. It were impiety to sully them with a tear. To cherish their memory, to embalm them with our praises, and so far as we can to emulate your bright example, will be the truest mark of our respect, the best tribute we can offer. Your wife will thus preserve the memory of the best of husbands; and thus your children will prove their filial piety; by dwelling constantly on your works and actions, they will have an illustrious character before their eyes; and not content with the bare image of your mortal frame, they will have what is more valuable—the form and features of your mind. Busts and statues, like their originals, are frail and perishable. The soul is formed of finer elements, and its inward form is not to be expressed by the hand of an artist. With unconscious matter our manners and our morals may, in some degree, trace the resemblance. All of you that gained our love and raised our admiration still subsist, and will ever subsist, preserved in the minds of men, the register of ages; and the records of fame of others who figured on the stage of life, and were the worthiest of a former day, will sink for want of a faithful historian into the common lot of oblivion, inglorious and unremembered. But you, our lamented friend and head, delineated with truth and fairly consigned to posterity, will survive yourself and triumph over the injuries of time."

Rev. E. H. Gray, D.D., pastor of the E-street Baptist Church, closed the solemn services with prayer.

At the conclusion of this sermon the corpse was removed to the hearse, which was in front of the Executive Mansion, and at 2 o'clock the procession was formed. It took the line of Pennsylvania-avenue. The streets were kept clear of all encumbrances, but the sidewalks were densely lined with people from the White House to the Capitol, a distance of a mile and a half. The roofs, porticos, windows and all elevated points were occupied by interested spectators. As the procession started minute guns were fired near St. John's Church, the City Hall and the Capitol. The bells of all the churches in the city and of the various engine-houses were tolled.

First in the order of procession was a detachment of colored troops, then followed white regiments of infantry and bodies of artillery and cavalry, navy, marine and army officers on foot; the pall-bearers in carriages next; the hearse, drawn by six white horses—the coffin prominent to every beholder. The floor on which it rested was strewn with evergreens, and the coffin covered with white flowers. Then followed physicians of the late President, then the grand hearse and the guard of honor and the pall-bearers, Capt. ROBERT LINCOLN and little TAD, the President's favorite son, in a carriage, and TOMMY behind. Mrs. LINCOLN was not present at either the ceremony or in the procession, illness preventing. The mourners, the delegations from Illinois and Kentucky, came next in order, and then President JOHNSON in a carriage, with Hon. PRESTON KING and the Cabinet Ministers. The carriages on this part of the line were flanked by a strong cavalry guard, with drawn sabers. Then came carriages with the Diplomatic Corps, Judges, Senators and others; then members of the House of Representatives on foot; the officers of the House; the New York delegation; the Massachusetts delegation, delegations from other States, Masons, Knight Templars, Perseverance Fire Company of Philadelphia, Catholic clergy, nine delegations, department clerks two thousand strong, Gen. MEIGS and staff and the Quartermasters department brigade, a regiment of Fenians, the Treasury regiment, Gen. McCallum and staff, and a brigade of the employes of the United States military railroads, all wearing an appropriate badge. Next a large delegation from Alexandria, with a car on which was painted, "Alexandria mourns the national loss." Then followed one of the saddest scenes in the entire column, a battalion of scarred and maimed veterans, with bandaged limbs and heads, with an arm or leg gone, but hobbling along on crutches, determined that their homage to their chief should be as sincere as that of their companions. Then more firemen and Sons of Temperance, with a battalion of soldiers, in full regalia of the Sons; then Coloied Benevolent Associations with their banners draped and their walk and mein the very impersonation of sorrow.

The procession was almost two hours in passing a given point, and the head of it had begun to disperse at the Capitol before the rear of the column had passed beyond the Treasury Department.

On the arrival at the eastern gate of the Capitol, the remains were conveyed into the rotunda, where a catafalque like that in the Executive Mansion had been erected to receive them. Here the attendants assembled, and amid profound silence Rev. Dr. Gurley read the burial service.

The vast assemblage then began to disperse. During the entire afternoon the bells in the city and in Georgetown and Alexandria were tolled, and minute guns fired from the fortifications.

Remarking upon the solemn scenes of the day, the *New York Times* said: "In point of sad sublimity and moral grandeur, the spectacle was the most impressive ever witnessed in the national capital. The unanimity and depth of feeling, the decorum, good order, and complete success of all the arrangements, and the solemn dignity which pervaded all classes, will mark the obsequies of ABRAHAM LINCOLN as the greatest pageant ever tendered to the honored dead on this continent. The day has been delightfully warm and pleasant, and thus contributed to swell the throng of spectators, which was by far the greatest that ever filled the streets of the city."

While this solemn spectacle impressed the people of the National Capital, similar spectacles were witnessed and participated in by the people of a very large majority of all the villages, towns, and cities of the Nation, and there was heartfelt mourning in a majority of the homes of our land.

LYING IN STATE IN THE CAPITOL.

When the remains of Mr. Lincoln were placed upon the *catafalque* in the rotunda of the Capitol, Major General Meigs, Quartermaster General, had control of the military arrangements for their protection until they were taken in charge by the guard of honor detailed for that duty, composed of the following

ARMY OFFICERS.

Brig. Gen. John P. Slough, Brevet Brig. Gen. William Gamble, commanding 1st separate brigade, 22d Army Corps, Fairfax Court House, Capt. R. C. Gale, A. A. G., Surgeon F. W. Mead, Surgeon Hard, Capt. Wickersham, A. A. G., Capt. H. C. Lawrence, A. Q. M., Capt. Brown, A. A. G., Lieut. Gamble, A. D. C., Lieut. Pearson, A. D. C., and Lieut. More, A. D. C.

NAVAL OFFICERS.

Lieut. Com'g Edward E. Stone, Monitor Montauk, Lieut. Com'g A. Ward Weaver, Monitor Mahopac, Lieut. N. H. Farquahar, Lieut. A. R. McNair, Lieut. B. F. Day, and Lieut. E. M. Shepard.

A detachment of the Twenty-Fourth Regiment Veteran Reserves was placed upon guard duty at the entrance of the rotunda and at the gates of the Capitol.

As soon as the doors were thrown open on the morning of the 20th, the throng of visitors began to press forward. All were required to enter at the main eastern entrance, and, passing in two lines on either side of the *catafalque*, to go out at the western door of the rotunda. None were permitted to linger. A strong guard was placed across the lower steps of the eastern entrance, and a line of guards in close order on either side marked the avenue left for the people who desired to pass in. About ten o'clock a heavy rain storm partially checked the crowd; but, notwithstanding the rain, the procession of saddened faces came pressing forward at the rate of three thousand persons per hour.

The catafalque was better arranged to afford a view of the features of the honored dead than at the White House. The features were little changed.

The rotunda, which was lighted only by a sort of twilight hue, was filled with solemn stillness, unbroken save by the rustling of the dresses of the female mourners, and occasionally a deep sigh from some of those passing the coffin.

At six o'clock the doors of the Capitol were closed to visitors, and the officers who had been on duty during the day as a guard of honor over the remains, were relieved by Brigadier General James A. Hall and staff—Captain Edwin H. Nevin, Jr., Lieut. Terrence Riley, and Brigadier General J. A. Ekin and staff, Maj. D. C. Welch and Capt. Charles Powers.

THE JOURNEY FROM WASHINGTON TO SPRINGFIELD AS PRESIDENT MARTYRED, 1865.

DEPARTURE FROM WASHINGTON.

At about six o'clock on the morning of April 21st, the members of the Cabinet and other distinguished individuals who had been invited to be present, or who had acted as pall bearers, assembled in the rotunda, and the Rev. Dr. Gurley offered a brief prayer, which was the only ceremony at the Capitol. At the conclusion of the prayer, at twenty minutes before seven o'clock, the coffin was taken from the *catafalque* by twelve orderly sergeants, and placed in the hearse, which was in waiting to receive it in front of the Capitol. The procession was then formed, and escorted the remains to the depot of the Baltimore and Ohio Railroad Company, on New Jersey avenue, where the funeral train had been prepared for their reception and that of the party which had been invited to accompany them to their final resting place. In the advance of the procession marched a detail of two hundred men of the Veteran Reserve Corps, under command of Lieuenant-Colonel T. M. Bell; following them came the hearse with the coffin, beside which were a guard of honor composed of a detail of twelve orderly sergeants from the Veteran Reserve Corps, under the immediate command of Captain J. M. McCamley of the Ninth, and Lieutenants J. R. Durkee, of the Seventh, E. Hopy, of the Twelfth, and E. Murphey, of the Tenth Regiment Veteran Reserve Corps. Immediately following the hearse, on foot, came Lieutenant General Grant, Brigadier General Hardie, Brigadier Generals Barnard, Rucker, Ekin, Howe, Eaton, Townsend and McCallum, and Major Generals Hunter and Meigs, Admiral Davis and Capt. W. R. Taylor, of the navy, and Major Field, of the marine corps. Following them were several carriages, in which were Secretaries Stanton, Welles and McCulloch; Postmaster General Dennison and Attorney General Speed; Major B. B. French, Commissioner of Public Buildings; Commissioner Dole, of the Indian Bureau; Holloway, of the Patent Bureau; Captain Newman, of the Capitol Police; Governor Oglesby, Senator Yates and ex-Senator Browning, of Illinois; the Illinois delegation, which takes charge of the remains on behalf of that State, and a number of other Senators and members of Congress. President Johnson's carriage was also in the procession, accompanied by the President's body guard, mounted, which closed the procession.

Notwithstanding the early hour, and inclement weather, a large number of citizens had collected for the purpose of rendering a last mark of respect to the mortal remains of one whom they had loved and reverenced as the second Father of his Country. The assemblage increased in numbers very rapidly during the march from the Capitol to the depot, until on its arrival at the depot thousands were assembled. The space immediately in front of the depot was cleared by the military; the detachment of the Veteran Reserves, which escorted the remains, was drawn up fronting the main entrance and the line covering the entire front, while the guards kept back all but those who immediately assisted in the demonstration, or those who were actually intending to take passage in the half-past seven A. M. train.

The coffin was carried into the depot, followed by the distinguished gentlemen, civil and military, before mentioned, and deposited in the car which had been prepared for its reception. At the door of this car the Rev. Dr. Gurley again briefly addressed the God of the living and the dead in a solemn and appropriate prayer. Ten minutes before eight o'clock a pilot engine was started to ascertain that the track was clear, and at precisely eight o'clock the funeral train was put in motion.

The military escort remained in line in front of the depot until the train started, and as it commenced to move presented arms, as a last token of respect. As the train moved off by the Soldiers' Rest, which is immediately in the rear of the depot, the Eighth Regiment United States colored artillery, were drawn up in line and presented arms until it had passed.

The remains of little Willie Lincoln, who died in the White House, December 21st, 1862, at the age of twelve years, was placed in the interior of the hearse car, immediately in front of those of his father. Mrs. Lincoln requested that no display be made of her son's remains, but that they might be privately removed to Springfield.

THE GUARD OF HONOR.

The following is a list of the gentlemen prominent in civil and military life, officially appointed to accompany the Funeral Train:

RELATIVES AND FAMILY FRIENDS.

Judge David Davis, United States Supreme Court.

C. M. Smith and N. M. Edwards, brothers-in-law of Mrs. Lincoln.

General John B. S. Todd, cousin to Mrs. Lincoln.

Charles Alexander Smith, brother of C. M. Smith.

GUARD OF HONOR.

Major General David Hunter.

Brigadier General E. D. Townsend.

Brigadier General Charles Thomas.

Brigadier General A. D. Eaton.
Brevet Major General J. G. Barnard.
Brigadier General G. D. Ramsey.
Brigadier General A. P. Howe.
Brigadier General D. C. McCallum.
Brigadier General J. C. Caldwell.
Rear Admiral C. H. Davis, United States Navy.
Captain Wm. R. Taylor, United States Navy.
Major T. H. Field, United States Marine Corps.

GENTLEMEN ON DUTY.

The following named gentlemen accompanied the train in an official capacity:

Captain Charles Penrose, Quartermaster and Commissary of Subsistence of the entire party.
Ward H. Lamon, Marshal of the District of Columbia.
Dr. Charles B. Brown, Embalmer.
Frank T. Sands, Undertaker.

MEMBERS OF CONGRESS ACCOMPANYING THE REMAINS.

The following members of the Senate and House of Representatives had been specially invited to accompany the remains to Springfield:

Mr. Pike, Maine.
Mr. Rollins, N. Hampshire.
Mr. Baxter, Vermont.
Mr. Hooper, Massachusetts.
Mr. Dexter, Connecticut.
Mr. Anthony, R. Island.
Mr. Harris, New York.
Mr. Cowan, Pennsylvania.
Mr. Schenck, Ohio.
Mr. Smith, Kentucky.
Mr. Julian, Indiana.
Mr. Ramsay, Minnesota.
Mr. T. W. Terry, Michigan.
Mr. Harlan, Iowa.
Mr. Yates, Illinois.
Mr. Washburne, Illinois.
Mr. Farnsworth, Illinois.
Mr. Arnold, Illinois.
Mr. Shannon, California.
Mr. Williams, Oregon.

Mr. Clarke, Kansas.
Mr. Whaley, West Virginia.
Mr. Nye, Nevada.
Mr. Hitchcock, Nebraska.
Mr. Bradford, Colorado.
Mr. Wallace, Idaho.
Mr. Newell, New Jersey.
Mr. Phelps, Maryland.
Geo. T. Brown, Sergeant-at-Arms of the Senate.
N. G. Ordway, Sergeant-at-Arms of the House of Representatives.

THE DELEGATES FROM ILLINOIS.

The following are the names of the delegates from Illinois appointed to accompany the remains to their last resting place:

Gov. Richard J. Oglesby.
Gen. Isham N. Haguie, Adjutant General Illinois.
Col. Jas. H. Bowen, A. D. C.
Col. M. H. Hanna, A. D. C.
Col. D. B. James, A. D. C.
Maj. S. Waite, A. D. C.
Col. D. L. Phillips, U. States Marshal of the District of Illinois, A. D. C.
Hon. Jesse K. Dubois.
Hon. T. J. Stuart.
Col. John Williams.
Dr. S. H. Melvin.
Hon. S. M. Cullom.
Gen. John A. McClernand.
Hon. Lyman Trumbull.
Hon. Thomas A. Haine.
Hon. John Wentworth.
Hon. S. S. Hayes.
Col. R. M. Hough.
Hon. S. W. Fuller.
Capt. J. B. Turner.
Hon. J. Lawson.
Hon. C. L. Woodman.
Hon. G. W. Gage.
G. H. Roberts, Esq.
J. Connisky, Esq.
Hon. L. Talcott.
Hon. J. S. Fredenburg.
Hon. Thomas J. Dennis.
Lieut. Gov. William Bross.
Hon. Francis E. Sherman, Mayor of Chicago.

GOVERNORS OF STATES.

Governor O. P. Morton, of Indiana; Governor John Brough, of Ohio; Governor William Stone, of Iowa, together with their aides.

THE VETERAN RESERVE GUARD.

The Veteran Reserve guard consisted of—

Captain J. McCamby, 9th Veteran Reserve Corps.
First Lieut. J. R. Durkee, 7th " " "
Second Lieut. E. Murphy, 10th " " "
Second Lieut. E. Hoppy, 12th " " "
First Sergt. C. Swinehart, Co. D, 7th V. R. C.
J. R. Edwards, E, 9th Veteran Reserve Corps.
S. Carpenter, K, 7th " " "
A. C. Cromwell, I, 7th " " "
J. F. Nelson, A, 9th " " "
L. E. Bulock, E, 9th " " "
P. Callaghan, H, 9th " " "
A. K. Marshall, K, 9th " " "
W. T. Daly, A, 10th " " "
J. Collins, D, 10th " " "
W. H. Durgin, F, 10th " " "
Frank Smith, C, 10th " " "
G. E. Goodrich, A, 12th " " "
A. E. Carr, D, 12th " " "
F. Carey, E, 12th " " "
W. H. Noble, G, 12th " " "
J. Karr, D, 14th " " "
J. P. Smith, I, 14th " " "
J. Hanna, B, 14th " " "
F. D. Forehand, 18th " " "
J. M. Sedgwick, 18th " " "
R. W. Lewis, 18th " " "
J. P. Berry, A, 24th " " "
W. H. Wiseman, E, 24th " " "
J. M. Pardun, K. 24th " " "

Of the escort that accompanied Mr. Lincoln from Springfield to Washington, but three left Washington with the remains—Judge David Davis, of Illinois, Major-General David Hunter, and Ward H. Lamon.

THE FUNERAL TRAIN.

The funeral train consisted of nine cars, eight of them furnished in succession by the chief railways over which the remains were transported. The ninth car, containing the body, was the "President's car," built for the convenience of the President and other government officers in traveling over the United States Military Railroads. This contained a parlor, sitting room, and sleeping apartment. It had been richly draped in mourning within and without, the heavy black drapery being relieved with white and black rosettes, and silver fringes and tassels.

The windows were draped with black curtains, and the entire furniture shrouded in black. A plain stand covered with black cloth, was placed in the car, at one end, and on this the remains of the President rested. On a similar stand, at the other end of the car, was the coffin holding the remains of Willie Lincoln. The funeral car was in charge of Mr. John McNaughton, United States Military Railroad.

The other cars of the train were new and elegant, and tastefully draped in mourning. The locomotive was also heavily draped.

Brigadier-General McCallum had charge of the general arrangements for the running of the train.

A pilot engine, furnished by the several railway companies on the route, preceded the train over each line of the roads traversed.

OBSEQUIES AT BALTIMORE.

The funeral train ran from Washington to Baltimore without stopping, except at Annapolis Junction, where Gov. Bradford joined the mournful procession. Baltimore was reached at ten o'clock. A heavy rain fell, yet with unanimity, in that city never equaled, the citizens testified their high regard for the honored dead in every expressive mode. Work was suspended; the hum of traffic was hushed; all turned aside from their usual avocations to unite in the observance of the day, and in paying reverence to the great departed. Before daylight had fairly broken through the mist, the streets were thronged with citizens, hastening to the different localities assigned for the assemblage of the different clubs and associations, to join the procession. In spite of the inclement weather, people of all ages and both sexes, white and black, gathered about the Camden station of the Baltimore and Ohio Railroad, where the funeral cortege arrived from Washington. By eight o'clock the crowd was so great that it was almost impossible to move on any of the footwalks surrounding the depot buildings.

The depot buildings, engines, &c., were tastefully draped. Every arrangement had been made in this department by the Master of Transportation, William Prescott Smith, Esq., to insure no delay or interruption in the proceedings. Lieut.-Gov. Cox, with a portion of the Governor's staff, General Berry and staff, Hon. William B. Hill, Secretary of the State, Hon. Robert Fowler, the State Treasurer, with other officials of the State government, Mayor Chapman, the City Council of Baltimore, with the heads of departments of the city government, General Wallace, Brigadier-General Tyler, Commodore Downin, and many other officers of the army and navy, were assembled to receive the remains and escort them to the Exchange building, where they were to lie in state.

When the car bearing the body reached the depot, in charge of General McCallum and John W. Garrett, the coffin was removed by a guard of sergeants of the Invalid corps, and, surrounded by uncovered heads and saddened hearts, was escorted through the depot buildings by the State and city authorities to the hearse awaiting its reception on Camden street. The body of this hearse was almost entirely composed of plate glass, which enabled the vast crowd on the line of the procession to have a full view of the coffin. The supports of the top were draped with black cloth and white silk, and the top of the car itself was handsomely decorated with black plumes. It was drawn by four black horses. Owing to the presence of large detachments of the army in the Monumental City, the military escort was exceedingly imposing. The various commands were thoroughly equipped. The entire column was under command of Brigadier General H. H. Lockwood, attended by his staff. It formed a line on Eutaw street, the right resting on Conway street, and moved in reverse order a few minutes after ten o'clock. The rear of the escort was brought up by a large number of officers of various departments, including medical and other branches, all mounted. Among these were Major-General Lew Wallace and staff, Surgeon Josiah Simpson, Medical Director, General E. B. Tyler, Brig.-General D. R. Kenly, and Colonel S. M. Bowman.

A few moments before one o'clock, the head of the procession arrived at the southern front of the Exchange. As the head of the military escort reached Calvert street the column was halted, and the hearse, with its guard of honor, passed between the lines, the troops presenting arms, and the bands of music wailing out the plaintive tune, "Peace, Troubled Soul." The general officers dismounted and formed, with their staffs, on either side of the approach from the gate to the main entrance of the Exchange. The remains were then removed from the funeral car and carried slowly and reverently into the building, and placed on a catafalque prepared for them. After they had been properly placed and the covering removed, the officers present passed slowly forward, on either side of the body. The civic part of the procession followed, and the general public was then admitted.

The catafalque was erected immediately beneath the dome. It consisted of a raised dais, eleven feet by four at the base, the sides sloping slightly to the height of about three feet. From the four corners rose graceful columns, supporting a cornice extending beyond the line of the base. The canopy rose to a point fourteen feet from the ground, and terminated in clusters of black plumes. The whole structure was richly draped. The floor and sides of the dais were covered with black cloth, and the canopy was formed of black crape, the rich folds drooping from the four corners and bordered with silver fringe. The cornice was adorned with silver stars, while the sides and ends were similarly ornamented. The interior of the canopy was of black cloth, gathered in fluted folds. In the central point was a large star of black velvet, studded with thirty-six stars—one for each State in the Union. The floor of the dais on which the body of the illustrious martyred patriot rested, was bordered with evergreens and a wreath of spiral azaleas, calla lilies, and other choice flowers.

But a small portion of the throng in attendance were able to obtain a view of the remains. At about half-past two o'clock, to the regret of thousands, the coffin was closed, and, escorted by the guard of honor, was removed to the hearse. The procession then re-formed and took up its mournful march to the depot of the Northern Central Railway Company.

BALTIMORE TO HARRISBURG.

The funeral train from Baltimore to Harrisburg was under the immediate charge of the Superintendent of the Northern Central Railway, Mr. Du Barry. At every point along the entire route significant tokens of sorrow and respect were manifested by large concourses of people. At the Pennsylvania State Line, Gov. Curtin met the train, accompanied by his staff, consisting of Adjutant-General Russell, Quartermaster-General Reynolds, Inspector-General Lemuel Todd, Surgeon-General James A. Phillips, and Colonels R. B. Roberts, S. B. Thomas, Frank Jordan and John A. Wright. Governor Curtin was received by Governor Bradford, who was in the front car with his staff, consisting of Adjutant-General Berry, General Edward Shriver and Lieutenant-Colonels Thomas J. Morris, Henry Tyson and A. J. Ridgeley. General Cadwalader, commanding the Department of Pennsylvania, accompanied Governor Curtin. The General's staff consisted of Major W. McMichael, A. D. C., and Captain L. Howard.

At York, a scene worthy of special record occurred. The ladies of that city asked permission to lay on the President's coffin a wreath of flowers. Asst. Adjt.-Gen. Townsend, of the United States Army, granted the request, with a modification that six ladies might perform the service. During the performance of a dirge by an instrumental band the flowers were brought forth and carried in procession to the funeral car, while the bells tolled, and all the men stood uncovered. The ladies—namely, Mrs. Samuel Smalley, Mrs. Henry E. Miles, Mrs. David E. Smalley, Miss Plover, Miss Louisa Ducks, Miss Susan Smalley and Miss Jane Lattimore—entered the car, three on each side of the coffin; and the wreath having been handed to them they placed it in the centre of the coffin and then retired, those who witnessed the scene bitterly weeping. The bells continued to toll and the band to sound its mournful strains. The wreath was very large, about three feet in circumference. The outer circle was of roses, and alternate parallel lines were composed of white and red flowers of the choicest description. The hand of affection could not have contributed a more choice and delicate tribute to departed worth.

HARRISBURG.

The obsequies at the Capital of Pennsylvania were after night. The funeral train arrived at eight o'clock. In despite of a severe rain storm the streets were densely thronged. A large military escort, accompanied by an immense procession of the people, followed the President's remains to the State House, amid the sound of minute guns, where the corpse was exposed to the view of the public until midnight. On the following morning, the doors of the Capitol were opened at seven o'clock, and immediately a compact mass of people, in double lines, began to move through the rotunda, which had been appropriately draped. Thousands of citizens of the neighboring towns and adjoining counties swelled the procession of mourners. At nine o'clock the coffin was closed, and at ten o'clock the procession was re-formed and began its march of escort to the depot. Almost without exception tokens of mourning were displayed from the dwelling-houses and places of business in all quarters of the city. The Governor's residence, the residence of Simon Cameron, and those of several of the officers of the State, attracted marked attention.

The procession was composed of eight divisions, and marched in the following order:

First, with slow and solemn music, came the Carlisle Barracks Band. Then a regiment of infantry from Camp Curtin, with arms reversed; drum corps, playing the

"Dead March;" Sixteenth Veteran Reserve Corps, with Colonel commanding escort; drum corps, with muffled drums; battalion of artillery, with pieces shrouded with crape; mounted infantry, Co. F, 201st Pennsylvania Regiment, who had just arrived from the border, Captain Thomas F. Maloney commanding; battalion of cavalry; Chief Marshal, Colonel Harry McCormick ,and aids; clergy of Harrisburg.

PALL-BEARERS.	PALL-BEARERS.
Hon. A. L. Roumfort.	Hon. Jno. J. Pearson.
Hon. David Fleming.	George Bergner, Esq.
Hon. W. F. Murray.	Hon. V. Hummel, Sr.
Hon. Jno. C. Kunkel.	R. A. Lamberton, Esq.
Herman Alricks, Esq.	A. B. Hamilton, Esq.
Dr. C. Seller.	Henry Thomas, Esq.
Capt. George Prince.	Henry Gilbert, Esq.
Geo. Trullinger, Esq.	Dr. Geo. Bailey.

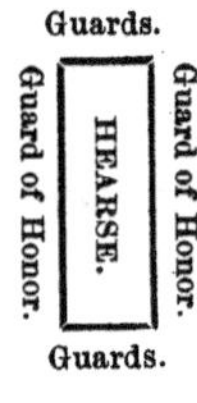

Following the hearse came the relatives of the deceased and a delegation of mourners from Illinois; Gov. A. G. Curtin; Major-General Cadwalader and staff; Major-General Heintzelman and staff; Rear-Admiral Davis, and other distinguished men, in carriages; Adjutant-General A. L. Russell, Colonel Samuel L. Thomas and others of the Governor's staff, on horseback; Pennsylvaia Legislature, there being only twenty-five or thirty members in the procession; 201st Regimental Band, Pennsylvania Volunteers; Pittsburg Delegation, numbering fifty individuals; Philadelphia Delegation; Citizens; Friendship Fire Company; Ex-Mayor Kepner; Hope Fire Company, with locked arms, three abreast; Mount Vernon Hook and Ladder Company; Paxton Fire Company; Sons of Malta, richly caprisoned, with swords draped in mourning; Free Masons; Odd Fellows; Salem Lodge, I. O. B. B.; Attaches of the Quartermaster's and

Provost Marshal's Departments; Young Men's Christian Association.

At precisely twelve o'clock the funeral train left the depot for Philadelphia. Between Harrisburg and Philadelphia thousands of men, women and children assembled at depots and along the line of the railway, to pay respect to the services and the memory of the patriot around whom their affections and their hopes had clustered; and for many miles before the cars reached Philadelphia, either side of the railway was completely lined with people who stood with uncovered or bowed heads as the funeral car passed.

PHILADELPHIA.

The *Philadelphia Enquirer* of April 24th said: "A grand, emphatic and unmistakable tribute of affectionate devotion to the memory of our martyred chief was that paid by Philadelphia on the arrival of his remains on Saturday evening. No mere love of excitement, no idle curiosity to witness a splendid pageant, but a feeling far deeper, more earnest, and founded in infinitely nobler sentiments, must have inspired that throng, which, like the multitudinous waves of the swelling sea, surged along our streets from every quarter of the city, gathering in a dense, impenetrable mass along the route prescribed for the procession. * * * * The myriads of expectant faces gathering around the depot at Broad and Prime streets, and lining the route of the procession for hours before the arrival of the funeral train; the various civic associations marching in orderly column, with banners draped in mourning, to take their assigned places; the bands leading such associations, and making the city vocal with strains sweet but melancholy; the folds of sable drapery drooping from the buildings, and the half-masted flags, with their mourning borders; all were striving to express the same emotion. It was this alone which gave them interest or significance, and this alone which makes them worthy of being recorded."

Between three and four o'clock P. M., the military escort, under Brigadier-General O. S. Ferry, arrived at the depot, and formed in line along Broad street. On the right were three regiments of infantry, and next to them two batteries of artillery, and below them was the City Troop of Cavalry, mounted on their chargers, conspicuous afar off by their brilliant uniforms and fur-crowned helmets. Below these, in a long succession, were the various civic associations, all drawn up in line along the east side of the street, and waiting to fall into their places in the column as the procession moved by, constantly swelling in its progress. Many of these associations displayed tasteful and appropriate banners.

As the time for the arrival of the train approached, the throng in the street grew rapidly larger and denser, and the eagerness of the people to obtain positions from which a good view could be obtained, rendered it necessary for the police to use considerable exertion to keep clear the space necessary for the passage of the pall-bearers and escort from the door of the building to the hearse. The Committee of Arrangements were at the station in readiness to receive the remains and the party accompanying them on behalf of the city, as also the special escort of military and naval officers detailed by order of General Cadwalader as a special guard of honor.

The following are the names of the gentlemen comprising the committee: Fred. A. Van Cleve, Chairman; James Armstrong, Thomas Barlow, James Freeman and Joshua Spering, on the part of Select Council; and Alexander Harper, Samuel Willets, Joseph F. Marcer, Geo. Nichols,

Thomas H. Gill, on the part of the Common Council, together with the Presidents of both chambers.

The special guard of honor in behalf of Philadelphia consisted of twenty-four officers, among whom were: Commodore H. A. Adams, Commodore S. C. Rowan, U. S. Navy; Brevet Brigadier-General Alexander Cummings, Col. George H. Crosman.

The hour announced for the arrival of the train was 4:30 P. M., but it did not arrive until twenty minutes later. Almost simultaneously with its entrance to the depot the report of a cannon announced the fact to the entire city, and the firing of minute guns was continued during the entire progress of the procession. The escort or guard of honor above mentioned went in to meet the car containing the body, and forming in two lines, between which passed the pall-bearers with the coffin and the guard on either sides (sergeants and soldiers of the Veteran Reserve Corps), fell in behind it and followed it with bare heads and solemn step to the hearse, which was waiting in front of the building.

The hearse, especially constructed for the occasion by the Committee of Reception, was an imposing structure, well adapted for its purpose, which was to display the coffin to view as prominently as possible. It was drawn by eight black horses, with silver-mounted harness.

At fifteen minutes past five the hearse, followed by the special city guard of honor, on foot, and the carriages bearing the funeral party and members of the Philadelphia Committee, commenced to move, the military escort taking its place in advance, keeping time to the slow, solemn music of the bands and the melancholy tolling of the bells. The procession was ordered in eleven divisions, and was one of the largest and most imposing which in any city on the route between Washington and Springfield paid tribute to Mr. Lincoln's memory.

It was nearly eight o'clock when the hearse arrived opposite the southern main entrance to Independence Square. The Union League Association had been detailed to receive the body at that point, and superintend the work of having it placed in its proper position in Independence Hall. The members of the League assembled at Concert Hall, about five o'clock, and proceeded from thence to Independence Square, accompanied by a band of music, and colors draped in black. They were dressed in full suits of black, and wore white gloves. On reaching the Square the members of the association took up position on either side of the main thoroughfare; they were formed in two ranks, and filled the Square from one end to the other. The band was placed in the State House steeple, and prior to the arrival of the remains performed a number of dirges.

When the hearse reached the main entrance to the Square, the coffin was removed and taken within the inclosure, when the line of procession was formed, consisting of the body guard and pall-bearers, and the solemn cortege moved slowly to Independence Hall. The members of the Union League stood with uncovered heads, and the band in the steeple performed a mournful dirge. The Square was brilliantly illuminated with Calcium Lights, about sixty in number, composed of red, white and blue colors, which gave a peculiar and striking effect to the melancholy spectacle.

Amid a breathless silence, broken only by the slow and mournful strains of the band, grief-stricken citizens standing uncovered, sorrow depicted on every countenance; amid the tolling of bells and the sound of minute guns fired in the distance, the coffin of the murdered Executive was conveyed within the classic shades of Independence Hall.

The body was placed on an oblong platform in the centre of the Hall, covered with black cloth, and lay north and south, the head towards the south, and directly opposite old Independence bell. The lid of the coffin was removed far enough to expose to view the face and breast of the deceased. An American flag, the one used to cover the coffin during the funeral procession, was thrown back at the foot of the coffin, and a number of wreaths of exotics laid on it.

At the head of the coffin was suspended a highly wrought cross, composed of japonicas, with a centre consisting of jet black exotics. The device contained the following inscription:

"To the memory of our beloved President, from a few ladies of the United States Sanitary Commission."

On the old Independence bell, and near the head of the coffin, rested a large and beautifully made floral anchor, composed of the choicest exotics. This offering came from the ladies of St. Clement's Church. Four stands, two at the head and two at the foot of the coffin, were draped in black cloth, and contained rich candelabras with lighted wax candles. To the rear of these were placed three additional stands, also containing candelabras with burning tapers; and, again, another row of four stands, containing candelabras also, making in all eighteen candelabras and one hundred and eight burning wax tapers.

Between this flood of light, shelving was erected, on which were placed vases filled with japonicas, heliotropes, and other rare flowers. These vases were about twenty-five in number.

A delicious perfume stole through every part of the

8

Hall, which, added to the soft yet brilliant light of the wax tapers, the elegant uniforms of the officers on duty, etc., constituted a scene of solemn magnificence seldom witnessed.

The Hall at large was completely shrouded with black cloth, arranged in a very graceful and appropriate manner. The old chandelier that hangs from the centre of the room, and which was immediately over the coffin, was entirely covered, and from it hung in every direction festoons of black cloth, forming a sort of canopy over the entire room. The walls of the room presented the appearance of having been papered with black. The celebrated historical pictures which ornament the Hall were, with few exceptions, hid from view. The statue of Washington, at the east end, stood out, however, in bold relief against the black background. The only pictures visible were the full-length portraits of William Penn, Lafayette, Washington, and Chevalier Gerard, and the smaller ones of Martha Washington, Stephen Decatur, and one or two others. Wreaths of immortelle were hung on the black drapery that covered the walls, and were placed about midway between the floor and ceiling.

At ten o'clock the doors of the Hall were thrown open, and from that hour until midnight an unbroken stream of people passed through the building into Independence Square, entering the room where the body lay in state by the southern door, and passing out by steps erected over a window at the south end of the room. During the hours stated a band, stationed near the Hall, performed a great number of dirges and other funeral selections.

A cordon of police, under charge of High Constable Harry Clark, were stationed from the outer door of the State House building, to the ballustrade that surrounded the coffin, and through the avenue formed by them the visitors passed to view the remains. Mayor Henry occupied a position at the head of the coffin, surrounded by the committee having the body in charge.

So great was the anxiety of the citizens to view the body of their beloved Chief Magistrate, that hundreds of them remained around Independence Hall all night, waiting anxiously for the doors, or rather the windows, to be again thrown open.

From six o'clock on Sunday until one o'clock on Monday morning, the public was admitted. As soon as the day began to break, the people from all parts of the town began to flock to the neighborhood of Fifth and Chestnut streets. The crowd became most dense, and when the doors were opened, a double line of applicants was formed, extending as far west as Eighth street, and east to Third street. By 11 o'clock the lines extended from the Hall west as far as the Schuylkill, and east as far as the Delaware. The residents of West Philadelphia flocked across the Market Street Bridge by hundreds, while the Camden ferry-boats apparently brought across the Delaware about one-half of the population of New Jersey.

The entrances were through two windows in Chestnut street, and the exits through the windows facing on Independence Square, temporary steps having been placed in position for that purpose. By this arrangement two lines of spectators were admitted at a time, passing on either side of the coffin. The *Inquirer*, in its report of the scenes of the memorable day, said:

"Never before in the history of our city was such a dense mass of humanity huddled together. Hundreds of persons were seriously injured from being pressed in the mob, and many fainting females were extricated by the police and military and conveyed to places of security. Many women lost their bonnets, while others had nearly every particle of clothing torn from their persons. Notwithstanding the immense pressure and the trying ordeal through which persons had to pass in order to view the remains, but little disorder prevailed, every one apparently being deeply impressed with the great solemnity of the occasion. After a person was once in line, it took from four to five hours before an entrance into the Hall could be effected. Spectators were not allowed to stop by the side of the coffin, but were kept moving on, the great demand on the outside not permitting more than a mere glance at the remains, which were under military guard."

PHILADELPHIA TO NEW YORK.

At one o'clock on Monday morning, April 24th, the funeral procession began its march from Independence Hall. The escort consisted of the One Hundred and Eighty-seventh Pennsylvania Infantry, the city troops, guard of honor, and a detachment of soldiers to guard the body, Perseverance Hose Company, and the Republican Invincibles. A band of music played dirges on the march. The procession reached Kensington station at four o'clock. On the way thousands of citizens joined it.

At a few minutes past four o'clock the train left the Kensington station. Governor Parker came on board at the State line, at Morrisville, with his staff, consisting of Adjutant-General R. F. Stockton, Quartermaster-General Perrine, and others. They were accompanied by United States Senator John P. Stockton, Rev. D. Henry Miller, and Colonel Murphy, and were received by Governor Curtin, of Pennsylvania. There was also upon the train a committee from Newark, consisting of the mayor, Joseph P. Bradley, Esq., the President and other members of the Newark Council.

The Delaware river, which separates the State of Pennsylvania from that of New Jersey, was crossed at half-past five, and as the train passed through Trenton the bells of the city were tolled. Every hill-top on the line of the road and other advantageous points were occupied by throngs of spectators. The train stopped at the Trenton station thirty minutes. A detachment of the Reserved Veteran and Invalid corps, drawn up in line on the platform, gave the customary funeral honors. Music was performed by an instrumental band, minute guns were fired, and the bells continued to toll. Everywhere the emblems of mourning were prominent.

The train arrived at New Brunswick at about half-past seven o'clock, where it halted for half an hour. A large number of people visited it. Meantime minute guns were fired and the bells tolled. At eight o'clock the train was again in motion.

At Rahway and Elizabeth the emblems of mourning were numerous, and many flags draped. The tolling of bells and the firing of cannon were repeated. Near Elizabeth a party of young men displayed, on differently colored banners, the words, separately, "Victory," "Peace," "Union," "Grant," "Sherman," with the usual crape attachments.

At Newark the private residences and public buildings and stores and workshops were elaborately draped, guns were fired, and the bells tolled. All Newark, with the exception of those at the windows, seemed to be out of doors. Trees and house-tops, door-steps and car-trucks —in fact, all the highest attainable positions and points where an unobstructed view could be had, were occupied. The United States Hospital was suitably decorated. In front were a large number of soldiers, some of them on crutches. All the patients who could move themselves were drawn up in double file. Every one stood uncovered.

NEW YORK CITY.

At ten o'clock on the morning of the 24th of April, the Funeral Train reached the Camden and Amboy Railway Depot in Jersey City. The depot and surrounding buildings had beeen appropriately draped. Outside the depot, at every place along the track whence a view of the funeral train and its occupants could be obtained, a dense crowd collected. Immediately in front of the western entrance to the building there was a bank of spectators, piled up one above the other on the vacant cars left standing on the track, and on every salient point which promised a view of the proceedings. It was not an ordinary crowd—pushing, jostling and shouting. A reverential stillness prevailed.

Gen. John A. Dix had met the train at Philadelphia, and under his orders detachments of the Second and Sixth regiments, two hundred strong, under the command of Captain Livingstone and Brevet Major McLaughlin, escorted the New York State and city officers, assembled to remove the remains, and guarded the depot. The arrival of the train was announced by minute guns. When it had entered the depot, General Dix, the guard of honor and the Congressional delegation, alighted from the cars. General Sandford and the officers of New York State and city stepped forward, and the body was removed from the car by four sergeants of the Reserve Corps. As the richly-decorated coffin was exposed to view, five choral societies, numbering sixty-five voices, led by F. A. Stonge, began to chant the solemn and appropriate dirge known as *Integer Vita.* A body guard of twenty-five sergeants and veterans of the Reserve Corps, under the command of Captain Campbell, surrounded the corpse. Before the last notes of the funeral dirge were ended the coffin was raised on the shoulders of ten veterans, and the order of procession was formed. First walked General Dix and General Sandford; next four undertakers, and Colonel McMahon and Captain Lord, of General Dix's staff. Then came the corpse, flanked by the body guard, with drawn swords, and followed, in irregular order, by the Washington guard of honor and delegation; Hon. Chauncey M. Depew, Secretary of State of New York; the Mayor and Common Council of Jersey City; the delegations from Hoboken, Hudson City, Bergen and Greenville, and other officials and mourners. Moving down the north platform, at which the train was drawn up, toward the eastern end of the building, the procession wound round and moved up the next platform, and so out at the western entrance of the depot, the choral societies meanwhile singing the *chorale*, "Rest in the Grave." The reporter for the *New York Herald* said: "The thrilling impressiveness of the funeral dirge, the saddened aspect of the immense throng of mourners, were tributes which might well outweigh the obloquy and misapprehension of the past."

In the streets of Jersey City every housetop, every balcony, every window overlooking the road taken by the procession, from the depot to the ferry, was crowded with spectators. Slowly the corpse was borne, amidst the solemn booming of minute guns and the tolling of distant bells, to the ferry-boat, Jersey City, which was placed at the disposal of the committee to convey the remains of the honored dead to New York.

When the mournful procession wended its way through the gate leading on board the boat, not a sound was heard other than the booming of minute guns, which reverberated far and near. The procession was received by the Mayor of New York, and members of the Board of Aldermen and Board of Councilmen. These were ranged on either side of the boat. Each member bore appropriate insignia of mourning on the left arm.

The Jersey City was appropriately draped in mourning. The flags hung at half-mast. The officers of the boat were:—Pilots, Captain S. Decker and Edward Ashford; engineers, S. Barr and Louis Angel. In addition to the military gentlemen, the New York Common Council and different delegations which came with the remains, on board were representatives from the corporate bodies of Hudson, Hoboken, Bergen and other portions of New Jersey. The German singing societies of Hoboken, who had chanted a funeral dirge on the arrival of the train at Jersey City, were also of the party. Up and down the North River the scene was peculiarly impressive as the Jersey City slowly crossed. All the shipping had the emblems of mourning prominently displayed, while in many instances crowds occupied the rigging, and watched with mournful earnestness the little craft which carried upon its deck the remains of the nation's murdered Chief Magistrate. In several cases the vessels' sides were draped in mourning colors, the masts wreathed in black muslin, while all persons who happened to be on board stood with uncovered heads as the boat moved past. All the docks in the vicinity were filled with spectators. Thousands thronged to the extreme verge of the piers and watched with breathless curiosity the movements of the Jersey City as she neared her destination.

When within a few hundred yards of the dock, at the foot of Desbrosses street, the German societies commenced a funeral ode from the first book of Horace, which produced a thrilling effect upon all who heard it. The solemn notes of the song as they burst forth from nearly one hundred voices gave touching inspiration to the sorrow of the time as they were wafted on shore by the gentle breeze. The boat being moored fast to the dock, and all arrangements completed, Generals Dix and Sandford left the boat, when the hearse, together with those composing the procession, followed.

The scene at the foot of Desbrosses street, could not fail to make a lasting impression upon the thousands who were congregated on the housetops and awnings for several blocks on each side of the ferry. Every available spot was occupied along Desbrosses street, from West to Hudson streets. The window sashes of all the houses were removed in order that the occupants might have an unobstructed view of the procession, and as far as the eye could see there was a dense mass of heads protruding from every window in the street. The fronts of the houses were tastefully draped with mourning, and the national ensign was displayed at half-mast from almost every housetop.

The Seventh Regiment National Guard, Col. Emmons Clark, had been selected as the escort. The procession started from the boat in the following order:—

Police.
General Dix, General Sandford, Alderman Ryers, and other Military Officers and Civilians.
Band.
Seventh Regiment.
Sergeants of the Invalid Corps.

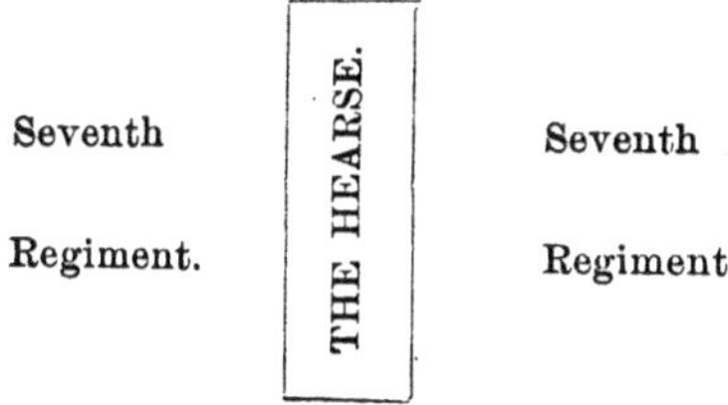

Sergeants of the Invalid Corps.

Seventh Regiment.

Then following was the guard of honor and the Washington Delegations accompanying the remains. Next to this came

His Honor Mayor Gunther.

Presidents of the Board of Councilmen and Aldermen.

United States Officers.

German Singing Society.

Police.

The sides and back of the hearse were of plate glass, and on the top were eight large plumes of black and white feathers. Around the edge of the roof and the lower portion of the body were American flags folded, draped in mourning, gracefully festooned, and fastened with knots of white and black ribbons. It was drawn by six gray horses covered with black cloth, each led by a groom dressed in mourning.

The route of the procession was from Desbrosses street through Hudson to Canal street, thence to Broadway and down Broadway to the City Hall.

Urns and other emblems of sorrow, in white and black cloth, and mottoes showing the grief of the people for the death of their beloved Chief Magistrate, were displayed from nearly every house, in the mournful shades of white and black. The stores were all closed and business suspended everywhere. Along the entire line of march as the hearse approached, the people uncovered their heads. The most creditable order prevailed. The silence of the immense crowds was expressively and impressively solemn. The *New York Herald* said: "No one could behold the scene, in all its impressive solemnity, earnestness and sincerity, without feeling satisfied that the funeral *cortege* of Abraham Lincoln was a triumphal procession greater, grander, more genuine, than any living conqueror or hero ever enjoyed.

The escort marched in files on each flank of the funeral

car, and in platoons on the front and rear. Then came the rest of the procession according to the arrangement of the programme. After them came the people by thousands, in solemn and orderly demeanor, from Desbrosses and Hudson streets in a vast throng, following in the rear and reaching from curb to curb on Canal street. This column increased as it went, and, with uncovered heads and sad and steadily persistent steps, followed the remains of the lamented Chief Magistrate to Broadway, and in many cases to the City Hall. Many people, seeing that the procession had passed, still remained in their positions in the street, as if scarcely satisfied that what they had watched and waited for was past.

Hours before the arrival of the body, masses of people gathered in the City Hall Park, along Broadway and Chatham street, and in and on the buildings overlooking the plaza in front of the City Hall, where the ceremony of receiving the body was to be witnessed. The police, by strenuous exertions, kept the streets cleared, but the sidewalks and the Park were filled with men, women and children, while the trees in the Park were loaded with adventurous urchins. Along the line formed by the police guard in front of the Hall, and the fences of the Park in Chatham street and Broadway, the crowd remained quiet, patiently awaiting the appearance of the hearse; but in the interior of the triangle of human beings thus formed the crowd swayed restlessly from side to side, but without the noise which usually accompanies such confusion. During the entire ceremony the people were orderly and quiet; each individual appeared to be impressed with the solemnity of the occasion. At the time of the appearance of the procession at the City Hall at least twenty thousand citizens were assembled, watching the ceremony with solemn interest.

The procession guarding the body filed into the Park a few minutes after half-past eleven o'clock, and the hearse, guarded by two companies of the Eighth Regiment, New York State National Guard, stopped before the door of the Hall. The coffin was immediately taken from the hearse, and carried up the stairs to the catafalque prepared for its reception in the Governor's Room, amid a solemn dirge, played by the Liederkranz band. Details from the Eighth Regiment were placed as guards around the building, and were soon solemnly pacing their beats.

While these preparations were being made, the several German singing clubs, under the direction of Mr. Paney, of the Liederkranz Society, and numbering nearly a thousand voices, sang several solemn dirges. As their swelling tones murmured their way through the closed windows of the Governor's Room, and surged amid

> The silken, sad, uncertain rustling
> Of each sable curtain,

the undertaker commenced the task of removing the lid of the coffin and disclosing the features of the deceased.

There was no trace of the interior architecture to be seen on the rotunda of the City Hall. Niche and dome, balustrade and panneling were all veiled. From the dome to the base there was a wall of crape, relieved by shrouded ensigns and semi-circular folds of paramatta. All these were arched with festoons, which fell gracefully over the combined display of flags and mourning—the symbols of the life of the republic and the death of its ruler. The light which fell upon the scene of death was modified. Across the oriels of the dome a black curtain was drawn, and the rays thus conducted fell subdued on the sad and imposing spectacle. The catafalque graced the principal entrance to the Governor's Room. Its form was square, but it was surmounted by a towering gothic arch, from which folds of crape, ornamented by festoons of silver lace and cords and tassels, fell artistically over the curtained pillars which gave form and beauty to the structure. The arch seemed lost in the dark labyrinths from which it rose. A spread eagle was perched above it. Beneath this aerial guardian was a bust of the dead President in sable drapery. Then came a ubiquitous display of black velvet, studded with beautiful silver stars in filagree lace, which reflected light over the suits of woe and gloom of which they were the national ornaments. On either side Roman urns were located, like those of old, near the distinguished dust of which they were the guardians. The interior of the canopy was in graceful harmony with the outside. The frontal arch, as it met the black ceiling of the catafalque, was relieved by a lining of white silk which skirted it. The walls were hung with solemn black, and the light of the great windows of the Governor's Room and that of the dome struggled vainly to illuminate it. There was nothing to vary the dark monotony of black cloth but the welcome trimming of silver lace, which gave limit to the gloomy aspect and grace to the display. The ceiling was formed of fluted folds of velvet, fretted with silver stars. Beneath the canopy, near the honored dead, were busts of Washington, Jackson, Webster and Clay—all resting on high pedestals. The vicinity of the catafalque was also the scene of elaborate and artistic mourning. All the furniture, the statues and the portraits of the Governor's room were in character with the sad scenes around them. "Washington's writing desk," the portraits of Presidents, Governors, and men distinguished in the State and city governments, were covered with crape. The statue of Washington, near which Mr. Lincoln received his friends four years previous, was elaborately draped, and the chandeliers were covered with black cloth.

The lid of the coffin having been removed, various floral offerings were laid upon it. General Hunter and Colonel O'Bierne then took their positions respectively by the side of the coffin, and, shortly after, the entrance below was opened, and the expectant crowd were admitted into the Hall. The solemn procession commenced at one o'clock. Scarcely had the interest to view the mournful *cortege*, as it wound its slow length within the railings of the Park, abated with the consignment of the honored remains to the care of the municipal authorities specially appointed for the reception, than a line began to be formed of those who desired to be among the first to look their last upon the mortal dead. Thousands formed that line, which, like a river receiving many contributions nearing its debouchment, gradually lessened, till away up in the Bowery, three-quarters of a mile off, it narrowed as it were at its source, still, however, receiving fresh supplies as an onward movement to the front gave a chance of nearing the object all so desired to look upon. Throughout the long early summer day, beneath the fervid rays of the sun, which shone almost uncomfortably warm, into the cool hours of the evening, and away through the chilly hours of the night, till dawn was almost again breaking, the seemingly ever unbroken line of people kept its ground persistently—to gratify the earnest desire which had brought them together. From distant points throughout the State, remote from the line of travel which took the President to his last bourne in Illinois, thousands of people flocked to the city in the hope of gaining a view of his bier. From Brooklyn, Jersey City, Williamsburg and neighboring localities, there was throughout the day a constant stream of people crossing in the ferry-boats, many of whom joining in the line remained for several hours, till at last they reached the goal of their desires. The eastern gate in the Park row was selected as the general entrance, the small gate, on the western side of the Park, being the entrance for those who had received special tickets. Down as far as Pearl street the line was double, or rather quadruple, that is, a double file of men, and on their right a double file of women, all anxious, and all determined to go through with it. The arrangements for the passage of the crowd were admirable, and a strong feeling of courtesy was mingled with the necessary adherence to duty of the various officials.

The deportment of the people was very different from that of the crowds which usually assemble in great cities. No gladsome laugh, no familiar greeting, no passing jests. Grief was denoted on every countenance. Many would have pressed close to the coffin, if but to touch it with their fingers, were they permitted. Frequent attempts were made by ladies to kiss the placid lips of the corpse.

But, notwithstanding the immense number which had passed during the day, the throng was at its greatest about midnight. As the clock tolled the hour of twelve, the members of the German singing societies, who had taken their places in the corridor beneath the rotunda, commenced the *Inter vitæ*. Heard from the neighborhood of the catafalque, the music had a most thrilling effect. Then followed the *Grabus heehe*, which was rendered with remarkable precision. The chorus consisted of seventy voices, under the direction of Mr. Loyer. The clubs represented were the Quartette, of Hoboken; the German, Harmonia and the Concordia. All the members wore appropriate mourning badges.

On careful calculations at various times during the day and night it was estimated that on an average eighty persons passed the coffin in a minute—that is, forty on either side. This would allow for the entire number passed up to midnight not much under sixty thousand.

Not till the first shadows of morning began to steal over the heavy folds of the drapery, lending additional melancholy to the scene, was there any break in the monotonous chain of onlookers. And then the torrent was stayed only for a few moments. Fresh arrivals, many of them from the country, began to take the place of the pallid-faced, wearied watchers who had waited all through the night to get their turn. As the day advanced the crowd increased, and by eight o'clock the approaches to the City Hall were more crowded than they were the day before. In the mournful throng were veterans, bearing the scars of many well fought battles; smart young soldiers who had evidently not long taken the bounty; aged women whose mourning garments betokened a husband or a son sacrificed on the altar of his country; blooming girls; sedate city merchants and prosperous professional men; country folks in eccentric costumes; dapper city clerks; old men, gray headed and feeble; every class of life found its representatives in the throng which encompassed the body of the dead.

It was evident from the earliest hour that half those who were so patiently standing on the footpaths in Broadway and Centre street could not possibly get a view of the body within the time assigned for the lying in state. Still they remained in the ranks, hoping, apparently against hope, that some unlooked for diversion might lessen their distance from the wished for goal. Soon after ten o'clock the military began to assemble. First came a company of the Seventh regiment, and afterwards a detachment of the old Washington Grays, their officers attired in full mourning. Very soon the bugle call to assemble resounded through the corridor, where the dead was lying in its silent state, and the tramp of military feet varied the stealthy footsteps of the passing spectators. Several companies of the Seventh regiment, upon whom had devolved the duty of maintaining guard at the City Hall, passed by to view the body. After them followed a number of officers and veterans of the war.

The steamboat Granite State, from Hartford, brought down over three hundred passengers, who marched from the boat to the City Hall to view the body. One of their number placed a cross, two feet in length, upon the coffin. It was composed entirely of white camelias, rosebuds and azalias. There was one bud for each of the United States and one azalia to represent each year of the deceased's life. It was made in Hartford from flowers culled from the choicest private conservatories, and was the handiwork of Warren H. Burr, local editor of the Hartford *Daily Post.*

Captain Parker Snow, the commander of the arctic and antarctic exploring expeditions, presented to Gen. Dix, with a view of their being interred in the coffin with the President, some interesting relics of Sir John Franklin's ill-fated expedition. They consisted of a tattered leaf of a Prayer Book, on which the first word legible was the word "Martyr," and a piece of fringe and some portions of uniform. These relics were found in a boat lying under the head of a human skeleton.

At twenty minutes to twelve o'clock the doors of admission were closed to the general public, and though for some hours past the people had been admitted at the rate of nearly one hundred a minute—and over one hundred and fifty thousand persons must have seen the body—there yet remained immense crowds who were sent away disappointed. With practised fingers the undertaker,

Mr. F. G. Sands, and his assistant, Mr. G. W. Hawes, removed the dust from the face and habiliments of the dead; the flowers laid upon the coffin were taken charge of by the officials, and the lid was silently screwed down without form or ceremony, and with none but a few officers and orderlies and a couple of reporters as witnesses. The appointed bearers, eight in number, sergeants of the Veteran Reserve, stationed themselves on each side of the coffin, and remained there motionless as statues awaiting further orders.

The Governor's Room, when all but the military and those immediately connected with the obsequies, had withdrawn, presented a brilliant appearance. All the foreign Consuls dressed in their diplomatic uniforms, Governor Fenton, General Dix, accompanied by his staff, and several distinguished Generals were present. When all was in readiness the order was given and six of the body guard raised the coffin upon their shoulders, and, while a sergeant at each end steadied it to prevent the possibility of accident, bore it slowly down the spiral staircase and out of the City Hall, the whole assemblage following.

At ten minutes to one o'clock the hearse, which was specially constructed to carry the remains through the city, was brought in front of the Hall. When it had been placed in its proper position Major General Dix, who stood with cap in hand on the steps of the hall, gave the signal for the remains to be carried out. The coffin then appeared, borne by the guard of honor from the Veteran Reserve corps. All in the immediate vicinity instinctively uncovered. The band of the Seventh regiment played a mournful dirge, the City Hall bell tolled, the military presented arms, and, amid unbroken silence among the multitude, the mortal remains of Abraham Lincoln were borne to the hearse.

The Seventh regiment and other portions of the procession contiguous to the City Hall steps were then formed, Sergeants of the Reserve corps, with drawn sabres, stood round the remains, while the military dignitaries, Congressional delegations and other bodies ranged themselves in the order marked out for them. The time appointed for the procession to move was one o'clock, but the hour hand pointed to two before it slowly marched off with steady, solemn pace, amid a muffled roll of drums and saddened strains of funeral dirges from a number of bands.

This procession was the grandest—the most imposing ever organized in the United States. It marched in eight divisions, which embraced military and civic associations representing all the lines of martial service, and all the various walks of official and business life.

The First Division composed the military escort which preceded the hearse. The *New York Herald* said: When the history of the New York militia is written there will be two pages in their annals more interesting, more creditable and more gallant than all the others, and these will record their prompt response to the call of President Lincoln to defend the national capital in 1861, and the unanimity, force and order with which they turned out to escort the remains of that same great and good President on their passage through New York on the 24th and 25th of April, 1865. The military pageant yesterday—if such so solemn and mournful a display can properly be denominated—exceeded any thing in the military order that ever occurred in the city of New York. There were eighteen city regiments in the parade, and they averaged fully five hundred men each, thus making a total of nine thousand troops, besides the batteries, guns and their staffs, escort and so forth, amounting to one thousand more, which made the whole number of city militia in the parade at least ten thousand men. The United States troops and the Brooklyn regiments numbered five thousand more, so that the entire force of military in the procession reached the grand figure of fifteen thousand men.

Immediately following the military escort came Major General John A. Dix and staff, preceding the guard of honor, which consisted of a detachment from the Seventh regiment, formed two deep and in hollow square, inside of which marched the Veteran Guard. In the centre of the square was the hearse bearing the remains of the illustrious dead. It was fourteen feet long at its longest part, eight feet wide and fifteen feet one inch in height. On the main platform, which was five feet from the ground, was a dais six inches in height, at the corners of which were columns holding a canopy, which, curving inward and upward toward the centre, was surmounted by a miniature temple of liberty. The platform was entirely covered with black cloth, drawn tightly over the body of the car, and reaching to within a few inches of the ground, edged with silver bullion fringe. Over this hung graceful festoons of the same material, spangled with silver stars, and edged also with silver bullion. At the base of each column were three American flags, slightly inclined, festooned, covered with crape. The columns were black, covered with vines of myrtle and camelias. The canopy was of black cloth, drawn tightly, and from the base of the temple another draping of black cloth fell in graceful folds over the first; while from the lower edges of the canopy depended festoons, also of black cloth, caught under small shields. The folds and festoons were richly spangled and trimmed with bullion. At each corner of the canopy was a rich plume of black and white feathers.

The Temple of Liberty was represented as being deserted, having no emblems of any kind in or around it save a small flag on top, at half-mast. The inside of the car was lined with white satin, fluted, and from the centre of the roof was suspended a large gilt eagle, with outspread wings, covered with crape, bearing in its talons a laurel wreath, and the platform around the coffin was strewn with laurel wreaths and flowers of various kinds.

The car was drawn by sixteen gray horses, with coverings of black cloth, trimmed with silver bullion, each led by a colored groom, dressed in the usual habiliments of mourning, with streamers of crape on their hats.

When the gilded top of the temple surmounting the hearse was seen in the distance along the line of march, there was a general pushing and crowding in the dense throng on the sidewalks for good positions. At its nearer approach a simultaneous hush seemed to come over the entire crowd; the men reverently lifted their hats, and all eyes, many of which were moist with tears, were fastened on the hearse and coffin from the time of its appearance till it passed out of sight.

Many waited to see no more of the procession as it passed on in its regular order, which was the guard of honor, followed by a troop of cavalry as escort to Brigadier-General Hall, Grand Marshal, with his aids.

The Second Division, which comprised the representatives of the State, county and city governments of New York and other cities and States, representatives of foreign nations, &c., formed a prominent feature of the grand procession.

The carriages provided for the foreign representatives and delegations from the States and Territories of the

United States, were formed in line in Chambers-street, the right resting on Broadway, and the federal officers of the Custom House, Surveyor's Office, Post Office, and the collectors, assessors and deputies of the United States interal revenue, United States marshals and the judges and officers of the United States courts, formed on Centre-street, the head of the line resting on the corner of City Hall-square and Tryon-row. The carriages stood two abreast in the following order:

First—Occupied by Governor Fenton, of New York, Mayor Gunther, and Generals Batchellor and Swayne, of the Governor's staff.

Second—Lieutenant-Governor Alvord; Judge Davies, of the Court of Appeals; Judge Advocate General Harvey and Quartermaster-General Merritt, of the Governor's staff.

Third—Senators, Cole, Christie, Laimbler, and Representative Ingraham, which constituted the joint committee of the Senate and Assembly.

Fourth—Charles Loosey, Consul General of Austria; C. F. Habicht, Swedish and Norwegian Consul; E. M. Archibald, C. B., Her Britannic Majesty's Consul; Pierrepont Edwards, Esq., Her Britannic Majesty's Vice-Consul.

Fifth—William A. Kobbe, Consul-General of Nassau; G. L. Avezzana, Vice-Consul of Italy; D. Aguiar, Consul-General of Brazil.

Sixth—R. C. Burlage, Consul General of the Netherlands; D. N. Botassi, Consul of Greece; Robert Schultz, Vice-Consul of Russia; Adolph Gosling, Consul-General of Hanover.

Seventh—Jose F. Sanchez, Consul of Venezuela; Leopold Schmidt, Vice-Consul of Saxony and acting Consul-General of Prussia; Erhardt Jansen, Vice-Consul of Oldenburg; Fred. Kuhne, Consul of Hesse.

Eighth—Geo. H. Siemon, Royal Bavarian Consul; Carlos Enrique Leland, Consul of Uruguay; F. W. Kentgen, Consul of Hesse Darmstadt; C. B. Richard, Consul of Schammelburg Lippe; Blas Bruzual, Envoy Extraordinary and Minister Plenipotentiary of Venezuela.

Ninth—Governor Oglesby, of Illinois; Hon; J. DuBois, Colonel John Williams, Major L. Wait and Colonel James H. Bowen, all of Springfield, composing the Illinois delegation.

Tenth—Hon. S. M. Cullom, General J. N. Haynie, Dr. S. H. Melvin, of Springfield, Illinois, and Governor William Pickering, of Washington Territory.

Eleventh—O. M. Hatch, Major Brown, Dr. Phelps and E. F. Leonard.

Twelfth—Senator Anthony, of Rhode Island; Senator Nye, of Nevada; General Farnsworth and Mr. Washburne, of Illinois.

Thirteenth—Governor Stone, Judge Loughbridge and Mayor Corkhill, of Iowa, and S. D. Ward, of Chicago.

Fourteenth—Mayor Wallach, of Washington; Marshal Phillips and C. A. Page, of Illinois; and U. H. Painter, of Pennsylvania.

Fifteenth—Hon. J. N. Arnold, of Illinois; Hon. Leonard Myers, of Philadelphia; Hon. A. H. Rice, of Massachusetts, and Samuel Hooper, of Boston.

Sixteenth—Mr. T. Pico de Villanueva, Consul-General of Spain; Mr. L. Borg, acting Consul-General of France; General Paez, of Venezuela, and N. Zeo, Vice-Consul of Spain.

Seventeenth—Senator Ramsay, of Minnesota; Senator Cowan, of Pennsylvania; General Schenck, M. C., of Ohio; Colonel Whaley, M. C., of West Virginia.

Eighteenth—Mayor Tyler, of New Haven; ex-Governor Newell, M. C., of New Jersey; Sidney Clarke, M. C., from Kansas; G. A. Newell and Alderman McKnight, of New York.

Nineteenth—Mr. Terry and Mr. Driggs, of Michigan; Mr. Phelps of Maryland, and Mr. Shannon, of California.

Twentieth—Mr. Wallace, Delegate from Idaho; Hon. Geo. H. Williams, Senator from Oregon; Hon. Anson Herrick, M. C., New York city; Dr. James T. Brown, assistant embalmer of the body of the late President, of Washington city.

Twenty-first—Senator Clarke and Governor Smith, of New Hampshire; Joseph Bailey, M. C., of Pennsylvania, and Senator Harris, of New York.

Twenty-second—George T. Brown, Sergeant-at-Arms of the Senate; N. G. Ordway, Sergeant-at-Arms of the House of Representatives, and their assistants.

The foreign representatives were dressed in full court costume, wearing on their persons the insignia of their rank. Many of them wore sidearms, and all wore the usual badge of mourning.

The whole division was in charge of N. B. Laban, assisted by William M. Tweed, Jr., as aid; the second in command being Colonel Van Brunt, W. R. Vermilyea, Jr., and S. R. Brunell, acting as aids.

The following is the order in which this division took its place in the procession:

The members of both Boards of the Common Council, twenty abreast, preceded by their Sergeant-at-Arms, all wearing the usual mourning badge on the left arm, and carrying in their hands their staves of office shrouded in crape, the *attachés* of both boards following in their proper places.

Next in order came the delegations that accompanied the remains from Washington, followed by delegations from the Common Councils of Washington, Baltimore, Philadelphia, Brooklyn, Jersey City and other cities.

Comptroller Brennan, City Inspector Boole, Commissioner Miller; Board of Croton Commissioners, headed by President Stephens; Counsel to Corporation, Devlin, with Robert A. Bradford, Esq.; City Chamberlain Devlin and clerks; Fire Commissioner Wilson, and colleagues of the Board of Fire Commissioners; Board of Appeals of Fire Department; Chief Engineer Decker and assistants; Supervisors, with their president and sergeant-at-arms; Commissioners Bell, Nicholson, Bowen and Brennan; Board of Police Commissioners, Messrs. Acton, Berger, McMurray and Bosworth, with their clerks; Board of Education, headed by President McLean; the faculty of the Free Academy, with the venerable President Webster at their head; the Central Park Commissioners; Tax Commissioners Brown, Purser and Woodruff, and clerks; Commissioners of Emigration; Coroners and their deputies, Recorder Hoffman and City Judge Russell; Board of Police Magistrates, Judges Bernard, Sutherland and Ingraham, and clerks; Judges Monell, Barbour,

McCunn, Moncrief, Robertson, Daly, Brady and Cardoza: these Judges were all attended by their clerks and officers, wearing appropriate emblems of mourning; District Attorney Hall and assistants, with clerks; County Clerk Conner and other county officials.

The Collector's office, in the absence of Mr. Draper, was represented by Deputy Collectors Clinch and Embury, accompanied by the Collector's private secretary and the officers of the department. Surveyor Wakeman and his deputies headed the revenue officers, who turned out a very fine looking body of men, all dressed in black, wearing crape on the left arm and mourning rosettes on the left breast; Naval Officer Dennison, deputies, clerks and other *attachés* of the office.

The Post-Office Department, headed by Postmaster Kelly, turned out a very large force. A very handsome black banner, fringed with silver lace and surmounted by a small gilt eagle, pendent from the beak of which was a small mourning wreath, was borne in front, with the name of the department in silver letters inscribed in the centre.

Collectors and assessors of internal revenue, with their officers, clerks and *attachés*, then followed. The United States Marshal's office was represented by Joseph Thompson, first deputy (Mr. Murray being absent). Captain Lansing and the officers of the old Independent Continental Guard, dressed in full uniform, formed the escort to the officers of the Marshal's office and the officers of the Federal courts and United States District Attorney's office. Judge Benedict represented the United States Court for the Eastern district of New York, and the United States Circuit Court was represented by Kenneth J. White, clerk, and United States Commissioner, and the other officers and *attachés* of the court.

The Sub-Treasurer, clerks and employes of the Assay

office took their place in the line after the officers of the United States courts. All these civic federal organizations marched twenty abreast, and formed a solid line extending from the front of the City Hall, through City Hall square, Centre and Chambers streets, to the office of the United States Marshal.

The officers of the United States Navy Yard of Brooklyn, headed by Captain Case and the ex-officers of the United States Army, and the officers and ex-officers of the United States volunteers, brought up the rear of this division. The time occupied by the division in passing a given point was nearly an hour, and at a moderate estimate there must have been nearly, if not quite, twelve thousand persons comprised in this part of the procession.

The Third division was led by Colonel Frank E. Howe, Grand Marshal, and his aids, J. A. Stevens, Jr., and Maj. James R. Smith. They were succeeded by the band and drum corps of the Twelfth United States infantry from Fort Hamilton, who were immediately in front of a detachment of about forty of the Hawkins Zouaves, carrying old battle flags, draped in mourning, under Lieutenant Jackson. This division composed the professional, literary, political and social associations of the city.

The Fourth division was composed exclusively of the Masonic fraternity, Odd Fellows and other orders. Attired in uniform black habilliments, and aided only by simple, unpretending mourning badges and sprigs of acacia—the emblem of immortality—their appearance was striking in the extreme, and appropriate to the mournful occasion. This division was headed by General Hobart Ward, Marshal, and his aids, and a brass band.

The Fifth division was composed of Irishmen. Green and gold, mingled with the solemn badge of the grave, were the devices which each man wore in the ranks. On arm, shoulder and breast each member of each Irish society wore some emblem expressive of sympathy for the dead. Even the little children, the sons of Irish parents, with their neat little green jackets slashed with gold, were provided by their patriotic fathers and mothers with badges suitable to the solemn occasion.

The Sixth division embraced the Mechanics' Associations and the New York Caulkers' Association, numbering one thousand strong. In front they carried a handsome obelisk, elaborately draped in mourning, with a dial on either side, stopped at twenty-two minutes past seven, and the inscription: "*A Dark Hour in History.*" About the centre of the obelisk was a mourning wreath, surrounding the name—"*Lincoln.*" In front, near the base, beautifully executed, was the inscription: "*In Memory of Departed Worth.*" Two American flags were crossed in the rear of the monument, thickly draped in mourning.

Other associations bore banners appropriately inscribed.

The Seventh division, consisting entirely of trades and societies, presented a sight exceedingly melancholy, bearing banners draped in excellent taste, and exhibiting mournful inscriptions—representing the sentiments of native born Italians, Germans, Scotsmen, as well as of native born American workingmen.

The Eighth division was composed of citizens and societies of Brooklyn, Colonel E. J. Fowler, Marshal. Aids, Dr. Jas. T. Farley, John Vliet, Henry Mitchell, and Chas. Carroll Sawyer.

Following the Eighth division were the colored population of New York, who, though deprived of an invitation to join the grand pageant, having formed in Reade street, patiently awaited the arrival of the left of the Eighth division, and then joined in the procession, numbering at least two thousand persons. They were preceded by a banner bearing the following inscription:—

"*Abraham Lincoln, our Emancipator.*" On the reverse side of which were the following words:—"*Two Millions of Bondsmen he Liberty Gave.*" All along the route, and particularly in Union square, the colored division was vehemently applauded by the crowded assemblages.

The *New York Herald*, describing the memorable scenes of the occasion and the conduct of the throngs of people which filled the streets and the public squares along the entire line of March up Broadway to Fifth Avenue, and hence along Twenty-sixth-street, thence to the Albany Depot, said:

"The entire mass, such as in size this city never before saw, seemed to be animated by one sentiment, and controlled by one impulse. High and low, rich and poor, native and foreign born, all seemed to be touched by the one sentiment of regret and sadness, that subdued the natural tendency of great masses to indulge in mild forms of mob violence, and made them as quiet, as peaceable, as orderly, as the congregation the country church bell calls to prayers on a mid-summer-day. The city never saw a greater throng, nor a more orderly one. The adventurous urchin that climbed the trees overlooking the Park, dropped for the time being his outlandish calls for his comrades with outlandish names, and sat solemnly and quietly and watched the funeral procession with a dignity and a seriousness rarely witnessed in the Park from furtive youths. There were no incidents, such as spring up and are garnered by the argus-eyed reporter on other occasions in the City Hall Park. The people were too sad and depressed to indulge in mirth or sportive tricks. No one was drunk to create a disturbance, and no one was elated enough to attract attention. So the people, with tearful eyes under the shadow of the great affliction, watched patiently and unmurmuringly the moving of the honored dead and mournful procession, and silently breathed over them their most heartfelt and fervent prayers, and saw it go from them with a pang at every heart and a sigh from every lip. Such an occasion, such a crowd, and such a day New York may never see again. The world never witnessed so grand a collection of well-dressed, intelligent, and well-behaved beings, male and female, as thronged the streets of New York yesterday and gathered around the bier of the leader of the nation. No outbreak, no violence, no feverish commotion marked the immense gathering. All was tranquil, free from disturbance, and as peaceable as the flow of the mighty Hudson. It was a proud day for New York, and a new evidence to the world of the well-founded strength of republican institutions."

The decorations along Broadway and Fifth Avenue were in such impressive harmony with the suggestions and lessons of the day, that many of them deserve permanent record.

On one of the columns between the doors of the store at 353 Broadway, was a miniature monument, and immediately beneath the following: "*Just in the fulfillment of his executive appointments—judicious in the selection of his state co-workers—wise in the administration of his governmental functions—he has established a reputation for truth, wisdom and justice, as stable in its continuance as it was exalting in its realization.*"

At No. 247 was the motto—"*The workman dies, but the work goes on.*"

At No. 303 a temporary framework was erected, which was covered with black, festooned and trimmed with white fringe and tassels, and on the top was an eagle, covered with crape, on either side of which was a small flag, also draped in mourning.

At No. 372 was the following: "*Your cause of sorrow must not be measured by his worth; for then there would be no end.*"

At 429 was a large banner inscribed as follows: "*His deeds have made his name immortal.*"

Then followed the lines of which our late President was so fond, commencing: "*Oh! why should the spirit of mortals be proud.*"

At 446 was the inscription—

"Let others hail the rising sun,
We bow to him whose race is run."

At 546 the following words appeared: "*The life, the right and truth of all this realm is fled to heaven.*"

Under the Metropolitan Hotel was a handsome monogram of A. L., and underneath the following:

———"He rose,
Till the plain tiller of the sod
Tower'd o'er his peers in mind and soul, a god.
The assassin's hand bestowed the martyr's crown,
And the wide, wide world now echoes his renown.
The insulted nation, bowed with bitterest grief,
Demands stern vengeance for her fallen chief."

At Stuyvesant Institute was the following motto: "*Semper honos, nomenque tuum, laudesque manebunt,*" surrounding the name "Lincoln;" and opposite, on the armory of the Ninth Regiment, was the following: "*Though the assassin has rendered inanimate the noble and generous heart, yet the spirit which God has called to Heaven still hovers around us, and its influence in the cause of Liberty and Union shall remain forever.*"

Immediately over this was a shield with the words—

"A time for weeping,
But vengeance is not sleeping."

Next door to the Institute were the following in white letters on a black ground:

"Statesman, yet friend to truth, of soul sincere;
In action faithful and in honor clear;
Who broke no promise, serv'd no private end;
Who gained no title and who lost no friend."

"Thou art the ruins of the noblest man
That ever lived in the tide of time.
Woe to the hand that shed this costly blood."

At Gurney's was the following tribute to the late President:

"Sleep, martyred hero, sleep!
Thy going to thy great and just reward,
Among the faithful and the good whose lives
Are stainless lives, hath left a gloom
Upon a nation's and a people's joy.
A silent city from its domes and towers,
With universal tears flings out its signs of woe.
Great husbandman, though lost to us,
Thou yet hadst time to scatter far the seeds
Whose future fruit shall yet
Adorn the times; and of thy tillage
Shall our annals speak
And make a record of thy deeds and name,
Eternal as our principle."

At 753 the black drapery over the windows was formed so as to leave a diamond-shaped space, in which were the following words on a white ground: "*In perpetuam rei memoriam.*"

At 757 both windows were covered with black; on one was the following: "A. *Justice to traitors is*"—and on the other—"L. *Mercy to the people.*"

At 763 was the inscription—

"The good and great to God belong
Of every age and time;
Columbia hath her sacrifice
Laid on the hallowed shrine.
Slavery's tyrant chain is broke;
The swarthy bondman now is free;
A nation's chieftain lowly laid,
Eucharist of Liberty."

Between the stanzas was a likeness of the late President, and on either side a couplet of draped flags.

On the northwest corner of Twelfth street a scroll bore this inscription: "*A glorious career of service and devotion is crowned with a martyr's death.*"

Next door to the above was the following, on a white ground: "*Well done, thou good and faithful servant.*"

At 823 was a scroll with this inscription: "*Barbarism of slavery, can barbarism further go?*"

Nearly opposite the Spingler House a new testimonial commanded general notice. The space which it occupied was about ten or twelve feet square, and a railing of the rustic order, partially Gothic in shape, surrounded it. It resembled a miniature monument, the pedestal and the column being of the ordinary model. On the former appeared the name—now too famous to be preceded by initials—"*Lincoln.*"

The panels of the pedestal bore appropriate sentences. On the first was the adieu to the departed: "*Good night! and flights of angels sing thee to thy rest.*"

The marble next this had the words of the late President: "*With malice towards none; with charity for all.*"

On the third was the inscription: "*There's a great spirit gone!*"

On the last panel was the quotation from Shakspeare:

> "His life was gentle, and the elements
> So mixed in him, that nature might stand up
> And say to all the world—
> This was a man."

From the base of the column above the panels four beautiful wreaths of *immortelles*, inlaid with crosses of jet, were suspended, giving grace and finish to the testimonial.

On the southeast corner of Seventeenth street and

Fifth avenue a tablet bearing the following inscription was suspended from the second story: "*The heart of the nation beats heavily at the portals of his tomb.*"

At the corner of Twenty-second street was the inscription: "*And the Lord blessed Abraham in all things.*"

And immediately underneath: "*Semper honor nomenque tuum laudesque manebunt.*"

And also:

"Oh, earth, so full of dreary noise!
Oh, men, with wailing in your voice!
Oh, delved gold, the wailers heap!
Oh, war—oh, curse, that o'er it fall!
God makes a silence through you all,
And giveth His beloved sleep."

At 176 was a shield, on which was inscribed a cross, and underneath the words: "*Martyr.*" "*Montez au ciel.*"

CEREMONIES IN UNION-SQUARE.

Shortly after the procession had passed through Union-square, a meeting was held for the purpose of rendering fitting testimonials of respect and reverence for the character of President Lincoln, and joining in appropriate religious exercises.

A large stand had been erected, which was decorated with the national colors draped in black, and a broken column, round the base of which a roll of black crape was placed. To the right of the stand, was a pedestal bearing a bust of President Lincoln, executed by Thomas D. Jones. It was draped in mourning, and attracted much attention. About two thousand persons collected in front of the stand, among whom were many ladies of Ohio, and the windows and doorways of the houses within sight and hearing distance of the stand were crowded.

On the stand were large representations of the clergy, and deputations from the Union, New York, Century, Atheneum, City, Union League, Eclectic, and other clubs.

Hon. John A. King presided. The exercises were opened with prayer by Rev. Stephen H. Tyng, during which the assemblage remained uncovered.

After the prayer, the band played the "Dead March."

Hon. George Bancroft then delivered the following oration:

MR. BANCROFT'S ORATION.

"Our grief and horror at the crime which has clothed the continent in mourning, find no adequate expression in words and no relief in tears. The President of the United States of America has fallen by the hands of an assassin. Neither the office with which he was invested by the approved choice of a mighty people, nor the most simple-hearted kindliness of nature could save him from the fiendish passions of relentless fanaticism. The wailings of the millions attend his remains as they are borne in solemn procession over our great rivers, along the seaside, beyond the mountains, across the prairie, to their final resting-place in the valley of the Mississippi. The echoes of his funeral knell vibrate through the world, and the friends of freedom of every tongue and in every land are its mourners.

"Too few days have passed away since Abraham Lincoln stood in the flush of vigorous manhood, to permit any attempt at an analysis of his character or an exposition of his career. We find it hard to believe that his large eyes, which in their softness and beauty expressed nothing but benevolence and gentleness, are closed in death; we almost look for the pleasant smile that brought out more vividly the earnest cast of his features, which were serious even to sadness. A few years ago he was a village attorney, engaged in the support of a rising family, unknown to fame, scarcely named beyond his neighborhood; his administration made him the most conspicuous man in his country, and drew on him first the astonished gaze, and then the respect and admiration of the world.

"Those who come after us will decide how much of the wonderful results of his public career is due to his own good common sense, his shrewd sagacity, readiness of wit, quick interpretation of the public mind, his rare combination of fixedness and pliancy, his steady tendency of purpose; how much to the American people, who, as he walked with them side by side, inspired him with their own wisdom and energy; and how much to the overruling laws of the moral world, by which the selfishness of evil is made to defeat itself. But after every allowance, it will remain that members of the government which preceded his administration opened the gates to treason, and he closed them; and when he went to Washington the ground on which he trod shook under his feet, and he left the republic on a solid foundation; that traitors had seized the public forts and arsenals, and he recovered them for the United States to whom they belonged; that the capital, which he found the abode of slaves, now the home only of the free; that the boundless public domain, which was grasped at, and, in a great measure, held for the diffusion of slavery, is now irrevocably devoted to freedom, that then men talked a jargon of a balance of power in a republic between Slave States and Free States, and now the foolish words are blown away forever by the breath of Maryland, Missouri and Tennessee; that a terrible cloud of political heresy rose from

the abyss, threatening to hide the light of the sun, and under its darkness a rebellion was rising into indefinable proportions; now the atmosphere is purer than ever before, and the insurrection is vanishing away; the country is cast into another mould, and the gigantic system of wrong, which had been the work of more than two centuries, is dashed down, we hope, forever. And as to himself personally: he was then scoffed at by the proud as unfit for his station, and now, against the usage of later years, and in spite of numerous competitors, he was the unbiased and the undoubted choice of the American people for a second term of service. Through all the mad business of treason he retained the sweetness of a most placable disposition; and the slaughter of myriads of the best on the battle-field, and the more terrible destruction of our men in captivity by the slow torture of exposure and starvation, had never been able to provoke him into harboring one vengeful feeling or one purpose of cruelty.

"How shall the nation most completely show its sorrow at Mr. Lincoln's death? How shall it best honor his memory? There can be but one answer. He was struck down when he was highest in its service, and, in strict conformity with duty, was engaged in carrying out principles affecting its life, its good name, and its relations to the cause of freedom and the progress of mankind. Grief must take the character of action, and breathe itself forth in the assertion of the policy to which he fell a sacrifice. The standard which he held in his hand must be uplifted again, higher and more firmly than before, and must be carried on to triumph. Above everything else, his proclamation of the 1st day of January, 1863, declaring throughout the parts of the country in rebellion the freedom of all persons who had been held as slaves, must be affirmed and maintained.

"Events, as they rolled onward, have removed every doubt of the legality and binding force of that proclamation. The country and the rebel government have each laid claim to the public service of the slave, and yet but one of the two can have a rightful claim to such service. That rightful claim belongs to the United States, because every one born on their soil, with the few exceptions of the children of travelers and transient residents, owes them a primary allegiance. Every one so born has been counted among those represented in Congress; every slave has ever been represented in Congress—imperfectly and wrongly it may be—but still has been counted and represented. The slave born on our soil always owed allegiance to the General Government. It may in time past have been a qualified allegiance, manifested through his master, as the allegiance of a ward through its guardian or of an infant through its parent. But when the master became false to his allegiance the slave stood face to face with his country, and his allegiance, which may before have been a qualified one, became direct and immediate. His chains fell off, and he stood at once in the presence of the nation, bound, like the rest of us, to its public defence. Mr. Lincoln's proclamation did but take notice of the already existing right of the bondman to freedom. The treason of the master made it a public crime for the slave to continue his obedience; the treason of a State set free the collective bondmen of that State.

"This doctrine is supported by the analogy of precedents. In the times of feudalism the treason of the lord of the manor deprived him of his serfs; the spurious feudalism that existed among us differs in many respects

from the feudalism of the middle ages, but so far the precedent runs parallel with the present case—for treason the master then, for treason the master now loses his slaves.

"In the middle ages the sovereign appointed another lord over the serfs and the land which they cultivated; in our day the sovereign makes them masters of their own persons, lords over themselves.

"It has been said that we are at war, and that emancipation is not a belligerent right. The objection disappears before analysis. In a war between independent powers the invading foreigner invites to his standard all who will give him aid, whether bond or free, and he rewards them according to his ability and his pleasure with gifts or freedom; but when at a peace he withdraws from the invaded country he must take his aiders and comforters with him; or if he leaves them behind, where he has no court to enforce his decrees, he can give them no security, unless it be by the stipulations of a treaty. In a civil war it is altogether different. There, when rebellion is crushed, the old government is restored, and its courts resume their jurisdiction. So it is with us; the United States have courts of their own, that must punish the guilt of treason and vindicate the freedom of persons whom the fact of rebellion has set free.

"Nor may it be said, that because slavery existed in most of the States when the Union was formed, it cannot rightfully be interfered with now. A change has taken place, such as Madison foresaw, and for which he pointed out the remedy. The constitutions of States had been transformed before the plotters of treason carried them away into rebellion. When the Federal Constitution was formed, general emancipation was thought to be near; and everywhere the respective legislatures had authority,

in the exercise of their ordinary functions, to do away with slavery; since that time the attempt has been made in what are called Slave States to make the condition of slavery perpetual; and events have proved with clearness of demonstration, that a constitution which seeks to continue a caste of hereditary bondmen through endless generations is inconsistent with the existence of republican institutions

"So, then, the new President and the people of the United States must insist that the proclamation of freemen shall stand as a reality. And moreover, the people must never cease to insist that the Constitution shall be so amended as utterly to prohibit slavery on any part of our soil for evermore.

"Alas! that a State in our vicinity should withhold its assent to this last beneficent measure; its refusal was an encouragement to our enemies equal to the gain of a pitched battle, and delays the only hopeful method of pacification. The removal of the cause of the rebellion is not only demanded by justice; it is the policy of mercy, making room for a wider clemency; it is the part of order against a chaos of controversy; its success brings with it true reconcilement, a lasting peace, a continuous growth of confidence through an assimilation of the social condition. Here is the fitting expression of the mourning of to-day.

"And let no lover of his country say that this warning is uncalled for. The cry is delusive that slavery is dead. Even now it is nerving itself for a fresh struggle for continuance. The last winds from the South waft to us the sad intelligence that a man who had surrounded himself with the glory of the most brilliant and most varied achievements, who but a week ago was named with affectionate pride among the greatest benefactors of his country and the ablest Generals of all time, has usurped more than the whole power of the Executive, and under the name of peace has revived slavery and given security and political power to traitors from the Chesapeake to the Rio Grande. Why could not he remember the dying advice of Washington, never to draw the sword but for self-defence or the rights of his country, and when drawn, never to sheath it till its work should be accomplished? And yet from this bad act, which the people with one united voice condemn, no great evil will follow save the shadow on his own fame. The individual, even in the greatness of military glory, sinks into insignificance before the resistless movements in the history of man. No one can turn back or stay the march of Providence.

"No sentiment of despair may mix with our sorrow. We owe it to the memory of the dead, we owe it to the cause of popular liberty throughout the world, that the sudden crime which has taken the life of the President of the United States shall not produce the least impediment in the smooth course of public affairs. This great city, in the midst of unexampled emblems of deeply seated grief, has sustained itself with composure and magnanimity. It has nobly done its part in guarding against the derangement of business or the slightest shock to public credit. The enemies of the republic put it to the severest trial, but the voice of faction has not been heard—doubt and despondency have been unknown. In serene majesty the country rises in the beauty and strength and hope of youth, and proves to the world the quiet energy and the durability of institutions growing out of the reason and affection of the people.

"Heaven has willed it that the United States shall live. The nations of the earth cannot spare them. All the worn out aristocracies of Europe saw in the spurious feudalism of slaveholding their strongest outpost, and banded themselves together with the deadly enemies of our national life. If the Old World will discuss the respective advantages of oligarchy or equality; of the union of church and state, or the rightful freedom of religion; of land accessible to the many or of land monopolized by an ever decreasing number of the few, the United States must live to control the decision by their quiet and unobtrusive example. It has often and truly been observed that the trust and affection of the masses gather naturally round an individual; if the inquiry is made whether the man so trusted and beloved shall elicit from the reason of the people enduring institutions of their own, or shall sequester political power for a superintending dynasty, the United States must live to solve the problem. If a question is raised on the respective merits of Timoleon or Julius Cæsar, of Washington or Napoleon, the United States must be there to call to mind that there were twelve Cæsars, most of them the opprobrium of the human race, and to contrast with them the line of American Presidents.

"The duty of the hour is incomplete, our mourning is insincere if, while we express unwavering trust in the great principles that underlie our government, we do not also give our support to the man to whom the people have intrusted its administration.

"Andrew Johnson is now, by the Constitution, the President of the United States, and he stands before the world as the most conspicuous representative of the industrial classes. Left an orphan at four years old, poverty and toil were his steps to honor. His youth was not passed in the halls of colleges; nevertheless he has received a thorough political education in statesmanship in the school of the people and by long experience of public life. A village functionary; member successively of each branch of the Tennessee Legislature, hearing with a thrill of joy the words, "The Union, it must be preserved;" a representative in Congress for successive years; Governor of the great State of Tennessee, approved as its Governor by re-election; he was at the opening of the rebellion a Senator from that State in Congress. Then at the Capitol, when Senators, unrebuked by the Government, sent word by telegram to seize forts and arsenals, he alone from that Southern region told them what the Government did not dare to tell them, that they were traitors, and deserved the punishment of treason. Undismayed by a perpetual purpose of public enemies to take his life, bearing up against the still greater trial of the persecution of his wife and children, in due time he went back to his State, determined to restore it to the Union, or die with the American flag for his winding sheet. And now, at the call of the United States, he has returned to Washington as a conqueror, with Tennessee as a Free State for his trophy. It remains for him to consummate the vindication of the Union.

"To that Union Abraham Lincoln has fallen a martyr. His death, which was meant to sever it beyond repair, binds it more closely and more firmly than ever. The blow aimed at him, was aimed not at the native of Kentucky, not at the citizen of Illinois, but at the man who, as President, in the executive branch of the Government, stood as the representative of every man in the United States. The object of the crime was the life of the whole people; and it wounds the affections of the whole people. From Maine to the southwest boundary of the Pacific it makes us one. The country may have needed an imperishable grief to touch its inmost feeling. The grave that receives the remains of Lincoln, receives the martyr to the Union; the monument which will rise over his body will bear witness to the Union; his enduring memory will assist during countless ages to bind the States together, and to incite to the love of our one undivided, individual country. Peace to the ashes of our departed friend, the friend of his country and his race. Happy was his life, for he was the restorer of the Republic; he was happy in his death, for the manner of his end will plead forever for the union of the States and the freedom of man."

The delivery of the oration was frequently interrupted by applause.

Rev. Dr. Joseph P. Thompson was introduced, and read President Lincoln's last inaugural address in a very impressive manner. This was followed by the reading, by Rev. W. H. Boole, of the 94th Psalm, which was pronounced by the inspired Psalmist against the enemies of his country. Rev. Dr. Rogers then pronounced a prayer, in which he thanked God that our late President had been removed from among us without even a shadow on his name, and that a Joshua had been raised up to replace him. After appropriate music by the band, Rev. Rabbi Isaacs, of the Broadway Synagogue, read a selection from the Scriptures and delivered a short prayer.

Rev. Dr. Samuel Osgood then read the following hymn, composed only a few hours previously, by William C. Bryant:

ODE—ABRAHAM LINCOLN.

O, slow to smite and swift to spare,
  Gentle and merciful and just,
Who in the fear of God did'st bear
  The sword of power, the nation's trust.

In sorrow by thy bier we stand,
  Amid the woe that hushes all,
And speak the anguish of a land
  That shook with horror at thy fall.

Thy task is done, the bond are free—
  We bear thee to an honored grave,
Whose noblest monument shall be
  The broken fetters of the slave.

Pure was thy life—its bloody close
  Hath placed thee with the sons of light,
Among the noblest host of those
  Who perished in the cause of right.

Dr. Osgood also read the following composition of Mr. Bryant, which he said had not yet been published:

FUNERAL HYMN

"Thou hast put all things under his feet."

O North, with all thy vales of green,
  O South, with all thy palms,
From peopled towns, and fields between,
  Uplift the voice of psalms;
Raise, ancient East, the anthem high,
And let the youthful West reply.

Lo! in the clouds of heaven appears
  God's well-beloved Son;
He brings a train of brighter years—
  His Kingdom is begun;
He comes, a guilty world to bless
With mercy, truth, and righteousness.

O Father, haste the promised hour
  When at his feet shall lie
All rule, authority and power
  Beneath the ample sky;
When He shall reign from pole to pole,
The Lord of every human soul.

Archbishop McClosky being unavoidably absent, the benediction was pronounced by Dr. Hitchcock, and the assemblage then dispersed.

DEPARTURE FROM NEW YORK.

At three o'clock, the head of the procession having reached the Hudson River Railroad depot in Twenty-ninth street between Ninth and Tenth avenues, the column halted and formed in line facing to the west, to allow the hearse and escort of mourners to pass. At half-past three the approach of the hearse was made known by solemn refrains of bands and the muffled roll of martial drums. As it passed other bands and other drums caught up the melancholy notes, regiments brought their arms to a present, officers saluted with their swords and colors draped in the badges of mourning were lowered.

When the head of the procession reached the railroad station the rear of it had not passed Fourteenth street. It must have contained full sixty thousand men. After the delivery of the remains to the charge of the railroad authorities, it was hours before the rear of the procession ceased marching, and when the train, containing the body of the President, started from the depot at 4:15, the procession was still progressing up Broadway.

The funeral escort passed out of Ninth avenue into Twenty-ninth street in the following order:—

Mounted troop, Eighth regiment, New York.

Superintendent Kennedy.

Inspectors Carpenter and Leonard.

Broadway Squad.

Grand Marshal and Aids.

Grafulla's Band.

Seventh regiment.

General Dix and Guard of Honor, mounted.

Escort. HEARSE. Escort.

Naval officers.
The Mayor and Governor Fenton.
Carriages containing foreign representatives.
Color guard, Irish brigade.
General Dix's body guard.
Police.

The Seventh regiment marched on the sidewalk, and, forming into full battalion front, presented arms to General Dix as he passed by them.

The General and guard of honor dismounted at the second entrance and advanced to meet the hearse, which had halted midway between the upper and lower entrance to the depot.

A staircase with a top made so as to rest on the side of the hearse and reaching from the street, was then placed in position; the sergeants of the Invalid corps ascended it, and, raising the coffin descended with their burden to the sidewalk. The guard presented arms and all the spectators uncovered. The pall-bearers, preceded by General Dix, then marched through the entrance into the depot, where they were met by the guard of honor.

In an article upon the extraordinary character of the obsequies, and the unparalled conduct of the people the *New York Times*, said: "As a mere pageant, the vast outpouring of the people, the superb military display, the solemn grandeur and variety thrown into the procession by the numberless national, friendly, trade and other civic societies; the grand accompaniment of music; and, above all, the subdued demeanor of the countless multitude of onlookers, made the day memorable beyond the experience of the living generation.

* * * * * * *

"The tribute, unparalled as it has been, in its character and costliness, was not the heedless offerings of prodigality, but primarily a prompt, spontaneous and deliberate sacrifice by the industrious, the frugal, the pecuniarily responsible body of the people. Viewed as such, it forms not only the grandest oblation ever made on the altar of departed worth, as embodied in Statesman, President or Monarch, but it raises the character of the whole nation far above the imputation of sordidness, of persistent and unchangeable devotion to Mammon, so falsely urged against it by outside commentators, whose pleasure and privilege is uniform destruction. And we may also say that, in the presence of the ready self-sacrifice which our present bereavement has illustrated, the theory that republics are ungrateful may at least bear revision."

NEW YORK TO ALBANY.

Two locomotive engines were set apart by the Railway company for the conveyance of the funeral train to Albany, which were most beautifully and appropriately decorated with mourning symbols for the occasion. The "pilot engine" was the Constitution. The name of the locomotive which drew the train was the Union, and the decorations bestowed upon it were of the most elaborate and tasteful description. The Union conveyed the President from Albany to New York, while on his first triumphal progress from Springfield to Washington, in 1861. Mr. William Raymond was the engineer to the train, and Mr. J. M. Toucey, assistant superintendent of the road, acted as conducter, assisted by a carefully selected staff of breaksmen. The train was composed of eight cars, besides the funeral car, seven of which were furnished by the railroad company, including a baggage car. These cars were new, and neatly though not heavily draped in black.

While the historic group standing on the platform was superintending the depositing of the remains in the car, its number was added to by the unexpected appearance of Lieut.-Gen. Scott. The old General was simply attired in citizen's clothes, wearing a deep crape band on his hat, and was wrapped in a heavy regulation overcoat. He was greeted with great feeling by the knot of Generals who comprised the escort of honor, and replied to their inquiries after his health with cordiality. The General did not remain in the depot long, but after a cordial greeting and adieu to the funeral party, retired to his carriage, leaning on the arm of a friend.

The word was given, and the parties who were to accompany the remains entered the cars assigned to them. Governor Fenton was accompanied by Generals Batcheller, Merritt, Harvey and Swain; Judges Davies and Porter, of the Court of Appeals; Messrs. Dawson and Cassidy, representing the press; Colonel L. L. Doty, Lieutenant-Governor Alvord, with Senators D. A. Cole, W. F. Laimbeer and Robert Christie, and Assemblyman S. P. Ingraham. General Dix also formed one of the escort, accompanied by Colonel McMahon and Captain Lord, of his staff.

At 4¼ o'clock the depot bell rang, and in a few minutes the train began to move slowly off. As it passed down the platform every one standing upon it removed his hat. Outside of the gate of the depot yard, on Tenth avenue, the immense throng stationed there received in respectful and mournful silence the very brief and unsatisfactory glimpse they gained of the coffin. The usual hoarse clangor of the engine bell was deadened by the tongue being muffled, and as the train moved off it gave an indescribable air of mournfulness and of woe to the scene.

The train passed from New York to Albany without stoppage, except for a few minutes at Poughkeepsie, where a delegation from the city government of Albany met it. Along the entire route the respect and sorrow of the people were appropriately manifested. At Hastings, the home of Commodore Farragut, a striking memorial was erected near the depot. It consisted of a four columned arch, draped with mourning and flags, and bearing the following inscription: "*We will cherish the memory of Abraham Lincoln by supporting the principles of free government, for which he suffered martyrdom.*"

At one place a hundred school girls, dressed in white, came down to the roadside. At another the track was arched high over the cars with tablet flags and drapery, and the inscription "*The Nation mourns a Nation's loss.*" At a third a young lady, representing the Goddess of Liberty, knelt upon a dais, in sorrowing attitude, one hand grasping the flag whose folds, clad in transparent black, fell by her side, while the other rested upon and held fast to a floral anchor. Before her, on the same dais, was a small monument, deeply and darkly clad, inscribed simply "*Abraham Lincoln.*" At West Point the Cadets were drawn up in line, half minute guns were fired, and the bands discoursed funeral dirges. After dark torches at each station lighted up the scene for the throngs who stood by, and bonfires blazed from jutting rocks at many points.

ALBANY.

The funeral train arrived at Albany at eleven o'clock. The remains were received at the depot by the appointed committees and deposited in the hearse, which was drawn by four gray horses draped and plumed. Carriages were in attendance to receive the Governor and Joint Committee. The city officials and many citizens of distinction, with members of the Legislature, were also present to join in the mourning train. The night was murky, dry, starlight, still and pleasant. From the depot the cortege moved to the ferry boat, and crossed to the west side of the Hudson from East Albany. About a dozen fire companies had assembled at the Albany landing, bearing their lamp torches. Three companies of militia from the Tenth Regiment, and one from the Twenty-fifth, were in attendance as escort. The streets were thronged as they had never been before. A profusion of sable drapery prevailed at the depot, on the boat, and at every point along the route, from the landing at Albany to the platform where the remains lay in state in the Assembly Chamber. The smoke and glare of the torch-lights, the silent tramp and the perfect hush of the people, as the cortege moved on its way through the capital of the State, was very impressive.

A large band led the procession with a dead march. The Governor and committee, with the other attending mourners in carriages, followed the hearse, the Guard preceding and following, while the firemen, making a flanking line on either side, comprised the order of the procession to the Capitol.

At one o'clock on the morning of April 26th, the coffin was opened and the face of the martyred President exposed to view in the Capitol of New York. The coffin rested upon a simple platform, covered with black velvet, with silver bullion; a silk flag of the Union was wound around it. It was prepared and placed there by Thurlow Weed's daughter. The Assembly Chamber was simply but tastefully draped in mourning; one inscription, in black relief, extended over the Speaker's desk, in the words of Lincoln—"*I have sworn a solemn oath to preserve, protect and defend the government.*"

The people were admitted in two lines, and passed the corpse in unbroken lines until two hours after mid-day, when the doors were closed and the procession formed, which escorted the hearse and its honored burden to the Central Railway Depot. A reporter, who witnessed the tribute of the people paid to the memory of Mr. Lincoln at the Capital of the Empire State, said:

"All day the streets have been crowded with people to see the remains of the late beloved President. They reached from the Assembly Chamber at the Capitol to the foot of State-street, in a prolonged and patient line four deep. However enthusiastic and earnest the feeling kindled in the great cities through which the funeral procession had passed, its approach through the State to the great masses of the rural population of the interior indicates a power of feeling and unanimity of sentiment which must present permanent results in the public opinion of the country for generations."

Soon after two o'clock, the procession having been formed under Grand Marshal Franklin Townsend, commenced to move over the prescribed route. It was composed of the 10th and 25th Regiments of Albany, the 24th and the Light-Horse Battery of Troy, the State and city authorities, the Fire Department, and a large number of civic societies. State-street, from the Capitol to Broadway, and Broadway, from State to Lumber streets, altogether a distance exceeding a mile, was densely packed during the march. Such a mass of human beings (probably not less than 60,000) was never before seen in the streets of Albany. There were four bands, each with a full drum corps, in line; and as the procession moved down the hill, the bands playing "Love Not," "Auld Lang Syne," "Come and let us worship," the effect was thrilling. All the buildings along the route were draped with mourning. Among the most touching mottoes on house fronts were the following: "*The heart of the Nation throbs heavily at the portals of the tomb.*" "*Let us resolve that the Martyred dead shall not have died in vain.*"

ALBANY TO BUFFALO.

The funeral train, under the immediate charge of Conductor Homer P. Williams, the General Superintendent, H. W. Chillinden, accompanying it, moved from the Albany Depot at four o'clock. In all the cities, towns and villages along the thickly populated line of the Central railway, demonstrations were made as appropriate and suggestive as any which had been witnessed on the journey from Washington. The reporter for the *New York Tribune* wrote "that a funeral in each house in central New York would hardly have added solemnity to the day."

The following-named gentlemen accompanied the funeral procession through the State of New York, by invitation of Gov. Fenton: Judges Davies and Porter, of the Court of Appeals; Hon. Chauncey M. Depew, Secretary of State; Gens. Alex. W. Harvey and George S. Batchellor; E. Merritt and S. E. Marvin, Staff Officers; Col. L. L. Doty, of the Military Bureau; George Dawson, of the *Albany Journal*, and Wm. Cassady, of the *Argus and Atlas*. Gov. Fenton himself could not attend the party, owing to the fact that the Legislature was on the eve of adjournment.

In addition to the usual tokens of respect, processions, firing of guns, solemn music, sable drapery, there were several in central New York entitled to permanent record. At Schenectady ladies were seen shedding tears. The signal men bore in their hands white square flags, bordered with black. At Little Falls a note, of which the following is a copy, was presented in behalf of the ladies:

LITTLE FALLS, *Wednesday* April 26.

The ladies of Little Falls, through their committee, present these flowers and the shield, as an emblem of the protection which our beloved President ever proved to the liberties of the American people.

The *cross*, of his ever faithful trust in God, and the *wreath* as the token that we mingle our tears with those of an afflicted nation.

Mrs. S. M. RICHMOND,
Mrs. E. W. HOPKINS,
Mrs. POWERS GREEN,
Mrs. J H. BUCKLIN,
Miss MINNIE HILL,
Miss HELEN BROOKS,
Miss MARIA BROOKS,
Miss MARY SHAW,
Committee.

The floral emblems were deposited on the coffin, the band, meanwhile, performing a dirge. Women and men were moved to tears at this solemn exhibition of heart-felt regard.

At Syracuse, the sable decorations attracted especial attention. A company of veteran reserves were in attendance to pay honors to the illustrious dead; a band of music played a dirge as the train entered the depot, and a choir of an hundred voices sang appropriate hymns during the stoppage of the train. A small bouquet was handed to the delegate from Idaho (Hon. W. H. Wallace), upon which were the appropriate words—"The last tribute of respect from Mary Virginia Raynor, a little girl of three years of age. Dated Syracuse, April 26, 1865." It was laid on the President's coffin by Gen. Aken.

The train reached Rochester at twenty minutes past three o'clock on the morning of April 27th. On the north side of the railroad station were drawn up in line the Fifty-Fourth National Guard State troops, first company of Veteran Reserves, and hospital soldiers and a battery attached to the Twenty-Fifth brigade, and the first company of Union Blues. The Independent and new Marines regimental band played a funeral dirge. On the south side were the Mayor with twenty-five members of the common council of Rochester, together with Gen. John Williams and staff, Major Lee, commanding the post, with his corps of assistants, and Gen. Martindale and staff

The funeral party had been increased by the addition of Ex-President Fillmore, and Messrs. J. A. Verplank, J. Gallasten, James Sheldon, S. S. Jewett, Henry Martin, Philip Dorsheimer, J. P, Slivens, E. S. Prosser, John Wilkinson, Henry Morrison, N. P. Hopkinson, on behalf of the Mayor of Buffalo.

BUFFALO.

The firing of cannon and tolling of bells announced the arrival of the train bearing the remains of the assasinated Chief of the Nation at Buffalo, at seven o'clock A. M., April 27th. It was met at the depot by a large concourse of people.

The procession was formed between 7 and 8 o'clock and proceeded toward St. James' Hall, under a civil and military escort. The coffin was prominently in view of the very many persons who lined the streets through which the cortege passed. The hearse was heavily covered with black cloth, surmounted with an arched roof and tastefully trimmed with white satin and silver lace.

An extensive display of the military and civilians was omitted, in view of the fact that Buffalo had a funeral procession on the day the obsequies took place at Washington. The procession reached the Young Men's Association Building at 9:35 A. M. The body was taken from the funeral car and carried by soldiers up into St. James' Hall, and deposited on the dias in the presence of the accompanying officers, the guards of honor, and the Union Continentals, commanded by N. K. Hall. The remains were placed under a crape canopy, extending from the ceiling to the floor. The space was lighted by a large chandelier. In the gallery outside the canopy, was the Buffalo St. Cecelia, Society, an amateur American music association, who, as the remains were brought in, sang with deep pathos the dirge, "Rest, spirit, rest," affecting every heart and moving many to tears. The society then placed an elegantly formed harp, made of choice white flowers, at the head of the coffin as a tribute from them to the honored dead. Shortly after this the public were admitted. Ex-President Fillmore was among the civilians escorting the remains to St. James' Hall. Company D, Seventy-Fourth regiment, Capt. J. C. Bowles, which acted as an escort to President Lincoln four years previous, from and to the depot, on his way to Washington, took part in the funeral procession. The remains were visited through the day from half-past nine in the morning until eight in the evening by an immense number of persons. During the morning there was placed at the foot of the coffin an anchor of white camelias, from the ladies of the Unitarian Church of Buffalo. A cross of white flowers was also laid upon the coffin.

The procession, with the remains, left St. James' Hall about 8:45 o'clock, escorted to the depot by the military, followed by a large crowd. The train left at about 10 o'clock for Cleveland.

BUFFALO TO CLEVELAND.

Between Buffalo and Cleveland the people of New York, Pennsylvania and of Ohio, testified in great numbers and with tasteful symbols and elaborate demonstrations, respect which was heartfelt, and sorrow which sought close sympathy.

At Dunkirk, a group of thirty-six young ladies, representing the States of the Union, appeared on the railway platform, dressed in white, each with a broad, black scarf resting on the shoulder, and holding in her hand a national flag.

At Westfield, at one o'clock in the morning, a party of five ladies, namely, Mrs. Drake, wife of Col. Drake, killed at Cold Harbor; Mrs. F. B. Brewer, Mrs. L. A. Skinner, and Miss Abbie and Miss Elizabeth Tucker, brought in a cross and a wreath of flowers. On the cross were the words—"Ours the Cross; Thine the Crown." All of them were affected to tears, and considered it a sacred privilege to kiss the coffin.

At the line which separates New York from Pennsylvania, Major-Gen. Dix and staff took leave of the funeral procession, and F. F. Farrar, Mayor of Erie; George W. Starr, F. B. Vincent, E. P. Bennett, J. T. Walsher and Capt. F. A. Roe, U. S. N., came on board the cars.

Miss Leonora Crawford, aged 12 years, at this point presented a cross and wreath with the words "Rest in Peace," attached. The scene was illuminated by a large bonfire and Chinese lanterns.

At Wickliffe, Governor Brough, on behalf of Ohio, received the funeral party. At that point his staff joined him, consisting of Genl. B. R. Cowen, Adjt.-Genl.; Genl. Merrill Barlow, Q. M. Genl.; Genl. R. N. Barr, Surgeon-Genl.; Col. Sidney D. Maxwell, Aid-de-Camp; Lt.-Col. John T. Mercer, Asst. Adjt.-Genl.; F. A. Marble, Esq., Private Secretary.

Major-Genl. Joseph Hooker, commanding the Northern Department of Ohio, also joined the funeral party at Wickliffe, under orders from the War Department, to accompany the President's remains to Springfield, with his staff, including Col. Swords, Asst. Q. M. Genl.; Lieut. Simpson, U. S. Engineers; Lieut.-Col. Lathrop, Assist. Inspector-Genl.; Major Bannister, Chief Paymaster; Major MacFeely, Commissary, U. S. A.; and Capt. Taylor. United States Senator Sherman, Hon. S. Galloway, Hon. Octavious Waters and Major Montgomery, also met the remains at Wickliffe; together with a number of the prominent citizens of Northern Ohio, who had been appointed at Cleveland a committee to attend the funeral procession from the State line to that city.

There was a special feature about the running of the train from Erie to Cleveland that deserves notice. As far as possible, everything connected with the train was the same as on the occasion of Mr. Lincoln's journey over that road in 1861. The locomotive (the "William Case") was the same. The engineer, Wm. Congden, was dead, and the engine was run by John Benjamin. The fireman in 1861, George Martin, was engineer, but asked and obtained the privilege of again acting as fireman on the train. The same conductor, E. D. Page, had control of the train. Superintendent Henry Nottingham, as before, had the complete management. The pilot engine, "Idaho," which preceded the train ten minutes, was run by engineer J. McGuire, and fireman Frank Keehen.

CLEVELAND.

As soon as it was definitely ascertained that the remains of President Lincoln would pass through Cleveland on their way to Springfield, measures were taken to extend to them the honor due from a grateful people to their beloved Chief Magistrate. The first movement originated in the City Council, in the shape of a series of resolutions introduced by Amos Townsend, appropriate to the occasion, authorizing the appointment of a committee, with the Mayor as chairman, to make the necessary preparations. This committee consisted of George B. Senter, Mayor, Thomas Jones, Jr., President of the Council, and Joseph Sturges, Ansel Roberts and Amos Townsend, Trustees. It held its first meeting at the Mayor's office on Wednesday evening, April 19, when George B. Senter was chosen permanent Chairman, and Thomas Jones, Jr., permanent Secretary.

The Board of Trade took action on Thursday, and appointed Philo Chamberlin, R. T. Lyon, J. F. Freeman, S. F. Lester, W. Murray and A. J. Begges, a committee to co-operate with the committee from the City Council in all matters pertaining to the reception of the remains of the President. This committee met with the Council committee on Saturday evening, and on motion was incorporated with that committee.

The Council committee in the meantime had added to their number several prominent citizens, and the augmented committee took the name of the General Committee of Arrangements, and consisted of the following gentlemen:

Hon. George B. Senter, Chairman; Thomas Jones, Jr., and J. C. Sage, Secretaries; Ansel Roberts, Hon. R. P. Spalding, Gen. A. S. Sanford, Col. W. H. Hayward, W.

B. Castle, R. T. Lyon, W. Murray, S. F. Lester, A. Stone, Jr., L. M. Hubby, Joseph Sturges, Amos Townsend, Hon. H. Payne, Col. Jas. Barnett, Wm. Bingham, Philo Chamberlin, J. F. Freeman, A. J. Begges, H. M. Chapin, M. Barlow.

At the meeting of the General Committee of Arrangements on Saturday evening, April 22d, the following sub-committees were raised, and the Mayor authorized to designate the names of gentlemen to fill them: On Location of Remains, Reception, Procession, Military Entertainment, Music, Decoration and Carriages.

As filled by Mayor Senter the sub-committees were as follows:

On Location of Remains.—Philo Chamberlin, H. B. Payne, Ansel Roberts, Wm. Bingham, A. S. Sanford, and Amasa Stone, Jr.

On Reception.—George B. Senter, Chairman, Thomas Jones, Jr., Ansel Roberts, Joseph Sturges, Amos Townsend, Hon. David Tod, Hon. Wm. B. Castle, Hon. H. B. Payne, Hon. H. M. Chapin, Amasa Stone, Jr., Hon. E. S. Flint, Hon. R. C. Parsons, Hon. H. V. Willson, General M. Barlow, M. R. Keith, Hon. S. O. Griswold, Hon. F. J. Dickman, S. D. McMillen, Anson Stager, Hon. George Mygatt, Hon. John Brough, Hon. R. P. Spalding, Hon. S. Williamson, C. W. Palmer, Philo Chamberlin, Hon. F. T. Backus, Stillman Witt, W. H. Truscott, George A. Benedict, Hon. A. Everett, T. P. Handy, D. B. Sexton, T. M. Kelley, L. A. Pierce, Hon. Samuel Starkweather, Hon. John A. Foot.

On Procession.—Col. James Barnett, Wm. Bingham, Col. John P. Ross, Silas Merchant, Amos Townsend, Col. W. H. Hayward, Capt. F. W. Pelton, Capt. B. L. Spangler.

On Military.—Gen. A. S. Sanford, Col. Chas. Whittlesey, Wm. Bingham, Col. W. H. Hayward, Major J. D. Palmer.

On Entertainment.—Thomas Jones, Jr., Earl Bill, John A. Wheeler, Joseph Sturges, E. Cowles.

On Music.—B. Seymour, R. T. Lyon, R. Crawford, Daniel Stephan.

On Decoration.—John M. Sterling, Peter Thatcher, B. Butts, F. R. Elliott, T. Ross, Dr. E. Sterling, Wm. Beckenbach, Capt. Spaulding, Geo. Howe.

On Carriages.—Nelson Purdy, William Murray, David Price, Peter Goldrick.

To Meet the Remains.—Hon. R. P. Spalding, Gov. David Tod, Thomas Jones, Jr., Col. Anson Stager, Amasa Stone, Jr., Hon. H. B. Payne, Hon. John A. Foot, Hon. H. V. Willson, Stillman Witt, Ansel Roberts, William Bingham, Hon. Wm. B. Castle, Charles Hickox, John Martin, Hon. Wm. Collins, H. N. Johnson, Dr. G. C. E. Weber, Dr. Proctor Thayer, E. Cowles, H. B. Hurlbut, Jacob Hovey, James Worswick, George Willey, Lemuel Crawford.

At a subsequent meeting of the General Committee of Arrangements the following gentlemen were selected to act as a Civic Guard of Honor:

Fayette Brown, Chairman, H. F. Brayton, E. Simms, Charles Pettingell, John Bousfield, Geo. W. Woodworth, C. L. Russell, George W. Gardner, M. B. Clark, James Worswick, A. T. Brinsmade, E. Cowles, O. N. Skeels, Allayne Maynard, Samuel Starkweather, T. S. Beckwith, C. S. McKenzie, E. Chester, H. J. Herrick, K. Hays, Geo. Presly, J. W. Fitch, L. M. Pitkin, H. D. Ruggles, E. Rockwell, Ch. Glasser, John Hartness, A. E. Burlison, E. R. Perkins, John Huntington, S. H. Benedict, F. T. Wallace, Harvey Rice, Jacob Hovey, S. H. Mather, Geo. C. Dodge, D. W. Cross, James Pannell, James J. Tracy, R. K. Winslow, John E. Carey, G. W. Calkins, E. J. Estep, J.

P. Bishop, William Jones, H. K. Reynolds, F. C. Keith, H. C. McFarland, V. C. Taylor, Geo. B. Ely, S. Hyman, J. H. Morley, A. J. Wenham, L. L. Lyon, W. P. Fogg, J. C. Calhoun, Chas. Whitaker, E. J. Gorham, Moses Kelley, T. W. Leek, H. N. Raymond, M. L. Brooks, B. F. Piexotto, S. Thorman, Frank W. Parsons, E. S. Root, A. B. Stone, A. Chisholm, G. A. Hyde, H. C. Hawkins, R. E. Mix, C. C. Rogers, Augustus Thieme, Jacob Schroeder, Wm. Hart, C. A. Read, Reuben Becker, J. P. Robinson, S. M. Carpenter, James Hill, S. W. Crittenden, H. S. Davis, G. B. Murphey, C. A. Brayton, W. M. Crowell, Peter Thatcher, N. M. Standard, Wm. Melbinch, S. M. Strong, J. M. Perkins, T. J. Burrin, G. Herrick, J. C. Buell, Wm. J. Smith, Henry Blair, J. V. Painter, E. S. Willard, Thos. Quayle, James Mason, Joseph Perkins, William Collins, J. F. Clark, Thomas Burnham, John H. Gorham, W. J. Boardman, Arthur Quinn, Charles Hickox, H. G. Hitchcock, Robt. F. Paine, William Edwards, H. Harvey, S. L. Mather, H. B. Hurlbut, W. F. Otis, C. W. Coe, M. C. Younglove, A. G. Colwell, H. C. Blossom, W. V. Craw, B. Lampson, E. M. Peck, Frank Kelly, Geo. F. Marshall, E. P. Morgan, E. W. Sackrider, J. B. Glenn, C. S. Hobbs, J. A. Redington, J. A. Harris, H. G. Abbey, John F. Warner, D. P. Eells, John C. Grannis, Geo. H. Burt, C. W. Noble, F. J. Prentiss, C. A. Crumb, Addison Hills, Geo. A. Stanley, Geo. F. Armstrong, Joseph Randerson, Chas. Evatt, O. C. Scoville, P. Roeder, H. W. Leutkemeyer, C. J. Ballard, A. Rettberg, Louis Smithknight, B. Steadman, I. Buckingham, W. Lawty, W. Wellhouse, L. A. Benton, H. J. Hoyt, T. D. Eells.

The Guard was divided into six squads, under the direction of the following gentlemen:

1st Aid—J. Ensworth; 2d Aid—Louis Smithknight; 3d Aid—Robert Hanna; 1st Assistant—Peter Thatcher;

2d Assistant—H. F. Brayton; 3d Assistant—F. T. Wallace; 4th Assistant—J. P. Robinson; 5th Assistant—Geo. F. Marshall; 6th Assistant—Thomas Quayle.

The Committee on Location of Remains found no room or building, in which to place the remains, suitable to accommodate the vast crowd that would be present and wish to take the last look at their late President. The Committee therefore decided to erect upon the east side of the Park a proper structure. The Committee of Arrangements authorized the erection, and the building was immediately commenced, and on Thursday night was completed. It stood directly east of the Monument, and was an oblong structure twenty-four by thirty-six feet, and fourteen feet high. The roof was pagoda shaped, and over the centre of the main roof was a second roof, raised about four feet, and forming a canopy over the catafalque. The sides and ends of the building were open above the low breastwork, which was covered with black cloth. The roof was supported by pillars shrouded in black and white, and the open sides were elegantly draped with festoons of white and black, looped up with rosettes of white and black. The roof was of white canvas, the ribs supporting it being shrouded in black. The ends of the building were heavily draped with black cloth. Over each end of the building was a large golden eagle with the national shield. The sides supporting the second roof were covered with black cloth on the outside, on which were fastened beautiful evergreen wreaths and floral devices. At the east end of the building, where the procession entered, were six splendid regimental flags of silk. Eight immense plumes of black crape surmounted the sides of the building. Slender flag poles bearing crape streamers and mourning flags were ranged along the top of the building. Evergreen and floral wreaths were used to loop up the drapery and crown the capitals of the columns. Directly over the upper roof was a streamer stretched between two flag poles, bearing the inscription from Horace: "*Extinctus amabitur idem*" (Dead, he will be loved the same).

The inside of the building was in admirable keeping with the exterior decorations. Heavy drapery of black cloth, festoons of evergreen, and floral wreaths and bouquets completely shrouded the pillars and roof. In the centre was the catafalque, a raised dais, twelve feet long, four feet wide, and about two feet high to the underside of the coffin. The floor and sides of the dais were covered with black cloth and velvet. The floor was so inclined that on entering the building the visitors were able at once to see the remains and keep them in sight until nearly leaving the building. From the corners of the dais sprang four slender columns supporting a canopy draped with black cloth with silver fringe, and the corners of the canopy hung with silver tassels. The capitals of the pillars were wreathed with flowers. At the head and foot of the dais were several seats covered with black cloth, designed for the use of the Guard of Honor. The floor of the building was covered thickly with matting, so as to deaden every sound. The building was well lit with gas at night. The people entered from the east and passed through the broad passages on each side of the dais, going out on the west side. Cleveland was the first place on the route of the funeral cortege where a special building had been erected for the reception of the remains.

Mayor Senter appointed the following gentlemen as Pall Bearers:

Hon. John Brough, Hon. David Tod, Hon. John Sherman, Hon. R. P. Spalding, Hon. James M. Ashley, Hon.

J. C. Deven, Hon. Horace Foot, Hon. John Crowell, Hon. J. P. Robison, Hon. D. R. Tilden, Gen. R. P. Buckland, Gen. O. M. Oviatt.

Every train that arrived on the railroads during Thursday and Thursday night, was filled; all the hotels were crowded, and hundreds of persons were unable to procure even a sleeping place upon the floor.

The symbols of mourning were universal. Men, women and children, of all classes and conditions, wore some badge or symbol of sorrow. Toward evening of Thursday the citizens on Superior, Euclid, Prospect, Bank and other streets, and around the Square, commenced to drape their dwellings and places of business. Along the line designated for the passing of the procession, the draping was very elaborate, tasteful, and almost universal.

The following was the order of proceedings for the day, as promulgated by Col. James Barnett, Chief Marshal:

The following programme of arrangements is announced for the solemnization of the obsequies of Abraham Lincoln, late President of the United States, in this city, on Friday, the 28th inst.

The bells of the city will be tolled during the moving of the procession.

The shipping in the harbor, and the proprietors of public houses and others, are requested to display their colors at half-mast during the day.

It is earnestly requested that all places of business or amusement be closed during the day.

Vehicles of all kinds will be withdrawn from the streets through which the procession will pass, and none will be allowed in the procession except those designated.

Delegations will be promptly at their places of rendezvous, prepared to march at the appointed time, failing in which, they will be excluded from their positions, and will take their places on the left.

A national salute of thirty-six guns will by fired by the 8th Independent Battery, at 7 o'clock A. M., and half-hour guns thereafter until sunset.

The procession will move from the Euclid street station at 7:30 A. M., through Euclid street to Erie, down Erie to Superior, down Superior to the Park, where the remains will be deposited in the building erected for that purpose, and exposed to view until 10 o'clock P. M.

At daybreak on Friday morning the citizens were startled from their slumbers by a salute of artillery, and in a very short time the whole city was astir. By six o'clock the streets were crowded with people, some wending their way down to the Union depot, to the Park, or to other advantageous positions on the line of march, whilst throngs of people started for the Euclid street depot, from which the procession was to start. Thousands of people from the country and from other cities had arrived during the preceding days of the week, and all night the streets had been crowded. The weather was gloomy and threatened rain, and by the time the train arrived the rain began to fall steadily but not heavily. The city could scarcely have looked to better advantage, in spite of the rain, as the dust was laid, and the partly opened foliage, with its delicate green tint, lent beauty to the elegant dwellings and grounds along the avenues through which the procession was to pass.

The importance and solemnity of the occasion was evidently appreciated by every one. The dense crowds that lined the streets from the Euclid street depot to the Public Square, the numerous badges of mourning worn, the heavily draped buildings, and the uniform stillness and decorum of the immense gathering of people, testified to the respect and love borne to the deceased by the people of Cleveland and the surrounding country. The immense crowd was hourly added to by the trains and steamers arriving from different points.

Punctually at seven o'clock the funeral train ran into the Union depot. The sight as it passed down the Lake Shore track was impressive, and was witnessed by a great crowd of people on the bank. On reaching the depot, the locomotive of the Cleveland and Pittsburgh Railroad, tastefully draped, took the train in its reversed position and drew it to the Euclid Street station, arriving there about twenty minutes after seven o'clock. As the train moved up, a national salute of thirty-six guns was fired. As the train came up the Lake Shore track a very beautiful incident took place. Miss Fields, of Wilson street, had erected an arch of evergreens on the bank of the Lake near the track, and as the train passed appeared in the arch as the Goddess of Liberty in mourning.

On arriving at the Euclid Street depot the train was stopped so that the funeral car lay nearly across the road. The depot was heavily draped with mourning and flags, and a draped flag hung from a line stretched directly across the road. The Veteran Reserve Corps were drawn up around the funeral car, eight of them being ready to carry the coffin, whilst the others formed in line on either side with drawn swords presented. The Guard of Honor stood on one side, and Governor Brough and staff, with the leading members of the Committees and the Pall-Bearers, on the other. The Camp Chase Band stood in front of the depot, and the hearse was drawn up a few yards distant. The hearse was surmounted with large black and white plumes, and the national colors draped. The hangings were of black velvet, with heavy silver fringe and silver tassels, fastened up with crape rosettes, each with a silver star in the centre. A beautiful wreath of flowers hung at the head of the hearse, and the bed on which the coffin was to rest was strewn thickly with white blossoms. Six white horses, decorated with festoons of crape, looped up with crape rosettes and silver stars, drew the hearse, and were attended by six colored grooms, wearing crape and mourning rosettes. The decorations were arranged and executed by Mrs. R. F. Paine.

At a signal given, the band played a solemn dirge, and the coffin was taken out of the car and borne to the hearse on the shoulders of the Veteran Reserves, the other Veteran Reserves marching by its side with drawn swords, attended by the pall-bearers and guard. On the head of the coffin was a cross of white flowers, and a wreath of similar flowers at the foot.

The hearse, surrounded by the Veteran Reserve Guard, with the Pall-Bearers on either side, the Guard of Honor, mounted, following, and preceded by the band playing a dirge, passed up Wilson Avenue. The 29th O. N. G. was drawn up in line, and saluted the cortege as it passed. The Civic Guard of Honor met the hearse on Prospect street, and saluted it, when the cortege turned, and went back to Euclid street, when the procession was formed according to programme.

The crowd around the station was exceedingly large, but owing to the excellent police arrangements and the orderly character of the people, there was no trouble or confusion. The large space reserved was kept perfectly clear. When the coffin was brought from the car, so great was the anxiety of the people to see it, that numbers, most of them women, got under the train and remained there until warned off by the police to save their lives. The scene when the procession started was very solemn. A slight rain fell, dripping like tears on the remains of the good man in whose honor the crowd had gathered, but not enough to be heeded by the people assembled. The street was lined with a continuous wall of people, and the yards and houses were also crowded.

The long perspective of Euclid street stretched away in unrivaled beauty, and the procession, with its solid column, great length, and imposing display, made up a scene never equaled in Cleveland. There was scarcely any variation from the published order of the Chief Marshal in the formation of the procession.

First came the Military Escort, Colonel Hayward commanding, led by the Camp Chase Band. The escort consisted of the 29th Regiment Ohio National Guard, and the 8th Independent Battery, under the command of Lieutenant Grenninger. The escort was followed by Major-General Hooker and staff, and officers of the army, on horseback. Then came Governor Brough and staff, and the Pall-Bearers, in carriages. The Hearse came next followed by the Escort of Honor that accompanies the remains from Washington to Springfield. The General Committee of Arrangements, Civic Guard of Honor, and Clergy followed on foot. This closed the First Division, which was under the direction of Colonel O. H. Payne, Assistant Marshal.

The Second Division, under the direction of Amos Townsend, Esq., Assistant Marshal, was led by the Detroit City Band. In this division were the following societies and bodies: United States civil officers, Earl Bill, Marshal; a large number of returned veteran soldiers, under command of Captain James K. O'Reilly; City Council and other city officers; Cleveland Board of Trade, and members of Boards of Trade from other cities; a delegation of citizens from Meadville, Captain Derrick-son acting as Marshal.

George H. Burt, Esq., had charge of the Third Division, which was led by the Detroit Light Guard Band. The Knights Templar followed the band, dressed in full regalia, with their banners, etc., draped in mourning.

They acted as an escort to the Order of Free and Accepted Masons, some in regalia and others wearing a sprig of evergreen on their breasts. Bigelow Lodge, West Side, turned out eighty strong, in full regalia, with banners and emblems of the Order all appropriately draped. Following the Masons came the Order of Odd Fellows, about a thousand strong, also with regalia and banners dressed with weeds of sorrow. Among the Odd Fellows from outside the city, were Cataract Lodge No. 295, from Newburgh, and members from other places.

The Fourth Division was under direction of Major W. P. Edgarton, Assistant Marshal. Next to the Temperance Band, which was at the head of this Division, came the Father Matthew Temperance Society, very strong in numbers, wearing their sashes and carrying their banners, all clothed in mourning. The Fenian Brotherhood followed the Temperance Society, and after them came the Laboring men's Union, carrying a banner with the motto:—"We mourn the loss of our President; Labor is the Wealth of the Nation; United we Stand, Divided we Fall." The St. Bonifacius Society came next, followed by the Aurora Band, from the West Side. Following the Band were the St. Joseph Society, St. Vincent Society, St. Andrew's Society, St. George's Society, and Mona's Relief Society. All these Societies were in full ranks, bearing their distinctive banners and emblems.

The Fifth Division, in charge of Assistant Marshal Major Seymour Race, embraced the members of the Ancient Order of Good Fellows; Ohio City Lodge of Good Fellows; the Hungarian Association, with their national badges and colors; and Solomon and Montefiore Lodges I. O. B. B., under the marshalship of B. F.

Peixotto, Grand Master of the Order in the United States. Leland's Band led the Fifth Division.

The Sixth Division was under the direction of Captain Basil L. Spangler, Assistant Marshal. The first society represented in this Division was the German Benevolent Mutual Society. This Society was followed by Eureka Lodge No. 14 of Colored Masons; 1188 G. U. O. O. F., also colored. This Society carried a banner on which was inscribed: "We mourn for Abraham Lincoln, the True Friend of Liberty." The Colored Equal Rights League followed. Cleveland Division No. 275 and Forest City Temple No. 52, Sons of Temperance, came next, and the Seamen's Union closed the organized procession. The Union carried a small full-rigged bark, with flag at half-mast.

The Chief Marshal, Col. James Barnett, and his valuable assistants, Col. J. P. Ross, Silas Merchant, Col. O. H. Payne, Amos Townsend, George H. Burt, Maj. W. P. Edgarton, Major S. Race, and Capt. B. L. Spangler, formed and conducted the long procession with the most perfect order. There was no confusion, no noise, and all the different Societies and bodies fell into the places in the procession allotted to them on time and with the precision of clock-work.

After the procession started from the depot, it moved slowly and solemnly, without stop or detention, until it reached the Square. As it neared the western end of Euclid street, the number of people began to increase until the sidewalks and far into the street became a solid mass; but there was no noise or confusion in the crowd that lined the streets on the line of march. All seemed impressed with the deep solemnity of the occasion.

The draping of the houses and buildings in mourning along the route of the procession was almost universal.

There was not a house on Euclid street, from the Square to the Euclid street Depot, which did not display some symbol of grief. Prospect and many other streets were also very generally draped. The greatest display, however, was on Superior and Euclid streets, and around the Square. On City High School building was a large shield, surrounded by flags, intertwined with white and black mourning. At the residence of A. B. Stone, Esq., on Euclid street, was the following truthful motto: "His aims were for his God, his Country, and Truth. He died a blessed Martyr." At Rouse's Block, corner of Superior street and the Square, was a profuse display of festoons of white and black, flags, &c., and on the Square front the motto: "An Honest man—the noblest work." The County Court House, City Council Hall, the Government Building, and other places around the Square near the pavilion in which the remains reposed during the day, were all tastefully and appropriately dressed in mourning.

The entire front of E. I. Baldwin's store was covered with black, on which was the motto:—"A glorious career of service and devotion is crowned with a martyr's death." All the other prominent business buildings were tastefully and elaborately decorated. The ladies connected with the Soldiers' Aid Society displayed much taste in the draping of the front of their rooms. Their windows were covered on the inside with a white background, on which was neatly arranged folds of black, and on the outside were many rosettes and small flags, also appropriately arranged. All the hotels, telegraph offices and express offices were appropriately draped.

There were over six thousand in the procession of organized societies. After the main procession passed a given point, the citizens fell in behind and followed it through the pavilion, in the same good order as characterized the proceedings. There was a considerable crush at the entrance gate on Superior street, but no boisterous actions. The admirable arrangements of the Committee for preserving order in the neighborhood of the building where the remains were to be placed prevented confusion. The procession entered the enclosure by the East gate, and after the removal of the body to the building, filed out at the Rockwell street gate. The 29th O. N. G. occupied positions inside the enclosure, and were stationed as sentinels at numerous points. The hearse was driven up to the south side of the pavilion, and the coffin borne on the shoulders of Veteran Reserves to the place prepared for it under the canopy. As the body passed the band played a dirge. As soon as the coffin was placed on the dais, a committee of ladies advanced and placed on it a number of floral ornaments and evergreens, wreathed in the forms of crosses and coronals. The embalmer and undertaker opened the coffin and inspected the remains. The Right Reverend Charles Pettit McIlvaine, Bishop of the Diocese of Ohio, advanced to the coffin and read from the Burial Service of the Episcopal Church :

"I am the resurrection and the life, saith the Lord; he that believeth in me, though he were dead, yet shall he live; and whosoever livith and believeth in me shall never die.

"We brought nothing into the world, and it is certain we can carry nothing out. The Lord gave, and the Lord hath taken away; blessed be the name of the Lord.

"Man that is born of a woman, hath but a short time to live, and is full of misery. He cometh up, and is cut down, like a flower; he fleeth as it were a shadow and never continueth in one stay.

"In the midst of life we are in death; of whom may we seek for succor, but of thee, O Lord, who for our sins art justly displeased?"

Bishop McIlvaine then offered an eloquent prayer, in which he prayed that this great affliction may be of good to the people. He prayed for blessing on the family of the deceased, and for health and blessing on Secretary Seward, whom the assassin tried, but failed to destroy. For President Johnson he asked that he might be led to follow the great example set him by his illustrious predecessor.

The religious services being concluded, the procession filed through the Pavilion, passing through both aisles. Many were affected to tears. The invalid soldiers from the military hospital, who were drawn up inside the inclosure previous to the arrival of the procession, passed through, and many a bronzed veteran's eyes were wet as he gazed upon him who had laid down his life for his country. After the procession had passed through, the public were admitted, and thousands poured in a steady stream, without haste or confusion.

The heavy rain which continued to fall from the first start of the procession down to the removal of the body from the building to the cars, seemed to have no effect in damping the eagerness of the people to take a last look at the remains of their beloved President. All day long the endless procession marched through without a break or pause, and when the lamps were lit the crowd thickened rather than diminished. The crowds seeking admission were formed by the police outside the inclosure into a column four deep, and those desirous of seeing the remains had to fall into the rear of the column and await their turn to enter. The column, on entering the inclo-

11

sure, passed up to the east end of the Pavilion, where it separated into two columns, each of two abreast, and marched through on either side of the catafalque, passing along, on emerging to the monument, where they either went westward forward toward Superior, or southward toward Ontario street. The military guard of officers appointed by General Hooker stood at the foot of the coffin and at the corners. One of the guard of honor of general officers stood or sat at the head of the coffin, Rear-Admiral Davis occupying that position in the forenoon. The civic guard of honor were ranged along the sides of the building, to pass the visitors on in proper order. A squad of the 29th O. N. G. was stationed at different points in the inclosure.

The most reverend silence and deep feeling were exhibited by all who passed through. The passage-way being ample, there was abundant facility for obtaining a good view of the remains. The features were but slightly changed from the appearance they bore when exposed in the Capitol at Washington.

At different times in the day an accurate count of those passing through within a certain length of time was taken. In the first four hours the rate was nine thousand per hour; then it fell to between seven and eight thousand, and increased in the evening and night. Until evening the visitors were nearly all from abroad, the city people holding back to give those a chance who would have to leave by the evening trains. At ten o'clock at night, when the gates were shut, over *one hundred thousand people* had visited the remains, and this without noise, disorder or confusion of any kind.

A distinguishing feature of the ceremonies and testimonials of the day was the profusion and beauty of the floral decorations and floral offerings. Besides the great number of flowers woven into the decorations of the Pavilion, a large number of beautiful floral devices were laid on the coffin. Among them were the floral offerings made by the ladies of the Soldiers' Aid Society of Northern Ohio, consisting of an anchor of white roses, azalias, and other white flowers, each fluke of the anchor being made of magnificent *calla;* a cross of beautiful red blossoms; and a wreath of blue flowers. The ladies decided to place the anchor in charge of Lieut.-Colonel Simpson, U. S. Engineers, for presentation to Captain Stephen Champlin, one of the survivors of the Battle of Lake Erie. The cross and wreath accompanied the remains from Cleveland.

A salute was fired on the arrival of the remains at the Square, and another at sunset. Half-hour guns were also fired during the day by the 8th Independent Battery, O. N. G. Five large and beautiful flags, draped in mourning, floated from the staff in the Park all day.

During the afternoon the bands from abroad and those belonging to Cleveland, were stationed on the balconies of the hotels and other prominent buildings, and played dirges, adding to the solemnity and impressiveness of the occasion.

A delegation of two hundred came from Meadville, and joined in the procession, under the marshalship of Capt. Derrickson. They wore a large badge upon the lappel of the coat with the word "Meadville." Also a delegation of about five hundred came from Detroit, to do honor to the memory of the President. Two bands, the Detroit City and the Light Guard, escorted them.

By invitation of Governor Brough the Illinois delegation and the general officers of the escort paid him a visit at his residence.

The following officers were detailed as a Guard of

Honor to the remains of the President, while in the Forest City:

First Relief—Rear-Admiral Davis; Major D. Bannister, Paymaster U. S. A.; Capt. Mix, U. S. Cavalry; Captain Meisner, V. R. C.; Major Perry, U. S. A.; Surg. Sternburg, U. S. A.

Second Relief—Capt. Taylor, U. S. N.; Lieut.-Col. Simpson, U. S. Eng.; Lieut.-Col. De La Vergne, U. S. V.; Capt. Rower, Vet. Guards; Lieut. Robinson, Vet. Guards.

Third Relief—Major-Gen. Barnard, U. S. Eng.; Col. Swords, A. Q. M.; Capt. J. J. Upham, U. S. A.; Capt. Voges, A. Q. M.; Capt. De Forest, N. G.; Capt. Tibbitts, N. G.

At ten minutes past ten the coffin was closed. Up to the very last moment there was a stream of people passing through the Pavilion, and if the remains had been exposed until twelve o'clock there would undoubtedly have been the same interest manifested to take one last look. At ten minutes past eleven o'clock the coffin was taken from the beautiful resting place of the day and placed in the hearse, preparatory to being conveyed to the funeral car. The escort was as follows: The 29th Regiment O. N. G., Colonel Hayward; the General Committee of Arrangements; the Military Guard of Honor in carriages; the Civic Guard of Honor bearing flambeaux; the Father Mathew Temperance Society; the Eureka Lodge of Masons. The cortege proceeded down Superior street, preceded by three bands playing a dirge, thence down Vineyard street, at the foot of which the funeral train had been placed. The coffin was placed in the funeral car, and at precisely twelve o'clock the train started for Columbus, under the direction of Superintendent Flint, with Charles Gale as Conductor.

About the time the remains were being removed from the Pavilion the rain poured down in torrents, and continued until after the train started. Notwithstanding this, the streets the whole length of the line of march were crowded with people, many of whom were ladies. Everything was conducted with the greatest order and decorum, and the citizens of Cleveland returned to their homes with the consciousness that they had paid the last tribute of respect to a great and good man in a proper manner.

The correspondent of the *New York Times* writing from Cleveland said: "Everywhere deep sorrow has been manifested, and the feeling seems, if possible, to deepen, as we move Westward with the remains to their final resting place."

CLEVELAND TO COLUMBUS.

The Funeral Train was preceded, between Cleveland and Columbus, by a pilot engine, the "Louisville," in charge of Assistant Superintendent Blee and Master Mechanic W. F. Smith, with E. Van Camp as Engineer and C. Van Camp as Fireman. The engine of the Funeral Train was the "Nashville," with Geo. West as Engineer and Peter Hugo as Fireman. Mr. T. J. Higgins, the Superintendent of Telegraph, accompanied the train with necessary telegraph instruments, to be used in case of accident. Gen. McCallum, who had temporary military possession of all the railroads from Washington to Springfield, had an efficient aid in G. P. Duke, of the Baltimore and Ohio Railroad Company, who carried out his superior's orders, as to the time of starting, &c., with a fidelity which commanded general admiration.

Evidences of grief were manifested along the entire line between the Forest city and the Capital. The people gathered at the depots and at other points in throngs, eager to pay tribute to the memory of him whom they had loved. From the time the train left Cleveland until it reached Crestline, the rain fell in torrents, notwithstanding which, bonfires and torches were lit, the principal buildings draped in mourning, bells tolled, flags floated at half-mast, and the sorrowing inhabitants stood in groups, uncovered and with saddened faces gazing with awe and veneration upon the cortege as it moved slowly by.

After daybreak, the rain having ceased, the demonstrations were more general but of a less impressive character. At Cardington an immense crowd of citizens assembled to do the customary honors. Bells were tolled, minute guns fired, and the station was tastefully festooned with the national flag draped with rosettes of crape. In front and over the doors and windows was a white banner on which was inscribed "He sleeps in the blessings of the poor, whose fetters God commanded him to break." At other villages similar devices were exhibited, and sadness and mourning, deep and solemn, prevailed in town and hamlet. Beside the track, about five miles above Columbus, stood an aged woman bare headed, her gray hairs dishelved, tears coursing down her furrowed cheeks, holding in her right hand a sable scarf and in her left a bouquet of wild flowers, which she stretched imploringly toward the funeral car.

THE CAPITAL OF OHIO.

In accordance with a call signed by a large number of the prominent and influential citizens of Columbus, a public meeting was held at the City Hall on the evening of April 17th, for the purpose of making arrangements for the suitable observance of the day appointed for the funeral of the assassinated President, at Washington, and to properly receive the remains at the Capital of Ohio. Hon. Samuel Galloway was selected as Chairman, and H. T. Chittenden as Secretary. Prayer was offered by Rev. C. E. Felton. The Chairman set forth, in a few appropriate remarks, the object for which the people had assembled. On motion of L. J. Critchfield, Esq., a committee of five was appointed to draft resolutions expressive of the sense of the meeting. The following gentlemen were appointed by the chair: L. J. Critchfield, Geo. M. Parsons, C. N. Olds, B. F. Martin, and Peter Ambos.

Rev. J. M. Trimble, Hon. Samuel Galloway and Hon. Chauncey N. Olds addressed the meeting. The committee on Resolutions reported a series declaring that treason embraced murder and all other crimes necessary to accomplish its ends; expressing grief and indignation at the assassination of the President—tendering to his stricken family heartfelt condolence — avowing confidence in Andrew Johnson, and resolving:

"That, in token of the public sorrow on account of this great calamity, and to the honor of the illustrious dead, the citizens of Columbus be requested to close their places of business on to-morrow, between the hours of eleven o'clock A. M. and three o'clock P. M., the hours of the funeral services at Washington, and that those having charge of the bells in this city, cause them to be tolled during that time."

The following resolution was then offered by W. G. Deshler, and adopted unanimously:

"*Resolved*, That a committee of nine be appointed to co-operate with the committee of the City Council, in any appropriate ceremonies, should the body of our late President be brought to our city; and also in conjunction with the City Council committee, to arrange for a public oration upon the life and services of Abraham Lincoln."

The Chair appointed the following committee in pursuance of this resolution: W. G. Deshler, David S. Gray,

J. E. St. Clair, W. Failing, Isaac Eberly, Rev. K. Mees, L. Kilbourne, C. P. L. Butler, and S. Loving. On motion, Hon. Samuel Galloway was added to the committee.

The meeting then closed with a benediction by the Rev. J. M. Trimble.

The City Council cordially co-operated with the citizens in the movement thus inaugurated. On motion of Cyrus Field, it was agreed that the Mayor, city officers and members of the City Council join in the procession to escort the remains of the late President, and, on motion, Messrs. Donaldson and Ross were appointed a committee to make the necessary arrangements for that purpose.

The Council had previously

"*Resolved*, That a committee of nine (one from each Ward) be appointed to act in conjunction with such committees as may be appointed by the State authorities, and the citizens generally, to make suitable preparations for the reception of the remains of the late President."

On the 24th of April the Adjutant-General of Ohio promulgated the following order:

GENERAL HEADQUARTERS, STATE OF OHIO,
ADJUTANT-GENERAL'S OFFICE,
COLUMBUS, April 23, 1865.

GENERAL ORDER, No. 5.

Major John W. Skiles, 88th O. V. I., is hereby appointed Chief Marshal of the ceremonies in honor of the remains of the late President Lincoln, in the city of Columbus, on the 29th inst. He will appoint his own aids, and will have entire control of the ceremonies and procession attending the transfer of the remains from and to the depot.

All societies, delegations, or other organizations, wishing to participate in the ceremonies, will report, by telegraph or letter, to the Chief Marshal, on or before 10 o'clock A. M. of Friday, 28th inst.

The headquarters of the Chief Marshal, during Thursday and Friday, 27th and 28th inst., will be at the Adjutant-General's office in the Capitol.

By order of the Governor:

B. R. COWEN,
Adjutant-General of Ohio.

James Patterson, chairman of the City Council committee, and W. G. Deshler, chairman of the citizens' committee, announced that the funeral train would arrive at Columbus on the morning of April 29th, at half-past seven o'clock—that the remains of the President would be escorted to the Capitol by a military and civic procession, where they would lie in state until six o'clock P. M., and that at three o'clock an oration would be delivered on the terrace on the east side of Capitol Square. The committee requested the general suspension of business, and described the general order of exercises, cordially invited societies and associations to join the procession, and announced the following officers of the day:

Chief Marshal—Maj. John W. Skiles.

Aids—Charles Scarrett, Ed. Fields, Carl Bancroft, Ed. Fitch, A. Greenleaf, W. W. Bailey, Theo. Butler, Capt. Jas. Grover, C. S. Dyer, John W. Doherty, C. W. Douty, R. S. Neil, Maj. S. Sullivant, Jno. Radebaugh.

Pall Bearers—Dr. John Andrews, Robert Neil, F. C. Kelton, John Field, Augustus Platt, Christian Heyl, E. W. Gwynne, W. B. Hubbard, Judge Taylor, Jno. Brooks, Wm. B. Thrall, D. W. Deshler, L. Goodale, Jos. R. Swan, Wm. T. Martin, Wm. M. Awl, G. W. Manypenny, John M. Walcutt, F. Stewart, John Noble, F. Jaeger, Sr., Amos S. Ramsey.

Executive Committee—W. G. Deshler, C. P. L. Butler, James Patterson, S. N. Field, F. Jaeger.

Finance Committee—B. Gilmore, W. Failing, Isaac Eberly, S. N. Field.

Escort Committee—Samuel Galloway, L. Kilbourne, S. Loving, James Patterson, John Miller, J. Reinhard.

Committee on Catafalque, Decoration, &c.—D. S. Gray, A. B. Buttles, Wm. Gaver.

Committee on Music and Printing—A. B. Buttles, Rev. K. Mees, B. Gilmore, Wm. Naughton.

Committee on Reception of Escort and Guests—W. Failing, B. Gilmore, J. E. St. Clair.

Committee on Carriages—C. P. L. Butler, Wm. Gaver.

As soon as committees and associations had made report to him, the Chief Marshal advertised the following

ORDER OF PROCESSION.

COLUMBUS, O., April 27, 1865.

1st. The remains of Abraham Lincoln, late President of the United States, will arrive in the city of Columbus, O., at 7 o'clock A. M., Saturday, the 29th instant, at the Union depot.

2d. The funeral escort will consist of the 88th O. V. Infantry.

3d. Officers of the army, not on duty with troops, are respectfully invited to participate in the obsequies. They will report to Major James Van Voost, 18th U. S. Infantry, at Headquarters, Tod Barracks, at 6 o'clock A. M., Saturday.

4th. Detachments of the army and volunteer organizations, not on duty with the escort, will be assigned positions on application to Capt. L. Nichols, Tod Barracks. They will appear with side arms only, and will report at 6 o'clock A. M., Saturday.

5th. All military officers to be in uniform, and with side arms. The usual badge of mourning will be worn on the left arm and sword hilt.

6th. In order to prevent confusion at the entrance gate, all who are not in line of procession will form after the left of the procession has entered the Capitol Square in two ranks, on the outside of the Square fence, on High street, running north to Broad, south to State, thence east on Broad and State streets, for extent. They will enter the west gate four abreast, in regular order, by inward march of each rank, AND IN NO OTHER WAY.

It is desired to pass ALL through the Capitol, and in order to accommodate each person the public must preserve order and follow the programme as adopted.

A sufficient guard, composed of the 18th U. S. Infantry, will be stationed at the depot to prevent any delay or confusion in transferring the remains to the catafalque, and in seating the escort accompanying the remains.

7th. All delegations who have reported and have been assigned to positions in line of procession, will report promptly at their designated places, and will be moved by Assistant Marshals in charge.

MILITARY ESCORT.

Eighty-eighth O. V. Infantry, under command of Lieutenant-Col Webber.

ORDER OF PROCESSION.

1st. Officiating clergyman and orator in open carriage.

2d. Undertaker in buggy.

3d. Pall Bearers in carriages; carriages three abreast.

V. R. C., Guards of Honor.	HEARSE.	V. R. C., Guards of Honor.

4th. Pall Bearers in carriages; carriages three abreast.

5th. Escort accompanying remains from Washington in open carriages, three abreast, in charge of Assistant Marshals Theodore Comstock and Henry Wilson.

6th. Major-General Hooker and staff, mounted.

7th. Brevet Brigadier-General W. P. Richardson and staff, mounted.

8th. A. A. Provost-Marshal General Col. Wilcox and staff, mounted.

9th. Brigadier-General Wager Swayne and staff, in open carriage.

10th. Officers of the army on duty, and temporarily at this post, on foot, Major James Van Voost, 18th U. S. Infantry, commanding.

11th. Soldiers at this post not on duty with escort, Capt. Levi T. Nichols commanding.

12th. Governor Brough and suite.

13th. Camp Thomas Band.

14th. Committee of Arrangements on foot.

15th. Chief Marshal John W. Skiles, and Special Aids Charles Scarritt and Theo. H. Butler.

FIRST DIVISION.

Assistant Marshals—E. G. Field and John Radabaugh.

16th. Reverend Clergy, City and State, will form on Depot street, right resting on Exchange Hotel.

17th. Heads of Departments, State of Ohio, will form north of railroad track, in open carriages, right resting opposite of Exchange Hotel.

18th. Mayors of Cincinnati and Columbus, and Presidents of City Councils of said cities, in open carriages.

19th. City Councils of Cincinnati and Columbus, on foot, forming on North Public Laue, right resting on High street.

20th. Judges and officers of the United States Court, in open carriages.

21st. Judges and officers of Supreme Court of State of Ohio, in open carriages.

22d. Judges and officers of Franklin and other County Courts, on foot, forming with right resting north of railroad track, in rear of carriages.

SECOND DIVISION.

Assistant Marshals—Carl Bancroft and E. A. Fitch.

23d. Masonic Order will form on West North street, right resting on High, left extending north on Front street.

THIRD DIVISION.

Assistant Marshals—A. Greenleaf and J. W. Doherty.

24th. Independent Order of Odd Fellows, right resting on East North and High, left extending on South Front street.

FOURTH DIVISION.

Assistant Marshals—C. W. Douty and C. H. Olmsted.

25th. United Ancient Order of Druids, right resting on corner of High and West Spring streets, left extending on North Front street.

26th. Tod Barracks Band. Fenian Brotherhood, right resting on corner of East Spring and High streets, left extending south on Third street.

27th. Mechanics' Association will form with right resting on the left of Fenian Brotherhood, Third street.

28th. St. Martin's and St. John's Benevolent Associations, right resting on corner of West Long and High streets, left extending north on Front.

The Butchers' Association will form with their right resting on the left of the St. Martin's and St. John's Benevolent Associations.

FIFTH DIVISION.

Assistant Marshals—Colonel J. Wing and W. W. Bagley.

29th. Fire Department, right resting on corner of East Long and High streets, left extending on Long. Colored Masonic Order's right resting on corner of East Gay and High streets, extending east on Gay. Colored Benevolent Association will form with their right resting on left of Colored Masonic Fraternity.

30th. All delegations from a distance will form with right resting on West Gay and North, left extending on North Front.

The different delegations are hereby directed to form in four ranks.

ROUTE OF PROCESSION.

The procession will move promptly from south of the depot at 7:30 A. M., south on High street to Broad, east on Broad to Fourth, south on Fourth to State, east on State to Seventh, south on Seventh to Town, west on Town to High, north on High to west front of the Capitol.

A mounted cavalry force will be stationed at all the intersections of High street north of Town street, for the purpose of preventing all vehicles from entering on High street—that it must be kept clear during the movements of the procession.

At 6 P. M. the Capitol will be closed. The procession will re-form in the following order to escort the remains to the depot.

Military escort.

Escort accompanying the remains.

Pall Bearers.

Masonic Fraternity will form on East State street, the right resting on High.

Independent Order of Odd Fellows will form on East Broad street, right resting on High.

All other organizations will form on West Broad street, right resting on High.

All carriages, except those appropriated to the Escort Committee, will be under the charge of Assistant Marshals C. S. Dyer and H. M. Neil.

The guard at the Capitol will be under charge of Captain M. C. Wilkinson, 15th V. R. C.

JOHN W. SKILES,
Major and Grand Marshal.

Fourteen days from that on which the American people were shocked by the intelligence that a President, honored and loved for services more precious than any rendered by a Chief Magistrate since Washington retired to private life, had been assassinated, the remains of that President were brought to the Capital of Ohio. A heavy rain fell on the night previous, and the early morning was gloomy, but about the hour appointed for the arrival of the funeral train the clouds broke away and the rain ceased. At the appointed hour the funeral train entered the Union Depot, amid the ringing of muffled bells, and stopped so that the funeral car lay nearly across High street. An immense crowd of spectators was congregated in the vicinity of the depot. Bands of music, assembled with the military in procession, played solemn dirges while the coffin was taken from the car and laid in the hearse by a portion of the Veteran Reserve Corps, the other Veteran Reserves marching by its side with drawn sabres, attended by the pall bearers and military guard of honor.

The procession was then formed according to the programme, and was the most imposing and the most impressive which ever marched through the streets of Columbus. The slow measured tread of the troops, the muffled drum, the dead march, the enshrouded colors, told their own tale of the fearfully solemn occasion on which they were passing in review before the assembled thousands who had congregated as witnesses.

The hearse was the great centre of attraction. All along the line of march it was preceded and followed by hundreds, of all ages, sexes and conditions, striving to keep as near as possible to the sombre structure. It was 17 feet long, 8½ feet wide, and 17½ feet from the ground to the apex of the canopy. The main platform was four feet from the ground, on which rested a dais for the reception of the coffin, twelve feet long by five wide, raised two and a half feet above the platform. The canopy resembled in shape a Chinese pagoda. The interior of the roof was lined with silk flags, and the outside covered with black broadcloth, as were the dais, the main platform and the entire hearse. Black cloth, festooned, depended from the platform within a few inches of the ground, fringed with silver lace, and ornamented with heavy tassels of black silk. Surrounding the cornice of the canopy were thirty-six silver stars, and on the apex and the four corners were five heavy black plumes. The canopy was appropriately curtained with black cloth, lined with white merino. On each side of the dais was the word "Lincoln," in silver letters. The hearse was drawn by six white horses, covered with black cloth, which was edged with silver fringe. The heads of the horses were surmounted with large black plumes, and each was led by a groom dressed in black, with white gloves and a white band round his hat. On the dais, nearly in the centre of the hearse, the coffin was placed, in full view of the multitudes on the streets.

Every window, housetop, balcony, and every inch of the sidewalk on either side of High street was densely crowded with a mournful throng, assembled to pay homage to departed worth. In all the enormous crowd profound silence reigned. Conversation was carried on in whispers. The completeness of every detail of the procession was remarked by all, and much praise awarded the committee of arrangements. The display made by the various Orders and Associations in the procession elicited universal commendation. The Fire Department was the subject of especial notice and praise. The neat, clean uniforms of the officers and men, the splendid condition of the steamers and hose-carts, and the decorated car, filled with forty-two young ladies habited in deep mourning, were among the noticeable incidents of the day. A very impressive feature of the occasion was the singing by the young ladies in the mourning car of the Fire Department, of 1027th hymn of the Methodist Episcopal collection, commencing with :—

"Great Ruler of the earth and skies,"

and the 1018th hymn, commencing with—

"Behold, O Lord, before Thy Throne."

The route of the procession was south on High street to Broad—east on Broad to Fourth—south on Fourth to State—east on State to Seventh—south on Seventh to Town—west on Town to High—north on High to the west front of the Capitol. Along the entire line of march, dwelling houses, shops, stores, and other places of business, as well as all public buildings, were tastefully and solemnly decorated. It is proper to mention, on East Broadway, the offices of the Adams and American Express Companies, and the military offices in the Buckeye Block. The Seminary Hospital was adorned with mottoes in wreaths of evergreens, a draped picture of President Lincoln, and draped flags, and when the procession passed it the invalid soldiers strewed flowers before the hearse. The headquarters of Provost Marshal General Wilcox, on State street, were very handsomely decorated. The north end and east front of the Market House, the Odd Fellows' Hall, and the Gwynne Block, were each appropriately dressed in mourning. On the large front of Kelton, Bancroft & Co.'s Wholesale Dry Goods House the national colors hung in heavy rich folds from the top of each of the windows, shrouded in black, and most tastefully arranged with President Lincoln's initial letters in the centre. The various engine houses of the Fire

Department were draped and adorned with appropriate mottoes. The towers, gable, offices, baggage rooms and lamps of the Union Depot were heavily draped, as was also the office of the Little Miami Railroad Company. Among the most noticeable displays on High street, we mention the First National Bank building, the store rooms of Bain & Son, Blynn, Smith & Conrad, Randall & Aston, Thrall & Benham, F. D. Clark, Griffin & Champion, Naughton, Fay, and J. D. Osborn & Co. The great feature of the decoration was found at the Clothing House of Marcus Childs, in the Neil House building. Thousands of persons were attracted by the beauty and appropriateness of the designs, and the very elegant manner in which they were carried out. Beginning at the south window, we find them each draped with black cloth, relieved by white stars at regular intervals, and in established order. This window was adorned with the following mottoes:

"Servant of God, well done,
Thy race is o'er, thy victory won."

"The last Martyr for Freedom."

"Heaven but tries our virtues by affliction."

"East, West, North and South mourn,
The greatest friend of suffering humanity is gone."

"The President dies, we mourn;
The Nation lives, we rejoice."

The next window north—

"Our Country, Washington, Lincoln, Memoriori Eterna!"

"Memento Mori, Born Feb. 12th, 1809, Died April 15, 1865."

"Too good for Earth, to Heaven thou art fled,
And left the Nation in tears."

"He was a good man, and a just one"

The third window—

"Our Chief has fallen."

"In mourning tears the Nation's grief is spent,
Mankind has lost a friend, we a President."

"The Nation mourns."

"His memory, like the Union he preserved, is not for a day, but for all time."

"Weep, nature, weep, put on thy mourning garb."

The north window—

"We mourn our loss."

"We loved him, yes, no tongue can tell
How much we loved him, and how well."

"Fear not, Abraham, I am thy shield; thy reward shall be exceeding great."

"Only the actions of the just
Smell sweet and blossom in the dust."

"His noblest motive was the public good."

At the base of the front windows a draped portrait of Mr. Lincoln was exhibited, and each doorway was hung in heavy festoons of black cloth. Over all a draped flag was extended.

The west gateway of the Capitol Square was arched, and bore the simple inscription, "*Ohio Mourns.*" The columns at the west front of the Capitol were tastefully draped in spiral turns of mourning cloth from top to bottom. Immediately over the entrance (west front) was placed the inscription, "*God Moves in a Mysterious Way,*" and over the cornice of the columns was placed a quotation from President Lincoln's last inaugural address:—"*With Malice to none; with Charity for all.*" Each of the windows in the west front was heavily draped.

At about nine o'clock the head of the procession arrived at the west entrance of Capitol Square. The 88th O. V. I. acting as special escort, passed in immediately, forming lines in two ranks on each side of the passway from the gate to the steps of the Capitol. During the momentary delay the silence and deep feeling manifested by the people in the procession, by those crowding the streets in every direction, and by those gazing from every available window, was without precedent. The gaze seemed to alternate between the coffin being removed from the hearse containing the man dead and his striking living utterance, "With malice toward none, with charity for all," looking down upon them from the architrave of the Capitol. As the coffin, borne upon the shoulders of eight of the sergeants constituting the Veteran Guard, passed toward the archway, the bands gave expression to the solemn emotions of the hour in a dirge, the high officials in attendance assumed their places as escort, and thousands of bowed heads said as plainly as the letters arching the entrance, "OHIO MOURNS." Slowly and solemnly the escort, headed by General Hooker and staff, and Governor Brough and staff, passed to the Capitol entrance, and reverently the coffin was lowered from the shoulders of the veterans to the flowery bed awaiting it. The officers named, with their attendants, Major-General Hunter and staff, the General officers in charge of the corpse from Washington, General Wager Swayne and staff, the Pall-Bearers, and members of Committees, assumed their proper places around the catafalque with uncovered heads; the guard from the Veteran Reserve Corps formed in line on each side, and, as soon as the corpse was in place, Rev. C. E. Felton offered an appropriate prayer. Impressive as was this scene, it was surpassed by the one that followed immediately on the opening of the coffin. Amid silence almost painful the lid was raised—a sigh from those present—a slight movement by the undertaker—and for minutes all was again as still as death. The veteran officers and soldiers, with bowed heads, seemed immovable as statues, unconsciously every face mirrored the contending emotions of the heart, and the grouping around the dead of citizens and soldiers, seen by those forming the head of the procession at the foot of the western stairway, formed a scene never to be forgotten, and not to be described. Mrs. Hoffner, representing the Horticultural Society of Cincinnati, the only lady present, stepped softly forward and placed at the foot of the coffin an anchor composed of delicate white flowers and evergreen boughs, a wreath of the same upon the breast of the dead, and a cross at the head. Instructions were given more by signs than words, and arrangements made for the people to look upon the remains.

The Rotunda of the Capitol, well calculated for display, grand in its loftiness, and much the resort of our people, was transformed into a gorgeous tomb. The column of light streaming down from the lofty dome, made distinct and impressive each feature of the solemn scene below. There was no stiffness to jar with softened feeling, no unwonted display to mar the solemnity, but beautifully and simply grand as was the character of him whose mortal remains were to repose therein, the rotunda of Ohio's Capitol emblemed the sorrow of Ohio's people. The entrance ways and the corresponding panels were uniformly draped with black cloth, falling in heavy folds from the arches to the floor. In the panels the drapings were gathered to the sides equidistant from arch to floor, and then allowed to fall in full volume, and closing at the bottom as at the top. In three of these central spaces thus formed, were grouped the war-worn battle flags of veteran Ohio regiments. In the other panel, the one between the north and east entrances, tastefully mounted and appropriately draped, was Powell's painting, "Perry's Victory;" the grouping of characters and the sublimity of the scene represented, adding much to the general and impressive beauty of the rotunda. Above the panels, entirely round the dome, were three rows of festoons with black and white pendants, the whole joining appropriately the general drapings below.

On a platform with a base of 21½ by 28 feet, rising by five steps until it presented a top surface perhaps one-half as large, was placed the dais for the reception of the coffin. This platform, tastefully carpeted, the rise of each step dressed in black, was ornamented with emblematical flowers and plants in vases so arranged as to present, with their impression of beauty, the sorrow for the dead. At the corners facing the west entrance, were large vases containing beautiful specimens of amaranth, and midway between them a grand central vase glowing with the richness and beauty of the choicest flowers of the season. A similar disposition of vases faced the east entrance, from the corner ones the flowers of the emblematical Justitia, reaching to the hight of the dais. Around these large vases, were grouped smaller ones, rising in gradations of beauty with the steps of the platform. The dais was most properly the crowning beauty of the structure, and in a brief description it is impossible to do it justice. Rectangular in form, with a side elevation of two feet, it was without canopy and beautifully ornamented. The sides were covered with black broadcloth, over which drooped from the top festoons of white merino, and tassels of white silk. The end facing the west entrance bore inscribed, on a black panel with white border, in silver letters, the word "Lincoln." From the festooning at the top, rose in graceful swell a bed of white roses, immortelles and orange blossoms, the pure white relieved only by the deep fresh green of the leaves and sprigs accompanying.

The Guard of Honor was relieved by the following named officers, acting in the same capacity and under the immediate charge of Colonel J. A. Wilcox and Major L. S. Sullivant: Captain Douglas, 13th O. V. I.; Captain Stivers, U. S. A.; Captain Walker, 5th O. V. C.; Captain A. T. Wikoff, 91st O. V. I.; Captain McGroat, Captain Hull, 18th O. V. I.; Captain H. P. Wands, 22d Mich.; Captain Davis, 18th O. V. I.; Captain Hannal, 124th O. V. I.; Lieutenant Horringer, 2d O. V. C.; Lieutenant J. H. Orr, 109th O. V. I.; Lieutenant H. B. Freeman, 18th O. V. I.; Adjutant D. C. Patrick, and Lieutenants J. B. Dague, G. I. Davison, J. D. Wilson and Norris Killen, of the 88th O. V. I.

The officers, pall-bearers and committees, after looking upon the remains, retired, excepting those having the body in charge. The officers forming the guard were assigned their positions, and without delay the people commenced moving into the rotunda. First came the various military organizations of the procession, the men formed in four ranks, marching without noise upon a carpet to the catafalque, passing by twos on each side of the coffin—the face and upper part of the body being brought in full view of each individual—and then those on the right passing out at the south and those on the left turning to the north. Then followed in order the various delegations of the procession, succeeded by the people *en masse;* the same order being preserved throughout the day.

The impressive solemnity with which the ceremonies were inaugurated continued without interruption. The officers on duty firmly but courteously enforced every rule, and the people seemed imbued with such a spirit that they all moved as one person. Not an indecorous action, not a whispered word, not a frowning countenance marred the scene. The marked order, the seemliness of action, and the subdued demeanor of the countless multitude, composed of every class, age and color, during the entire day, form a feature of this more than pageant that speaks louder than the most eloquent and pathetic words the people's love for Abraham Lincoln.

By actual count it was found that over eight thousand passed in and out every hour from half after nine until four o'clock, and, making due allowance, 'tis thought that over fifty thousand people viewed the remains in that time. The unparalleled good order prevailing at all times must remain ever a source of pride to all participating.

Many scenes during the day were affecting and impressive, but to chronicle them would fill a volume. All felt the sorrow, and countenance and act mirrored it with striking plainness. Thousands of persons stood in line on High street, four abreast; the lines extending in either direction, north from the west gateway to Long street, and south from the west gateway to Rich street, patiently awaiting their opportunity. For more than six hours a steady stream of humanity poured through the channel, all eager to gaze at the martyred President on his bier.

THE AFTERNOON EXERCISES.

Long before the hour appointed for the delivery of the funeral oration the east terrace of the State House was crowded with men and women, who had gathered to hear the lessons which might be suggested from the exemplary life and violent death of Abraham Lincoln. A platform had been erected immediately in front of the entrance to the Capitol, and upon this platform, at three o'clock, appeared Maj. Gen. Hunter, Maj. Gen. Hooker, Maj. Gen.

Barnard, Brig. Gen. Townsend, Brig. Gen. McCallum, Col. Swords, Col. Simpson, Col. Lathrop, Capt. Taylor, Hon. T. B. Shannon of California, Hon. T. W. Terry of Michigan, Hon. Mr. Clarke of Kansas, the orator, Hon. Job E. Stevenson of Chillicothe, and Revs. E. P. Goodwin and C. E. Felton of Columbus. After appropriate music by military bands, and the singing of a hymn by a choir, under the direction of J. A. Scarritt, a prayer, impressive in thought and earnest in manner and word, was offered by the Pastor of the Congregational Church of Columbus, Mr. Goodwin. A solemn hymn was then sung by the choir. When Mr. Stevenson began his oration a mournful quiet pervaded the large assembly. It was broken during the delivery of the oration only when the orator, alluding to the great crime which rebellion had instigated, demanded that justice be done the criminals, and declared that conciliation of those who had murdered Mercy was condemned by the cries to heaven of thousands of soldiers murdered in rebel prisons—by bereaved homes in all loyal States. Mr. Stevenson's oration was substantially as follows:

THE OHIO ORATION.

"Ohio mourns, America mourns, the civilized world will mourn the cruel death of Abraham Lincoln, the brave, the wise, the good; bravest, wisest, best of men.

"History alone can measure and weigh his worth, but we, in parting from his mortal remains, may indulge the fullness of our hearts in a few broken words of his life and his death and his fame; his noble life and martyr's death, and matchless fame. A western farmer's son, self-made, in early manhood he won, by sterling qualities of head and heart, the public confidence, and was entrusted with the people's power. Growing with his growing State, he became a leader in the west.

"Elected President, he disbelieved the threats of traitors and sought to serve his term in peace. The clouds of civil war darkened the land. The President pleaded and prayed for peace, 'long declined the war,' and only when the storm broke in fury on the flag, did he arm for the Union.

"For four years the war raged, and the President was tried as man was never tried before.

"Oh, 'with what a load of toil and care' has he come, with steady, steadfast step, through the valley and shadow of defeat, over the bright mountain of victory, up to the sunlit plain of peace.

"Tried by dire disaster at Bull Run, where volunteer patriots met veteran traitors; at Fredericksburg, where courage contended with nature; at Chancellorsville, that desperate venture; in the dismal swamps of the Chickahominy, where a brave army was buried in vain; by the chronic siege of Charleston; the mockery of Richmond, and the dangers at Washington—through all these trials the President stood firm, trusting in God and the people, while the people trusted in God and in him.

"There were never braver men than the Union volunteers; none braver ever rallied in Grecian phalanx or Roman legion; none braver ever bent the Saxon bow, or bore barbarian battle-ax, or set the lance in rest; none braver ever followed the crescent or the cross, or fought with Napoleon, or Wellington, or Washington. Yet the Commander-in-Chief of the Union army and navy was worthy of the men—filling for four years the foremost and most perilous post unfaltering.

"Tried by good fortune, he saw the soldiers of the west recover the great valley, and bring back to the Union the Father of Waters, and all his beautiful children; he saw the legions of Lee hurled from the heights of Gettysburg; he saw the flag of the free rise on Lookout Mountain and spread from the river to the sea, and rest over Sumter; he saw the Star Spangled Banner, brightened by the blaze of battle, bloom over Richmond, and he saw Lee surrender. Yet, he remained wise and modest, giving all the glory to God and our army and navy.

"Tried by civil affairs, which would have taxed the powers and tested the virtue of Jefferson, Hamilton and Washington, he administered them so wisely and well, that after three years no man was found to take his place. He was re-elected and the harvest of success came in so grandly, that he might have said: 'Now Lord lettest thou thy servant depart in peace, for mine eyes have seen thy salvation.' Yet he was free from weakness or vanity.

"Thus did he exhibit, on occasion, in due proportion and harmonious action, those cardinal virtues, the trinity of true greatness—courage, wisdom and goodness;—goodness to love the right, wisdom to know the right, and courage to do the right. Tried by these tests and by the touch-stone of success, he was the greatest of living men.

"He stood on the summit, his brow bathed in the beams of the rising sun of Peace, singing in his heart the angelic song of 'Glory to God in the highest; peace on earth; good will to man.'

"'With malace toward none, with charity for all,' he had forgiven the people of the South, and might have forgotten their leaders—covering with the broad mantle of his charity their multitude of sins.

"But he is slain—slain by slavery. That fiend incarnate did the deed. Beaten in battle, the leaders sought to save slavery by assassination. Their madness presaged their destruction.

"Abraham Lincoln was the personification of Mercy. Andrew Johnson is the personification of Justice.

"They have murdered Mercy, and Justice rules alone—and the people, with one voice, pray to Heaven that justice may be done. The mere momentum of our victorious armies will crush every rebel in arms, and then may our eyes behold the majesty of the law. They have appealed to the sword;—if they were tried by the laws of war, their barbarous crimes against humanity would doom them to death.

"The blood of thousands of murdered prisoners cries to heaven. The shades of sixty-two thousand starved soldiers rise up in judgment against them. The body of the murdered President condemns them. Some deprecate vengeance. There is no room for vengeance here. Long before justice can have her perfect work the material will be exhausted, and the record closed.

"Some wonder why the South killed her best friend. Abraham Lincoln was the true friend of the people of the South; for he was their friend as Jesus is the friend of sinners—ready to save when they repent. He was not the friend of rebellion, of treason, of slavery—he was their boldest and strongest foe, and therefore they slew him—but in his death they die; the people have judged them, and they stand convicted, smitten with remorse and dismay—while the cause for which the President perished, sanctified by his blood, grows stronger and brighter. These are some of the consequences of the death of Abraham Lincoln. Ours is the grief—theirs is the loss, and his is the gain. He died for Liberty and Union, and now he wears the martyr's glorious crown. He is our crowned President. While the Union survives—while the love of Liberty warms the human heart, Abraham Lincoln will hold high rank among the immortal dead.

"The nation is saved and redeemed. She needs no aid from rebel hands to reconstruct the Union. The Union needs no reconstruction. It was not made by man; it was created by the God of Nations. It is vital and immortal. If it has wounds in the members of its body, they will heal, and leave no scar, without the opiate of compromise with treason. Let us beware of the Delilah of the South, who has so lately betrayed our strong man. Let the 'Prodigals' feed on the husks till they come in repentance, and ask to be received in their father's house—not as the equals to their faithful brethren, but on a level with their former servants. Then we can consider their petition, and discuss the question, not of the reconstruction of the Union, but of the formation of free States from the national domain. Until then let the sword which reclaimed their territory rule it, tempered by national law. Some cry conciliation, and say there can be no true peace by conquest. On the contrary, there is no enduring peace but the peace that is conquered. The peace of France is a conquered peace; the peace of England was conquered and conquered again; the peace of our fathers was a conquered peace; the peace of the world is a conquered peace; the peace of Heaven is a conquered peace; and thanks be to God, our peace is to be a conquered, and therefore a lasting peace. For a thousand years shall the people enjoy Liberty and Union in peace and security. The nation revived through all her members by the hand of free labor, prosperity shall fill and overflow the land—roll along the railways—thrill the electric wires—pulsate on the rivers—blossom on the lakes, and whiten the seas; and the imperial free Republic, the best and strongest Government on earth, will be a monument of the glory of Abraham Lincoln—while over and above all, shall rise and swell the great 'dome of his fame.'"

When the orator took his seat earnest and solemn manifestations of approval testified that he had appropriately and impressively spoken for the people.

Immediately there were cries for Hooker. Major Gen. Hooker rose from his seat, when the band began to play a dirge. He stood until the music stopped and then administered to those who called for him a just rebuke.

General Hooker said: "My friends, I thank you very much for the compliment you pay me by your call. If I do not respond by remarks, you will ascribe it to the inappropriateness of the occasion. Your call was dictated by curiosity as much as to hear a speech from me: that I grant you. Further you must excuse me."

This frank speech was received in the spirit which dictated it. The ceremonies were then concluded by the singing of the ode written by William Cullen Bryant, which formed a part of the funeral ceremonies in New York.

The hour for the removal of the coffin from the rotunda having nearly arrived, a majority of the people who had listened to the funeral oration quietly wended their way toward High street, which was densely thronged, until the cortege was reformed and moved to the depot.

At six o'clock in the evening the doors of the Capitol were closed, the bugle sounded the assembly, the soldiers took arms, and the procession began reforming for the final escort to the depot. As the body was being borne out to the funeral car at the west gateway of the Capitol grounds, a national salute was fired. Soon after, the procession moved, and the remains of the President were transferred to the funeral car at the depot of the Indiana Central Railway, for transportation to Indianapolis.

The committee superintending the catafalque in the rotunda determined to allow it to remain until the remains of Mr. Lincoln were consigned to the tomb at Springfield, and it is to be recorded as a memorable deed for the citizens of Columbus, that every morning until that of the 4th of May, fresh flowers were placed around the dais where the President's coffin had rested, and thousands of men, women and children visited and revisited the catafalque, and again and again with sad emotion viewed the symbols of grief which decorated the rotunda of Ohio's Capitol, in which, in February 1861, Mr. Lincoln had been given the most enthusiastic reception ever bestowed by the people of Ohio upon a citizen of the Republic.

FROM COLUMBUS TO INDIANAPOLIS.

The funeral train left Columbus at eight o'clock. B. E. Smith, Esq., President, and J. M. Lunt, Esq., Superintendent of the Columbus and Indianapolis Central Railway, accompanied it, giving personal attention to the wants and wishes of passengers. They had with them Messrs. Blemer and Cummings, chief track men, and William Slater, telegraphic operator, with all the necessary implements for immediate repair. S. A. Hughes, Esq., as Conductor, and Mr. James Gounley, Engineer, were in charge of the train.

At Pleasant Valley bonfires lit up the country for miles. A large concourse of citizens assembled around the depot. Two American flags, draped in mourning, were held in hand by two ladies. At Unionville about two hundred persons present, most of them sitting in wagons—the people having come in from the country. At Milford, assembled around bonfires, four or five hundred people waved flags and handkerchiefs slowly. About two miles from that place a farmer and his family were standing in a field by a bonfire, waving a flag. At Woodstock about five hundred people greeted the train. The ladies presented bouquets; one by Miss Villard, Miss Lucy Kimble and Miss Mary Cranston, on the part of the ladies of Woodstock; another by Miss Ann M. Currier; and another by Mrs. G. Martin and Miss Delilah Beltz, two sisters. These ladies were permitted to enter the President's car and strew flowers on the coffin. The Woodstock Cornet Band, U. Cushman, leader, played a dirge and hymn—"Dreaming, I sleep, love," and Playl's Hymn. The village bells slowly rang; men stood silent with uncovered heads. At Cable a very large crowd assembled around large bonfires. A soldier stood in the centre of an assemblage, holding a flag. All men stood uncovered.

Urbana was reached at ten o'clock forty minutes. Not less than three thousand people had gathered near the depot. On the platform was a large cross, entwined with circling wreaths of evergreens, which was worked under direction of Mrs. Milo G. Williams, President Ladies' Soldiers' Aid Society. From the top of the cross, and shorter arms, were hung illuminated colored transparencies. On the opposite side of the track was an elevated platform, on which were forty gentlemen and ladies, who sang with patriotic sweetness the hymn entitled "Go to Thy Rest." The singers represented the Methodist, Baptist, Episcopalian and Presbyterian Churches. Large bonfires made night light as day. Minute guns were fired. Ten young ladies entered the car and strewed flowers on the martyr's bier. One of the ladies was so affected that she cried and wept in great anguish.

At St. Paris were brilliant illuminations, by which could be seen a number of drooped flags, a large assembly present, who stood in silence as they looked on the moving train. A bouquet was presented and placed on the coffin by Mrs. Purron. The bouquet was a most artistic one, made by Mrs. Stouteymeyer. At Westville Station crowds were gathered to pay respect to the dead. At Conover a long line of people two deep stood in file; on the right little boys and girls, then young men and women, and on the left elderly people. In the centre, supporting a large American flag, were three young ladies, Miss Eliza Throckmorton, Miss Nora Brecount, and Miss Barnes. A patriotic religious song, with a slow and mournful air, was chanted by the flag-bearers.

At twenty minutes past twelve o'clock the train reached Piqua. Not less than ten thousand people crowded about it. The Troy Band and the Piqua Band played appropriate music, after which a delegation from the Methodist Churches, under Rev. Granville (Colonel) Moody, sang a hymn. Rev. M. repeated the first line, when it was then sung by the entire choir. Think of such actions at the midnight hour, when humanity is supposed to lay by its cares, and take its rest in the arms of repose. At Gettysburg was a large number of people around huge bonfires. Drooping flags and other evidences of mourning were displayed. There were like scenes at Richmond Junction and Covington.

At Greenville, Ohio, thirty-six young ladies dressed in white, slowly waving the Star Spangled Banner, greeted the cortege. Lafayette's Requiem was sung with thrilling effect by a number of ladies and gentlemen. About five hundred people were congregated on the platform. Company C, 28th Ohio Infantry, was drawn up in line, with fire arms reversed. The depot was tastefully decorated. On either side of the depot were two bonfires fifteen feet high, which shed most brilliant light all around the train and depot.

At New Paris great bonfires lit up the skies. A crowd

was gathered about, who stood with uncovered heads. A beautiful arch of evergreens was formed above the track, under which the train passed. The arch was twenty feet high and thirty feet in circumference. At Wiley's, New Madison and Weaver's Stations, hundreds of mourners were congregated.

Gov. Morton and suite, who had come from Indianapolis on a special train, met the funeral train at Richmond. The official personages and prominent citizens accompanying the Governor were Lieutenant-Governor Conrad Baker, Hon. T. B. McCarty, Auditor of State, Hon. John I. Morrison, Treasurer of State, Hon. D. R. Williamson, Attorney-General, Hon. Laz Noble, Clerk of the Supreme Court, Hon. Thomas A. Hendricks, Brig-General Tom. Bennet, Hon. H. S. Lane, Hon. G. S. Orth, Hon. Thomas N. Stillwell, Hon. David Kilgore, Hon. D. S. Gooding, Hon. D. C. Branham, Hon. J. A. Matson, Hon. Henry Secrist, Gen. Colgrove, Hon. J. F. Kibby, Hon. T. J. Cason, Hon. J. L. Miller, Hon. M. C. Culver, Col. R. N. Hudson, Col. R. W. Thompson, Col. Oyler, General Dumont, Hon. John U. Petit, Hon. Joseph E. McDonald, General John Love, Hon. Thomas Whitesides, Hon. Jer. Sullivan, Col. Jas. Burgess, Col. L. L. Shuler, Hon. H. C. Newcomb, Jos. J. Bingham, Alfred Harrison, Wm. Hannaman, Hon. Jas. N. Tyner, Captain H. B. Hill, Captain Stansifer, Hon. J. Y. Allison, Colonel C. D. Murray, Colonel Ira Grover, Colonel D. G. Rose, Colonel W. H. J. Robinson, Hon. David McDonald, Hon. J. D. Howland, Judge C. A. Ray, Judge Blair, Hon. John Hannah, Ex-Governor Dunning, Dr. Hendrix, Judge Gregory, J. H. McVey, E. J. Banta, D. E. Snyder, Chas. F. Hoagate, R. N. Brown, Esq., R. B. Catherwood, Esq., E. W. Halford, Esq., William Wallace, Esq., E. H. Barry, Esq., Hon. A. H. Connor, J. T. Wright, W. A. Bradshaw, Esq., J. J. Wright, Esq.,

E. W. Kimball, Esq., General Elliott, Major J. H. Lozier, Andrew Wallace, Esq., J. C. New, Esq., W. H. English, Esq., Captain Jas. Wilson, Mayor Caven and the Common Council, T. C. Phillips, J. P. Luse, Esq., J. H. Jordan, M. C. Garber, W. S. Lingle, Esq., R. J. Ryan, C. S. Butterfield, J. K. English, W. R. Manlove.

The funeral train reached Richmond at two o'clock on the morning of Sunday, April 30th. All the bells of that city rang out their solemn tones to awaken the citizens, and warn them to repair to the depot. Red, white, and blue lamps were suspended from the depot, and the arch spanning the track was lighted with the national colors. At least 5,000 persons stood in the solemn gloom of the night, reverently with uncovered heads. As the train, bearing the corpse and escort, slowly passed under the arch, a tableau of the Genius of Liberty weeping over the coffin of Lincoln, was formed, guarded on either side by a soldier and sailor, while a band played a mournful dirge, adding greatly to the impressive ceremonies.

A committee of ladies brought wreaths. One for Abraham Lincoln, bore the words "The nation mourns." The other, for Willie, had the following written upon a card: "Like the early morning flower he was taken from our midst." These floral gifts were deposited upon the respective coffins.

Centreville, the capital of Wayne county, did its whole duty, so far as decorations and a crowd of sorrowful spectators could be so accounted. The depot was very handsomely festooned with emblems of mourning, relieved by wreaths of evergreens. The building was illuminated vith two large chandeliers, and at least 2,000 people were formed on either side of the track, through which the train moved very slowly.

As the train reached Cambridge City at 4:15 A. M., it

was received with salvos of artillery. The darkness was dispelled by the burning of Bengal lights.

The loyal little village of Dublin had dressed its depot in mourning and evergreens, with portraits of Lincoln, Grant, Morton, Sherman and Sheridan. An arch spanned the railroad, and the track was lined with all the people the town and country could muster. Darkness was turned into day by large bonfires, around which the children were gathered in silence.

The depots at Lewisville, Coffin's Station, Ogden's and Raysville, were all appropriately dressed. At Lewisville each person on the train was given a circular, containing the sentiments of the people, as follows:

"We mingle our tears with yours. Lincoln—the Savior of his Country—the Emancipator of a Race, and the Friend of all Mankind—Triumps over Death, and mounts Victoriously upward with his old familiar tread."

Knightstown had erected funeral arches at each end of the depot, and festooned the building with the badges of sorrow. A choir chanted a solemn and beautiful hymn as the train moved leisurely between the files of mourning citizens. Charlotteville had not forgotten that the honored dead was the friend of the oppressed, and chief among the procession at the depot was a large body of colored people. Through the stations of Greenfield and Cumberland the funeral train passed the same scenes as at other stations.

The reporter for the *Indiana State Journal* wrote:

"Indiana is plunged into the depth of grief. Not by the magnificent demonstrations of her cities and towns is this shown, but all along the line the farm-houses were decorated, and their inmates had gathered in clusters, and by a light of bonfires caught a glimpse of the train that was bearing from their sight the remains of a man who had molded their opinions to the fashion of his own giant mind, and who in the first glimmerings of the twilight of Peace, had been snatched from the scene of his labors and his triumph to the reward of those 'who sink to rest, by all their country's wishes blest.'"

THE CAPITAL OF INDIANA.

The rain which fell early in the night did not prevent the outpouring of the people. After twelve o'clock the skies cleared and gave place to starlight. By the break of day the crowd began to gather about the depot, and at six o'clock all the avenues leading to it were closely packed with people. At seven the funeral train arrived. In the meantime the military had been drawn up in open order, facing inward, forming a line of bayonets extending from Illinois and Washington streets up to the State House doors. The general arrangements were under the direction of Major-Gen. Alvin P. Hovey, commanding the District of Indiana. The corpse was taken in charge by the local guard of honor, under command of Col. Simonson, and conducted to the hearse, the city band playing a sad and sorrowful dirge, called "Lincoln's Funeral March," composed expressly for the occasion by Charles Hess, of Cincinnati. Through the open ranks of soldiers standing at a present arms, the procession then took up its line of march to the State House. The rain had again began to fall, yet on either side, amid the sound of tolling bells, all along the entire line of march the citizens thronged the sidewalks, balconies and house-tops. The hearse conveying the remains was fourteen feet long, five feet wide and fourteen feet high, covered with black velvet. It was curtained with black and trimmed with silver fringe. The roof of the car bore twelve white plumes, with black trimmings. On the top, about the center, was an eagle, silver gilt. The sides were studded with large silver stars. The car was drawn by eight horses, with black velvet covers, and each bearing black and white plumes.

All the streets bore the usual badges and emblems of mourning, but Washington-street presented superior display. At all the intersecting streets were triple arches, adorned in part with evergreens and national flags, arranged in the most tasteful and beautiful manner.

The enclosure of the State House Square was hung with wreaths of arbor vitæ. At each corner on Washington street small arches trimmed with evergreen had been erected. The main entrance on Washington street was a structure of considerable size, combining a variety of styles of architecture. It was about twenty-one feet high, forty feet long, and twenty-four wide. Underneath was a carriage-way twelve feet wide, with a six-foot passage way on either side. The main pillars were fifteen feet high. Portraits of Grant, Sherman, Farragut and Morton were suspended from the pillars, while on the pedestals at the top rested handsome busts of Washington, Webster, Lincoln and Clay. The entire structure was beautifully shrouded in black and white, relieved by evergreens, with a display of flags. At the north side a simple gothic arch, decorated with the usual draping, had been erected. The pillars of the south front of the Capitol were spirally covered with alternate white and black cloth, the latter edged with evergreens, while the coat of arms of the State was placed in the pediment. During the performance of a funeral dirge, the tolling of bells and the sound of cannon, the coffin was conveyed to the interior of the State House in the presence of the military and civic escort. The decorations in the Hall, where the remains lay in state, reflected much credit upon those who designed and arranged them. Along the walls hung pictures of Washington, Lincoln, Johnson, Seward, Sheridan, Hovey, Morton, Douglas, Sherman, Grant, Colonel Dick O'Neill, and Edward Everett. Busts of Washington, Lincoln, Jackson, Webster, Clay and Douglas were placed at intervals, their brows bound with laurel. A bust of Lincoln, by T. D. Jones, of Cincinnati, stood on a pedestal at the head of the coffin, its brow encircled with a laurel wreath. The Hall was curtained with black, and brilliantly lighted with numerous chandeliers. The catafalque, on which the coffin rested, was covered with black velvet, and trimmed with silver fringe. The crowning glory of the interior decorations was the canopy overhanging and surrounding the catafalque. It was constructed of black material, in pagoda shape, with white cords and tassels, the ceiling being studded with golden stars. The coffin, as it rested upon the dais, was surrounded with flowers, and when the Veteran Reserve bearers placed it there, white wreaths and floral crosses were laid upon it, and a choir sung a funeral hymn.

The following named officers were detailed as the Indianapolis Guard of Honor:

First Watch, from 7 *A. M. to* 9 *A. M.*—Col. J. S. Simonson, U. S. A., Major C. S. Stevenson, Paymaster, Surgeon A. D. Gall, U. S. Volunteers, Captain T. Teneyck, 18th U. S. Infantry, Captain S. A. Craig, 17th V. R. C., Captain W. H. Thompson, 43d Regiment Infantry, Indiana Volunteers.

Second Watch, from 9 *A. M. to* 11 *A. M.*—Brevet Major General Alvin P. Hovey, U. S. Volunteers, Colonel Benjamin Spooner, Major J. W. Walker, A. A. G., Major

Will Cumback, Paymaster, Captain Hugh Middleton, A. D. C., Captain James Wilson, A. Q. M.

Third Watch, from 11 *A. M. to* 1 *P. M.*—Colonel Chas. D. Murray, 89th Infantry Indiana Volunteers, Lieutenant Colonel J. C. Major, 43d Regiment Infantry, Indiana Volunteers, Major William Bailey, Paymaster, Surgeon Charles J. Kipp, U. S. V., Captain F. S. Dunn, 12th U. S. Infantry, Captain J. B. Hager, 14th U. S. Infantry.

Fourth Watch, from 1 *P. M. to* 3 *P. M.*—Colonel A. J. Warner, 17th Regiment, V. R. C., Major V. C. Hanna, Paymaster, Surgeon J. S. Bobbs, U. S. V., Captain M. L. Ogden, 18th U. S. Infantry, Captain E. T. Wallace, 5th V. R. C., Captain William Sweeney, 43d Infantry, Indiana Volunteers.

Fifth Watch, from 3 *P. M. to* 5 *P. M.*—Brigadier General T. G. Pitcher, A. P. M. General, Major Marshall Grover, Paymaster, Major W. H. Norris, 43d Regiment Infantry, Indiana Volunteers, Captain Fergus Walker, A. A. I. G., Captain James Whittemore, Ordnance Officer, U. S. A., Captain J. P. Pope, A. C. S.

Sixth Watch, from 5 *P. M. to* 7 *P. M.*—Brevet Brigadier General A. A. Stevens, Col. 5th Regiment V. R. C., Major M. L. Bundy, Paymaster, Surgeon A. H. Fraser, 22d Regiment V. R. C., Captain J. D Taylor, Judge Advocate, Captain Eugene Pickett, 22d Regiment V. R. C., Captain T. B. Burrows, 18th U. S. Infantry.

Seventh Watch, from 7 *P. M. to* 9 *P. M.*—Lieutenant Colonel Allen Rutherford, 22d Regiment V. R. C., Major O. A. Blake, 12th Cavalry, Indiana Volunteers, Major C. M. Terrell, Paymaster, Captain James H. Rice, 5th Regiment, V. R. C., Captain M. H. Bailhache, A. A. G., Captain William T. Blanchard, 22d Regiment V. R. C.

Eighth Watch, from 9 *P. M. to* 11 *P. M.*—Colonel Wm. E. McLean, 43d Regiment Infantry, Indiana Volunteers,

Brevet Major H. K. Thatcher, 14th U. S. Infantry, Captain J. D. Russell, 5th Regiment V. R. C., Captain Wm. W. Jones, 22d Regiment V. R. C., Captain Christopher C. Becker, 17th Regiment V. R. C., Captain William L. Yelton, 43d Infantry, Indiana Volunteers.

Ninth Watch, from 11 *P. M. until departure.*—Lieutenant Colonel John H. Gardiner, 17th Regiment V. R. C., Lieutenant Colonel Gapin, 154th Infantry, Indiana Volunteers, Captain Samuel Place, 17th Regiment V. R. C., Captain Robert C. Hicks, 5th Regiment V. R. C., Captain Francis M. Welch, 43d Regiment Infantry, Indiana Volunteers, Captain John O. Neill, 22d Regiment V. R. C.

At nine o'clock the doors of the State House were thrown open, and the people, who had patiently waited for more than two hours, were permitted to view the corpse. Far down the west side of Washington street, reaching in fact to Illinois, the sidewalk was closely packed with people, jealously holding their places, frequently through great personal discomfort. Old men and young men, women with children in their arms, black people and white, indiscriminately associated, and animated by the same motive—not the gratification of a morbid curiosity, but an earnest, loving desire to gaze for the last time on the features of a great and good man, to whom they were grateful, doubly endeared by the atrocious act which destroyed his life. The touching solemnity of the Guard of Honor, ranged in solemn silence about the coffin—the sombre insignia of woe hung around the chamber of death—the sorrowful faces of the passing multitude, turned to catch one last glimpse of the features of the dead President, upon all who witnessed it, ineffaceably impressed the sadness of this "closing scene."

Notwithstanding the forbidding weather, a constant stream of people passed through the State House from nine o'clock in the morning till night. It was estimated that persons were passed through at the rate of one hundred and fifty per minute, and that fully one hundred thousand viewed the remains in the course of the day. The Sabbath School scholars of the different churches of the Capital constituted a most interesting portion of the mass of mourners. The colored Masons, in regalia, and colored citizens generally, visited the remains in a body. They formed a very respectable procession, at the head of which was carried the Emancipation Proclamation, and at intervals banners bearing the following inscriptions: "*Colored Men, always Loyal.*" "*Lincoln, Martyr of Liberty.*" "*He Lives in our Memories.*" "*Slavery is Dead.*"

Elaborate preparations had been made for a civic and military procession, but the rain fell so heavily that Gen. Hovey gave orders that it should not be formed. The *Indiana Journal* justly said:

"The unpropitious weather prevented the funeral pageant, but an offset to the disappointment of the people in this, was the increased facility given to view the remains as they lay in state at the Capitol. Every Indianian may feel that the honor of the State has been rather brightened than compromised by their reception of the remains of President Lincoln, and that the State where he passed some years of his youth, has rendered her full quota of honor to him as the Savior of his Country."

The ceremonies on the part of the State closed at ten o'clock with a procession of the Marshals around the coffin, after which the Guard of Honor and the Guard of

Sergeants filed in and took charge of the remains. At a few minutes past ten, while the band played the solemn air "Old Hundred," the coffin was lifted from the dais to the shoulders of the Sergeants, and by them carried to the hearse, whence, through a line of armed troops and torch bearers extending from the south entrance of the Capitol to the west end of the Union depot, the procession, headed by the carriages of Generals Hooker and Hovey, and composed of the civic and military escort, attended by Senator Lane and Representatives Orth, Stillwell and Farquhar, moved, amid the tolling of bells and thousands of uncovered heads, to place the coffin of Abraham Lincoln upon the train prepared by the Lafayette Railroad Company, to be transported to Chicago.

The City Councils of Louisville and Cincinnati, and a delegation from Covington, together with Gov. Bramlette, of Kentucky, and staff, were the guests of Indiana during the funeral ceremonies at its capital. Adjutant-General Terrill, General A. Stone, Colonel W. W. Frybarger and Colonel W. R. Holloway, of the Governor's staff, and C. P. Jacobs, General Mansfield, General Bennett and John M. Morton were detailed by Gov. Morton to accompany the funeral cortege from Indianapolis to Springfield.

INDIANAPOLIS TO CHICAGO.

At Indianapolis the funeral party was increased by the addition of Senator Lane, Representatives Orth, Stillwell and Farquhar, and the gentlemen of Governor Morton's staff. For the cortege the usual railway preparations had been made, N. N. Reid, the Superintendent of the Michigan Central Railroad, superintending them. The first places passed by the Funeral Train, after leaving Indianapolis at midnight, were small, yet the people had assembled by hundreds, many of them holding torches. Large bonfires were kept up at way points notwithstanding steady rain. At Lafayette, at three o'clock and twenty-five minutes on the morning of May 1st, the houses on each side of the railroad track were illuminated, and badges of mourning and draped flags were prominent. Bonfires blazed, the bells tolled, and the funeral strains of music were heard by thousands of mournful spectators. At Battle Ground, Brookston and Chalmers the people assembled in large numbers.

At eight o'clock and twenty-five minutes the train stopped at Michigan City, under a beautiful structure 12 feet wide, and the main columns 14 feet high. From these sprang a succession of arches in the Gothic style, 35 feet from the base to the summit. From the crowning central point was a staff with a draped national flag at half-mast. The arches were trimmed with white and black, and ornamented with evergreens and choice flowers. Numerous miniature flags fringed the curved edges, and portraits of the lamented dead were encircled with crape. At the abutments and at the ends of the main arch were the mottoes: "*The purposes of the Almighty are perfect and must prevail.*" "*Abraham Lincoln, the noblest martyr to freedom; sacred thy dust; hallowed thy resting-place.*" On each side of the arch were the words "*Abraham Lincoln,*" formed with sprigs of the arbor vitæ, with the mottoes, "*Our guiding-star has fallen;*" "*The nation mourns;*" and "*Though dead he yet speaketh.*" Near by this combination of arches stood sixteen young ladies dressed in white waists and black skirts, with black sashes. They sang "Old Hundred," concluding with the Doxology. Many persons were affected to tears. Large military and civil escorts were attentive and mournful listeners. Thirty-six young ladies occupied a tastefully-decorated platform, in white dresses with black scarfs. They held in their hands little flags. In their midst, and almost hidden in the folds of the national flag, was a lady representing the Genius of America. Meantime, guns were fired, and the subduing strains of music filled the air. Miss Colfax, a niece of the Hon. Schuyler Colfax, and fifteen other ladies entered the funeral car and laid flowers upon the coffin of the dead. At Michigan City the funeral party was joined by Schuyler Colfax, Senator L. Trumbull, and a committee of a hundred citizens of Chicago.

Near Lake Calumet, where the Train entered the State of Illinois, many people had assembled, and squads of soldiers were seen on the hill-sides. Minute-guns at 11 o'clock announced the arrival of the cortege at Chicago.

CHICAGO.

As the Funeral Train neared Chicago the gloomy pall of clouds rolled away and the sun broke through the rifts, enveloping all the pageant in a mellow flood of light. At every street and by-way, as the train rolled through the suburbs of the city, the crowd of expectant people increased, the men standing with heads uncovered. The brave boys of the Soldiers' Home of Fairview, some forty maimed heroes of the war, and a large representation from the troops on duty at Camp Douglas, gave the soldiers' salute and stood reverently as, with slackened speed, the train moved cityward. The Soldiers' Home was very beautifully decorated.

When the train arrived at the temporary station near Park Row, one mile north of the depot, guns were fired and the court-house bell tolled. From an early hour people had thronged the streets in the vicinity of and leading toward the station, and now on every side was a perfect sea of heads, unbroken save by the thin line of blank space running along the middle of the streets, hedged in by close ranks of waiting mourners. Every window was filled with faces, and every door-step and piazza filled with human beings, while every tree along the route was eagerly climbed by adventurous juveniles. The roofs of the houses too were covered. Every place that could by any possibility be used as seeing room was appropriated. The whole of the large space to the east of Michigan Avenue—Lake Park—was full even to the water's edge. Near the station stood military and navy officers, and prominent city officials; beyond them were the military lines, made up of three regiments—two the Veteran Reserve Corps from Camp Douglas. In the rear of these were nearly ten thousand children, from the public and private schools, and behind them the immobile spectators. Farther along the line, deep down the avenue as the eye could reach, extended the throng, the draped regalia of the different societies showing conspicuously, and setting against a solid background of marble palaces all fringed in mourning, and many of them elaborately decorated. Behind, was the still, clear surface of Lake Michigan, its waters, as the reporter of the *Chicago Tribune* said, "long ruffled by storm, suddenly calmed from their angry roar into solemn silence, as if they, too, felt that silence was an imperative necessity of the mournful occasion."

In the center of Park Place, facing east and west, a funeral arch had been erected. It was composed of one center and two side arches in treple Gothic form. The principal arch was twenty-four feet wide and thirty feet high to the summit; the side arches each eight feet wide and twenty feet high—the whole height forty feet. Each face was adorned with flags and draped with crape, the apex occupied by an eagle, that on the east side couching down to his rest; the one on the west side had her wings extended as in the act of taking flight. With this exception and the difference in inscriptions, the two faces were exactly alike. Each arch was supported by a cluster of hexagonal columns, resting on a single base, forming four sets of columns on each front. The intertices between the columns were fitted up as Gothic windows, draped in black and white. From each columnar group sprang five national flags, all draped in mourning and set in the American shield; other flags surmounted the arches, and the drapery fell in graceful festoons all around the arch, winding up to the central pinnacle. From the underside of the arches hung heavy drapery of velvet. On each central pediment was placed a bust of the President, above which the drapery took the form of the solar ray. Over each arch was an appropriate motto. Those on the east front were—"*An Honest Man's the Noblest Work of God.*" "*Our Union: Cemented in Patriot Blood Shall Stand Forever.*" "*The Poor Man's Champion—The People Mourn Him.*"

The mottoes on the west face were—"*We Honor Him Dead who Honored us while Living.*" "*Rest in Peace, Noble Soul, Patriot Heart.*" "*Faithful to Right: A Martyr to Justice.*"

Beneath the center arch was an inclined platform, up which the body was carried to be deposited in the hearse. The arch was designed and its construction supervised by W. W. Boyington.

The heavy rain which had fallen interfered with the proposed elaborate decoration of the city, but in spite of all embarrassment on that account, from dwelling and business houses were displayed many symbols expressive of deep mourning, and many appropriate mottoes and tasteful devices. In the vast crowd around the railway station there was no rush, not even an attempt at disorder. Every one in that sad crowd kept place. The figures were immovable, almost as if placed on canvass. At a quarter past eleven o'clock the coffin was lifted from the car and carried to the dais underneath the Funeral Arch by the Sergeants in attendance, the pall bearers forming in single file on each side; the Guard of Honor and Washington attendants were ranged on each side of the passage way, and all uncovered their heads in reverence as the corpse passed by. The coffin was laid on the dais, and the mourners gathered around it, the Great Western Light Guard Band taking up position in front and commencing the funeral march—"The Lincoln Requiem"—composed by Vaas for the occasion. After a short pause, thirty-six young ladies, High School pupils, dressed in white and banded with crape, came forward and walked around the bier, each depositing an immortelle on the coffin as she passed. The hearse was now brought up to the bier, and the procession prepared to move. It passed out of Park Row into Michigan avenue in the following order:

Police officers single rank, in uniform, wearing mourning rosettes on the left breast and crape bandage on the arm. Band of music, Great Western Light Guard, forty pieces, reed band, playing the "Lincoln Requiem." Chief Marshal, Col. R. M. Hough, and Major General Joseph Hooker. Assistant Marshals—Col. J. L. Hancock and Superintendent William Turtle. Major General Alfred Sully and staff; Brigadier General N. B. Buford and staff; Brigadier General B. J. Sweet and staff; Military band; Eighth Veteran Reserve Corps, Lieut.-Colonel Skinner commanding, 400 men, arms reversed, and in mourning; Military band; Fifteenth Regiment Veteran

Reserve Corps, Lieut.-Colonel Martin Flood commanding, 400 men, arms reversed, and in mourning; Sixth Regi ment United States Volunteers, Colonel C. H. Potter, commanding, 400 men, arms reversed, and in mourning.

PALL BEARERS.		PALL-BEARERS.
Hon. Lyman Trumbull,	HEARSE.	Hon. Thos. Drummond.
Hon. John. Wentworth,		Hon. Wm. Bross,
Hon. F. C. Sherman,		Hon. J. B. Rice.
Hon. E. C. Larned,		Hon. S. W. Fuller.
Hon. F. A. Hoffman,		Hon T. B. Bryan,
Hon. J. R. Jones,		Hon. J. Y. Scammon.

The hearse was eighteen feet in length, with an extreme height of fifteen feet from the ground. It consisted of a raised platform, surmounted by a canopy supported by four pillars. The form of the canopy, or roof, represented the intersection of two arches at right angles to each other. Each pillar was surmounted by a massive covered urn, draped with white and black crape, and festooned with white natural camelias. From every pillar was suspended a silken American flag, drooped and massively fastened with crape festoons. Each of the arches in the canopy was covered with rich black silk velvet, studded with thirteen silver stars, emblematical of the thirteen States in the original Federal Union. From the arches was hung broadcloth drapery, covered with black crape and trimmed with silver fringe thrown back to the corner pilasters and looped with heavy crape rosettes. The interior of the roof was of deep blue silk, studded all over with silver stars. At the head of the remains inside the car was a beautiful sunburst, constructed of white satin on a black velvet ground, also studded with silver stars and encircled by white crape *ruche.* Surmounting the car on the exterior of the canopy, stood an American eagle, draped with crape.

The coffin rested upon a dais elevated about fourteen

inches from the platform, and covered with black velvet ornamented with plaited white satin on the sides, overhung by black chenille fringe. On each side of the dais was inscribed in large letters the name "Lincoln," composed of white satin, each letter beautifully studded with silver stars. The lower part of the dais was heavily draped with black broadcloth, which fell in graceful folds over the sides of the hearse, perfectly concealing the wheels. From the position of the coffin it could be readily seen by every spectator.

The hearse was raised upon a light spring four-wheeled vehicle, to which additional springs had been placed to cause the remains to rest gently without any jarring. The hearse was drawn by ten black horses, each attended by a colored groom dressed in black, with crape hat band and crape badge on the left arm. The horses were draped in mourning, fastened with large black crape rosettes. The hearse was designed and constructed by Coan & Ten Broecke, of Chicago.

Following the hearse came the military escort—the Veteran Reserve Guard—and the delegations from Washington. They were succeeded by the Citizens' Committee of One Hundred, dressed in black, with crape hat bands and rosettes; the incoming and retiring Mayors of Chicago, with members of both old and new Councils—mourning badges; the Wisconsin delegation, consisting of Governor Lewis, General Fairchild, Secretary of State, Mr. Hastings, State Treasurer, Adjutant-General Gaylord, Hon. E. W. Keyes, Mayor of Madison, with full Board of Councilmen—also about one hundred citizens of Madison, Wisconsin; Judges of the Courts and Members of the Bar—two hundred gentlemen; the Reverend Clergy, numbering about fifty, each with a white cross on crape band; Col. Fred. Hurlbut, Marshal; officers of the Army and Navy, in service or honorably discharged, in uniform, about fifty, including many of the Illinois regimental officers.

The cortege slowly marched along the line, the band playing the solemn dirge, and the throng uncovering their heads as it passed by. Having gone through the open column of the military, who were formed in line on the avenue from Park Row to Hubbard Court, the band retired, and the regimental bands struck up the funeral strain.

The regular divisions of the procession then fell into line, as the cortege moved on, in the prescribed order. There were five divisions, and, excepting that of New York city, the procession was the grandest and most impressive by which the President's remains had been followed. In a careful article upon this grand feature of the pageant in Chicago, the *Tribune* of that city said:

"The procession was a solemn tribute to his memory, and evinced the devotion with which all classes looked up to Mr. Lincoln. Its composition was varied, and embraced all nationalities, all creeds, and all sects. Bronzed, war-worn and gray-bearded heroes of the army and navy; veteran soldiers, incapacitated for active service by honorable wounds; governors of States, and grave, thoughtful-faced counsellors of the nation; metropolitan officials irrespective of partisan differences; the children of the schools by thousands, unconsciously participating in a ceremony which in after years will be their most precious recollection; venerable judges of courts and the reverend clergy, all creeds merged in the one great sorrow—Protestant and Catholic and Hebrew—all moving side by side; Knights Templars and Masons, the mysterious symbols of their orders draped in mourning; Hollandish and Belgian, English and Scotch, Irish and Welsh, French and Norwegian, Danish and Spanish, Hebrew and Bohemian societies almost countless in numbers; the Arbeiter, Grueth Bildungs and Turnverein, of stalwart, phlematic Germans, pledged to liberty and humanity; associations, unions of every description; and last but not least, the men whom he has lifted from bondage and stamped with the dignity of manhood, the race which by one stroke of his pen he delivered from the task-master, and made forever free. For four long hours, they marched by with steady, measured tramp."

The line of march was from Park Row to Michigan avenue, along the avenue to Lake-street, down Lake to Clark, on Clark to the east gate of the Court-house square, and inside the square round to the south door of the Court-house, in which the coffin was deposited; the different parts of the procession filed through the Court-house, past the corpse, and left by the north door, breaking up into sections as they reached the street, and marching off to the places where they had gathered in the morning. The whole of the line of march was strongly guarded along the edge of the sidewalks. Inside these were formed the different components of the procession in double solid column; the sidewalks and open spaces being reserved for spectators. The people had room to pass, and owing to the very efficient measures taken to preserve order, there was no inconvenience among the immense crowds of people who thronged every avenue through which a sight of the mournful cortege could possibly be gained, and stretched far away back into the streets abutting on the line of march.

The head of the cortege reached the Court-house at

12:45 P. M. The military portion of the procession, under command of Brig.-Gen. Sweet, was formed by regiments in the Public Square, and as the hearse drew near the north entrance, they received it with a "present arms," and other military tokens of respect. General Hooker and his accompanying officers took a preliminary survey of the interior decorations of the Hall, and then returned to the north entrance. The coffin was borne into the Court-house upon the shoulders of soldiers, and attended by the pall-bearers and others who acted as chief mourners. While the coffin was being placed in position, a choir of many voices sang a dirge, sad and mournful as the occasion which called them together.

The court-house was elaborately decorated. From each window hung flags of black and white, and the dome was covered with mourning emblems, strips of white and black, and rosettes of the same general hue. The north door was heavily draped in black, and surmounting the whole was the inscription, in black upon a white ground, "*The beauty of Israel is slain upon her high places.*" On the south door was this inscription: "*Illinois clasps to her bosom her slain and glorified son.*" Upon entering the north door the visitor was struck with the air of intense gloom which pervaded the rotunda. The ceiling was draped with white and black cambric, gathered into festoons about the chandeliers, the last, except the globes, being covered with crape. The walls throughout the entire length, were covered with black crape, extending from the ceiling to the floor, closing altogether the stairways to the court-rooms above and the offices on the first floor. Above, on either side, were these inscriptions: "*We mourn. Liberty's Great Martyr has sunk to rest by his country blest.*" Upon the inner side of the south entrance was this inscription: "*He left us sustained by our prayers; He returns embalmed in our tears.*" The catafalque stood in the center of the rotunda, directly under the dome, with the head fronting the north entrance. The canopy was draped with rich black velvet, lined with white satin, and fringed and ornamented with stars and a border of silver. The dais was trimmed with the same materials, and liberally bespangled with silver fringes, stars and rosettes. The canopy was supported by four iron columns painted white, ornamented with trailing vines painted black, the whole covered with crape. At the head of the catafalque was an eagle executed in white marble, holding in its talon a miniature flag, and wearing around its neck a strip of crape. Directly in front of the catafalque and filling the space between the two front supporting columns, were six silk flags, crossing each other diagonally, artistically arranged, producing a singularly agreeable effect. The roof of the catafalque, inside, was a plain flat top of heavy cloth, in which were cut thirty-six stars. Over these were placed a layer of white gauze, and over this several brilliant reflectors, which caused the light to shine through the stars, upon the body below, with a softened, yellow mellow radiance. The effect was new and solemn. At each corner stood an Etruscan vase filled with the rarest natural flowers, which almost overpowered the visitor with their pungent perfume. Along the sides and ends of the dais were bouquets of flowers arranged in cruciform and basket shape. One of the most noticeable of these was a Greek cross made of camelias. Extending around the catafalque, about midway between the dais and the canopy, and looped in elegant festoons, was a wreath of evergreens and camelias, no inconsiderable part of the decorations. The designer of this elegant testimonial was J. M. Van Osdell, Esq., of Chicago.

After the coffin was placed upon the dais, the pall-bearers and the attendant officers retired, and then the entire procession passed through the rotunda in the same order in which they marched in the streets. The remains were not exposed. The people could only hurry past the catafalque and glance at the coffin and its surroundings. At five o'clock the remains were exposed to view, and the announcement made that the public would be admitted. Immediately the crowd, which was anxiously waiting outside the Public Square, began to file into the inclosure. The arrangements for exhibiting the body were excellent, and the visitors passed through the rotunda without confusion, taking time only to glance at the revered remains, at the rate of 7,000 an hour.

At intervals during the evening, dirges were sung, both solos and concerted pieces. Among others the following were performed: "Lord, I yield my spirit," and the choral, "Happy and blest," from the oratorio of St. Paul, "He that endureth to the end shall be saved," and "Farewell, father, friend and guardian"—the last, words by L. M. Dawn, and music by Geo. F. Root, composed expressly for this occasion. At midnight the Germans, numbering several hundred, chanted a beautiful and impressive dirge. It was one of the most interesting incidents of this long to be remembered day. A drizzling rain began to fall about nine o'clock, and yet it was long after midnight before there was much diminution in the crowds which sought to get a last look of the dead President. They surged through the rotunda as enduring and constant as a river. It is estimated that up to midnight at least 40,000 persons had looked upon the remains of Abraham Lincoln.

GUARD OF HONOR.

The following officers were appointed by Brig.-Gen. Sweet, to serve as the Chicago Guard of Honor over the coffin:

Lt.-Col. Martin Flood, 15th Regt,. V. R. C., commanding guard; Capt. E. C. Phetteplace, 8th Regt., V. R. C.; Capt. Samuel C. Gold, 15th Regt., V. R. C.; Capt. Jerry N. Hill, 15th Regt., V. R. C.; Capt. Edward Miller, 15th Regt., V. R. C.; Capt. J. L. Hill, 24th Ohio Battery; 1st Lieut. Nathan Cole, 13th Regt., V. R. C.; 1st Lieut. Frank D. Garrety, 15th Regt., V. R. C.; 1st Lieut. J. W. Crawford, 8th Regt., V. R. C.; 2d Lieut. J. S. Taylor, Adjutant, 15th Regt., V. R. C.; 2d Lieut. Samuel McDonald, 15th Regt., V. R. C.; 2d Lieut. W. L. Wood, 8th Regt., V. R. C.; 2d Lieut. W. R. McDaniel, 15th Regt., V. C. C.; 2d Lieut. S. W. Groesbeck, 15th Regt., V. R. C.

Fifty Illinois officers, formerly serving in the army and navy, through Gen. Julius White, offered to serve as Guard of Honor; and this offer was accepted by Adjt.-Gen. Townsend. They were appointed as follows:

First Relief.—Col. Daniels.
Second Relief.—Col. H. Davis.
Third Relief.—Lieut.-Col. Ducat.
Fourth Relief.—Capt. R. L. Law, U. S. N.

Each officer in command of the relief had under control nine officers who, for the time being, acted as the guard. The following is the full guard:

Col. Hasbrook Davis, Col. Edward Daniels, Major Jno. McCarty, Lieut.-Col. S. McClevy, Major W. B. Scates, Major Chas. Ehoon, Brevet Major L. Bridges, Capt. W. S. Swane, Capt. Jas. Duguire, Capt. F. Busse, Capt. Edward Went, Capt. Z. B. Greenleaf, Capt. Henry Kenkle, Capt. John McAssen, 1st Lieut. N. S. Bouton, Lieut. C. George, Capt. Sam'l A. Love, Lieut. W. P Barclay, Lieut. M. Shields, Lieut. J. S. Mitchell, Lieut. G. S. Bigelow, Lieut.-Col. A. C. Ducat, Capt. R. L. Law, U. S. N.; Maj. L. B. Kimball, Chief Eng. U. S. N.; Lieut.-Col. T. W. Grosvenor, Major M. Thieman, Capt. G. W. Hill, Capt. H. S. Goodspeed, Capt. R. N. Hayden, Capt. J. N. Leish, Capt. B. A. Busse, Capt. Ph. Adolph, Capt. J. G. Langgorth, Capt. C. G. Adoc, Capt. Wm. Cunningham, Lieut. R. J. Bellamy, Lieut. R. Sheridan, Lieut. Harry Briggs, Lieut. F. A. Munge, Lieut. J. H. Hill, Lieut. A. Russell, Lieut. C. H. Gladding.

It was calculated that 37,000 persons joined in the procession, and this was not one-third of the number who witnessed it. The *Chicago Tribune* deemed it safe to say that, including strangers and citizens who came upon the streets bordering the route of the procession, there were not far from 120,000 souls who participated in and witnessed the sad ceremonies.

In pursuance of orders issued by Brigadier-General Sweet, 400 members of the 15th Veteran Reserve Corps, 400 of the 8th Veteran Reserve Corps, and 400 of the 6th United States Infantry participated in the pageant, and detachments of the first two regiments performed guard duty during the afternoon and night. The 24th Ohio Battery was also in the city from Camp Douglas. One detachment served the minute guns at Park Place, while the remainder acted as mounted guards on the various parts of the line of march.

In the procession with the Chicago Board of Trade was Mr. Daniel Brooks, of New Hampshire, who, when a boy of sixteen, marched in the funeral procession of George Washington.

After midnight, persons anticipating the crowd of the forthcoming day, left their homes expecting to pass immediately into the rotunda where the corpse lay, but were disappointed in being compelled to take their places with others, some of whom had waited for hours. At noon, on the second of May, the line extended from the Court House to the corner of Washington and Lasalle streets, down the former street three blocks to State street, then one block south to Madison, and along Madison street down to Clark street—within a trifle of a mile in length.

Writing from Chicago on the morning of the 3d of May, the reporter of the *New York Tribune* said:

"A part of day before yesterday, all of night before last, and all day yesterday, the remains of the President lay in state amid the imposing funeral surroundings in the Court House, and still there was not sufficient time for all who sought the privilege to look upon his face. And when it was night, and the coffin was closed, and young ladies came to place upon it fresh flowers wrought into significant and touching emblems, and the last dirge was being chanted by the choir, and the guard of honor and the funeral escorts surrounded the bier, and the coffin was borne upon the shoulders of the veteran sergeants to the hearse in the street, between lines of flaring torches—even then, when the gates of the public square had been closed an hour, a long, dense column still waited in the vain hope of being admitted.

"Taken all in all, Chicago made a deeper impression upon those who had been with the funeral from the first than any one of the ten cities passed through before had done. It was to be expected that such would be the case; yet, seeing how other cities had honored the funeral, there seemed to be no room for more; and the Eastern members of the cortege could not repress surprise when they saw how Chicago and the North-west came, with one accord, with tears and with offerings, to help bury 'this Duncan' who had 'been so clear in his great office.' The last of these tributes was the escort of torches to the funeral train, showing the cortege as it passed to thousands who were themselves wrapped in darkness."

The Court House was closed at eight o'clock, and the coffin, with its honored contents, was escorted to the cars, which waited to convey it and its attendants to Springfield, in the following order:

Band.
R. M. Hough, Chief Marshal.
Colonel J. L. Hancock and Captain Turtle, Assistant Marshals.
Major General Hooker and staff.

Pall Bearers.  Pall Bearers.

[The members of the Common Council acting as Pall Bearers.]
Captain James McCauley, V. R. C., Lieutenants Durkee, Murphy and Hoppy.
Guard of Honor (in carriages, as before.)
Captain Perose, Col. Robinson, Captain Wyman, Illinois Delegation.
Congressional Delegation.

The cortege was flanked by torch-bearers, who marched parallel with it, and three feet from the sidewalk. The route of the procession was through Washington and Market streets to Madison street bridge, and thence to the depot of the St. Louis and Alton Railway.

The torchlight display was the most beautiful ever witnessed in the West, and when it reached the depot, the glare of its lights fell upon hundreds of people who had taken a last look of the corpse in the rotunda of the Court House, yet who were unwilling to be absent when it departed from the city.

Reviewing the suggestions and lessons of the solemn pageant which had arrested business, hushed all the noise and quieted all the rush of trade and commerce in the great City of the Lakes, the *Chicago Tribune* said :

"These streets, that five years ago this very month blossomed with flags and echoed the booming of cannon and the jubilations of assembled thousands, as the news was announced that Abraham Lincoln had been nominated as the candidate for the Presidency of the United States, are now clad in the parti-colored emblems of mourning, and echo only the solemn tolling of bells that then rang out glad peals, and the booming of minute guns that then gave forth the people's gladness. He went from among us the brave, earnest, hopeful, honest, Christian man, to save the country from the ruin which portended—the cloud, no bigger than a man's hand, that overspread the whole heavens, covered the whole land with darkness and deluged it with the pitiless storm. He went as an earnest, simple man, determined only to interpose the shield of justice and right between the threatened Republic and its enemies, to maintain the authority of the laws and the Constitution handed down by the fathers, and re-establish order and obedience. He comes back to us, his work finished, the Republic vindicated, its enemies overthrown and suing for peace; but alas! he returns with the crown of martyrdom, the victim of the dastard assassin. He left us asking that the prayers of the people might be offered to Almighty God for wisdom and help to see the right path and pursue it. Those prayers were answered. He accomplished his work, and now the prayers of the people ascend for help to bear the great affliction which has fallen upon them. Slain as no other man has been slain, died as no other man has died, cut down while interposing the hand of his great charity and mercy between the wrath of the people and guilty traitors, the people of Chicago tenderly receive the sacred ashes with bowed heads and streaming eyes."

"In Chicago he first laid deep and broad the foundation of his legal attainments. In the courts of Chicago he gained that distinction which made him peer among the ablest counsellors of the land. In that remarkable debate with the lamented Douglas, Chicago, more than any other city, aided to give his immortal utterances a wide-spread circulation throughout the land, and thus brought prominently before the country this hard working toiler, this acute thinker and logical reasoner, this unflinching and unyielding patriot. Chicago first summoned from his comparative obscurity, in a political sense at least, this man of men, and demanded that the country should recognize in him one fit to stand in high places—a safe counsellor in danger, a wise and prudent ruler in crises. And when, as the clouds were gathering thickly, and the mutterings of the approaching tempest were heard on the southern horizon, the servants of the people gathered together in this city to select the pilot who should stand at the helm, Chicago firmly demanded that that pilot should be Abraham Lincoln. * * * *

"His calm, sad face was ever turned westward, and already he had determined that, when he had fulfilled his glorious mission, full of honors, his course as rounded and complete as the orbit of a planet, *pater reipublicæ*, then laying aside the reins of government and sheathing the sword of justice, he would come to Chicago to spend the remainder of his days in the enjoyment of that ease he had so deservedly won, and go down to the grave in the quiet of home, peacefully and serenely. By the mysterious and inscrutable providences of Almighty God, that near desire of his heart was denied him. * * * *

"For all these reasons it was peculiarly appropriate that Chicago should do honor to his remains in a manner commensurate with his great abilities and his resplendent traits of personal character. That duty has been accomplished nobly and appropriately."

CHICAGO TO SPRINGFIELD.

The bells were tolled, a choir sang a dirge, and several bands of music performed solemn airs, as the funeral cortege left Chicago. Mr. Blackstone, the President, and Robert Hall, the Superintent of the Railroad Company, gave personal attention to the running of the train. Large accessions were made to the funeral party. Among them were the Springfield delegation appointed to escort the President's remains to the city from which he was called as Chief Magistrate. It was composed of the following named gentlemen: Governor Oglesby and staff; George H. Harlow, Private Secretary to the Governor; W. J. Conkling, A. L. Babcock, A. Johnson, W. D. Crowell, James C. Conkling, D. L. Gold, G. M. Brinkerhoff, N. W. Miner, A. Hale, A. A. Brackett, F. W. Tracy, H. G. Fitzhugh, T. A. Raysdale, G. H. Souther, E. L. Gross, E. B. Hawley, T. S. Whitehurst, A. B. McKenzie, Cyrus Vandever, S. M. Parsons, R. P. Johnston, Charles Dunn, J. E. Roll, S. D. B. Salter, B. Wright, Colonel William A. Smidt, E. L. Conkling, C. S. Zane, S. G. Nesbit, J. J. Lord, F. K. Whitmore, W. W. Watson, A. T. Barnes, P. C. Kennedy, John Armstrong, Joel Johnston, G. Keyes, J. M. Burkhardt, S. Holiday, Hon. James H. Beveridge, J. P. McCoy and Ed. S. Multimer.

Governor Bramlette and staff and a number of prominent citizens of Kentucky were also upon the train, embracing D. W. Lindsay, Adjutant General; S. E. Suddarth, Quartermaster General; W. T. Scott, Paymaster General; William H. Granger, Aid-de-Camp; A. G. Hodges, Aid-de-Camp; Rev. D. P. Henderson, Chaplain; W. T. Samuels, Auditor; James R. Page, Assistant Secretary; J. R. Duncan, Aid-de Camp; Hon. Wm. Kaye; D. R. Haggard, M.D.; W. B. Belknap, Esq.; A. B. Semple, Esq.; Arthur Peter, Esq.; B. F. Avery, Esq.; J. D. Orral, Esq.; R. C, Gwathmey, W. H. Goddard, T. C. Coleman, R. L. Post, A. J. Ballard, E. Slaughter, M. Redding, J. C. Nauts, W. B. Gurley, C. C. Hull, L. B. Todd, B. M. Patten, W. H. Kinney, E. N. Woodruff, W. D. Smith, J. H. Spear, Rev. C. Vansantvoord, Chaplain U. S. A.; Rev. T. Farver, do. do.; Major General J. M. Palmer, Commanding Department of Kentucky; Staff, Major L. Hammond, A. I. G.; Captain E. B. Harlan, A. A. G.; Captain H. Howland, C. Q. M.; Captain J. F. Herbert, Chief of Artillery; I. M. Wood, Orderly. There were also on the train a considerable number of the leading citizens of Michigan, Wisconsin and Minnesota.

At Bridgeport the people lighted bonfires, and with torches illuminated the track as the train slowly moved along. Passing Summit, Joyes and Lennox, crowds of spectators were seen. At Lockport, at 11:33, minute guns were fired. Many persons stood near the track holding torches, and in the background was an immense bonfire. Many of the houses were draped in mourning, and some were illuminated. One of the mottoes was: "*Come Home.*" The train passed all the stations slowly, the bells of the locomotives being tolled. At Joliet, near midnight, minute guns were fired and the bells tolled, and a brass band played a funeral air. Many ladies and gentlemen, arranged on a heavily draped platform, sang a hymn. It is said that 12,000 persons were assembled. The depot bore an illuminated portrait of the late President, with the motto: "*Champion, Defender, and Martyr of Liberty.*" Bonfires lighted up this interesting scene, and draped national flags were waved. It was raining, but this did not prevent even women and children from a participation in these outward marks of respect. The train moved beneath an arch which spanned the track. It was constructed of immense timbers, decked with flags, mottoes, and a profusion of evergreens, and surmounted by a figure of the Genius of America. "There is rest for thee in Heaven," was sung by male and female voices as the funeral car passed. At Elwood and Hampton the people had kindled immense bonfires. At Wilmington, at 10 o'clock on the morning of May 3d, at least a hundred people were drawn up in line on each side of the track, with torches. Minute guns were fired. Over two thousand persons surrounded the station, the men standing with their heads uncovered. At Gardner, all the houses were draped with mourning and illuminated. At Dwight, bells were tolled and minute guns fired. The American flag was draped. At Odell, Cayuga and Pontiac large crowds assembled, with the usual demonstrations, including minute guns; also at Lexington.

At Tonawanda, at half-past four o'clock, there was a large assemblage of people. At Bloomington a large arch bore the inscription, "*Go to thy rest.*" At other stations minute guns, the tolling of bells, singing by a choir of ladies, contributed with mournful effect to the sadness of the occasion which called out the inhabitants. At daylight the sky was clear, and the farm houses along the line exhibited badges and drapery of sorrow. Portraits of Abraham Lincoln were prominent in every direction. Thousands of people were assembled at Atlanta.

Minute guns were fired, and there was music of the fife and muffled drum. Among the mottoes was, "*Mournfully and tenderly bear him to his grave.*"

At Lincoln, reached at seven o'clock, named after Abraham Lincoln, and containing between two and three thousand inhabitants, the depot was handsomely draped. Ladies, dressed in white and black, sang as the train passed under a handsomely constructed arch, on each side of which was a picture of the deceased President, with the motto, "*With malice to none, with charity for all.*" The National and State flags were prominently displayed, and a profusion of evergreens, with black and white drapings, made up the artistic and appropriate arrangements.

At Broadwell and Elkhart, men stood with uncovered heads, and ladies waved little flags, which were handsomely draped. Eighteen miles from Springfield the cortege passed under an arch, with both large and small flags, mourning drapery and evergreens. Of the latter was formed a cross intertwined with black, bearing the motto: "*Ours the Cross: thine the Crown.*" At Williamsville all the houses were draped, and there were many flags and portraits. There was another arch, with the inscription: "*He has Fulfilled his Mission.*" At Sherman Station, eight miles from Springfield, many people assembled on the road, some on horseback and some in carriages, but the larger part on foot. The number increased as the train proceeded, until at nine o'clock —an hour beyond the schedule time—it reached Springfield.

SPRINGFIELD.

The correspondent of the *New York Tribune* wrote as follows of the suggestions and scenes of Abraham Lincoln's return to Springfield, from the service of his country and from martyrdom in that service:

"He said, in the few words of impressive farewell addressed to his friends on the 11th day of February, 1861, after he had stepped upon the platform of the car which was to bear him away, 'I must now leave you—*for how long I know not.*' Alas! those friends now know just how long. He said, too, 'I go to assume a task more difficult than that which devolved upon Washington.' And now the whole world whose central figure he has been from that day to this, must concede that he has acquitted himself of that task like another Washington. In the mellow air and bright sunlight of this May morning, sweetened by the rain of last night, when the prairies are clothed in flowers, and the thickets of wild fruit trees, and blossoming orchards are jubilant with birds, he comes back. His friends and neighbors are here to receive him, not with banners and triumphal music; not with congratulations and grasping of hands, as they had hoped to do; not so, but in mourning; and his oldest and dearest friends come to meet him, to be the pall-bearers at his funeral. The contrast between that other day and to-day, the contrast between what but for the assassin the day of his return should have been, and what that day actually is; these contrasts force themselves upon the mind, and will not be banished from our thoughts. The train that brought him to his long home moved slowly into the town, moved slowly through masses of 'plain people' who had come from all the country round about. These people had known him always, as the boy struggling for knowledge while he battled with poverty; as the young man who surveyed their lands, and read at night when perchance he stayed at their humble houses; as the rising young lawyer who plead the causes of the poor for only 'sweet pity's sake;' who upheld the weak against the strong for only justice's sake, and because oppression was hateful to him; as the politician, whose continual plea was, 'Let us see if this thing be right—if it be right let us have it, but if it be wrong let us put it away from us;' as the State legislator, who with one other, against an intolerant majority dared to file upon the records his protest against Slavery; as the Presidential Elector, who each four years spoke his convictions in every town in the State, though in a hopeless minority, for conscience sake, and yet never lost his temper or called bad names; as the candidate for Senator, who deliberately said, 'I will not be double-faced, I will utter the same opinions at both ends of the State, I will not be made Senator by a fraud;' and by and by he was made President and went from among them—and they watched him from afar, were proud that one of themselves had become in virtue and in station, 'the foremost man in all this world.' And then they saw him accomplish his great task; and now they were seized by a mighty longing to see him once more, and they made him promise that he would come in June; and then they heard of his most horrible murder, and behold, he comes in May, but he comes a dead man. Say, have not these people a right to mourn and to refuse to be comforted? Was he not peculiarly their own, and when you and all of us sorrow shall these not lament?

"The train stops. The pall-bearers, those old men, friends of his, lang syne, approach. The stillness among all the people is painful; but when the coffin is taken from the car, that stillness is broken, broken by sobs, and these are more painful than the stillness. The coffin is borne to the hearse; the hearse moves slowly, almost tenderly, away, followed by the mourners, and the pall-bearers walk by the side. The cortege, more solemn than any that had gone before, reaches the State House, where he was wont to speak face to face with his neighbors—where at this hour those neighbors press to behold his face locked in death. All night they will pass by with eyes searching through tears for resemblances and recognition of the features they knew so well. Many will not know the poor, chilled, shrunken features for his, for the beautiful soul that transfigured them into all loveliness no longer illumines this bit of clay—aye, but it shines at the Right Hand!

* * * *

"Springfield had been the home of Abraham Lincoln twenty-five years. With his companionable nature and open heart it followed that he was the personal acquaintance and friend of all the men, women and children in the city, and in all the region round about. Besides, Springfield was the political center of the State, and during twenty years Abraham Lincoln was the acknowledged State leader of a political party. That party, or the one that sprang from it, was finally successful, and rewarded him not merely with State honors, but with the headship of the nation. Such men as E. D. Baker, Lyman Trumbull, Richard Yates, S. T. Logan, David Davies, Owen Lovejoy, E. B. Washburne, Wm. H. Bissell, R. J. Oglesby, J. N. Arnold and John Wentworth—all these conceded his right to leadership, and cheerfully rallied beneath his standard. And yet more than the political leader, he was the popular townsman and good neighbor at his home in Springfield. Springfield, then, is his proper burial place."

The following had been announced as the Military Programme:

Special Orders, } HEADQUARTERS, DISTRICT OF ILLINOIS,
No. 86. } SPRINGFIELD, ILL., April 28, 1865.

The following programme for the funeral ceremonies of the late President of the United States is published for the information of all concerned:

1. On the first and third days of May, thirteen guns will be fired at dawn, and afterwards at intervals of thirty minutes, between the rising and setting sun, a single gun, and at the close of the day a national salute of thirty-six guns.

2. On the fourth of May, twenty-one guns at dawn, and afterwards single guns at intervals of ten minutes until the procession moves; firing will then cease until the close of the day, when a national salute of thirty-six guns will be fired.

3. Company E, 23d Regiment V. R. C., is designated as guard to the remains of the late President, while lying in state in the Hall of the House of Representatives.

4. The following troops will be drawn up in line, in full dress uniform, at the railroad depot, at least one hour prior to the time fixed for the arrival of the remains: 146th Illinois Volunteers; Company E, 23d Regiment Veteran Reserve Corps.

5. After the arrival of the remains at the depot, all of the 146th Illinois Volunteers in this city will be detailed for guard duty, and will be posted at such points as may be necessary.

6. At the earliest possible moment on the morning of the 4th proximo, the 12th Michigan Volunteers, and the battalion of the 14th Iowa Volunteers, at Camp Butler, will repair, under command of their respective officers, to this city, for duty as escort. After the conclusion of the funeral rites, they will return without delay to their station. Quartermaster's Department will furnish transportation.

7. The escort will consist of the following troops, and will be commanded by Col. C. M. Prevost, 16th V. R. C.: 24th Michigan Volunteers; 146th Illinois Volunteers; Company E, 23d Regiment V. R. C.; Company C, 42d Wisconsin Volunteers.

By command of Brig. Gen. John Cook.

B. F. SMITH, Asst. Adjt. Gen.

The Funeral Train was announced by the firing of cannon at nine o'clock. It passed into the depot through a dense crowd of expectant people, composed not only of the citizens of Sangamon county, but representing all the

States touching Illinois. The St. Louis delegation consisted of the Old Guard and Halleck Guards, members of the city government, of the Merchants' Exchange, Gov. Flëtcher and Staff, and Gen. Dodge, who commands the Department of Missouri, and his Staff, together with a number of private citizens, in all between five and six hundred persons. The procession was promptly formed in the following order:—Brigadier-General Cook and Staff; military escort; Major-General Hooker and Staff, on foot; the guard of honor; relatives and friends in carriages; the Illinois Delegation from Washington; Senators and Representatives of the Congress of the United States, including Speaker Colfax and their Sergeants-at-Arms; the Illinois State Legislature; the Governors of different States; delegations from Kentucky; the Chicago Committee of Reception; the Springfield Committee of Reception; the Judges of the different courts; the reverend clergy; officers of the army and navy; firemen of the city; citizens generally; colored citizens. The route of the procession was direct to the State House, and the President's remains were borne by the Veteran Sergeants into the Hall of the House of Representatives, in accordance with the rules which had governed the care of the coffin from the morning on which it was carried from the Capitol at Washington.

The principal decorations of the city were confined to the buildings on the four sides of the Capitol Square. At the First National Bank a wreath of evergreen and a portrait of the deceased President surmounted the motto:

> "He left us upheld by our prayers,
> He returns embalmed in our tears."

Over Wolf & Bergmann's was a portrait, and the motto:

> "An honest man now lies at rest,
> As ever God with his image blest;
> Few hearts like his with virtue warmed,
> Few heads with knowledge so informed."

Hammerslough Brothers displayed a portrait of Mr. Lincoln, with the motto: "*Millions bless thy name.*" The store of J. H. Holfer & Co. was decorated with drapery and a bust of Lincoln trimmed with evergreens. John McGriery's store was decorated with drapery and flags, and the motto: "*Revere his Memory.*" The headquarters of the Paymaster's Department were appropriately draped, and displayed the flag at half mast. L. Steiners & Co.'s store had the following motto: "*Weep, sweet country weep, let every section mourn; the North has lost its champion, the South its truest friend. Let every patriot halt at our country's altar, and drop a passing tear for departed worth.*" The Court House and the rooms of the State Agricultural Society were very beautifully draped. Little's store had the motto: "*He still lives in the hearts of his countrymen.*" G. W. Chatterton's store displayed the most elegant and tasteful decoration in the city. The building was profusely draped, and had on its front a monument against a black background, inscribed: "LINCOLN." "*With malice towards none, with charity for all.*" In the large window, which was heavily set in black, was an eagle holding in his beak a beautiful wreath of evergreens and immortelles, the whole surmounting a bust of the departed President, at the base of which was the motto: "*Ours in life—the nation's in death.*" Robinson & Banman's store had the motto: "*Our nation mourns.*" Smith & Bros.' store displayed a bust wreathed in evergreens, with the motto: "*How we loved him.*" J. H. Adams' store had a bust in the window, with the motto: "*A sigh the absent claim, the dead a tear;*" also, a portrait with the motto: "*Our martyred chief.*" The Odd Fellows' Hall displayed a portrait beautifully trimmed with evergreens. Other places of business and many of the private residences in the city were beautifully draped, among them the Executive Mansion, and the residences of ex-Governor Matteson and Colonel Baker of the *State Journal.*

The old residence of Mr. Lincoln was the center of mournful interest. The house, which was occupied by Lucien Tilton, was very heavily draped in mourning. The windows were curtained with black and white, the corner posts wreathed with evergreens, the cornice hidden by festoons of black and white looped up at intervals, and the space between the cornice of the door and the central window filled with the American flag gracefully trimmed. The law office which Mr. Lincoln had occupied in a block of three-story brick buildings, was draped in mourning, and at the door hung a portrait of the deceased.

The State House was decorated with superior taste and skill. The outside of the dome was deep black, and, together with the cornice and pillars on which it rests, was elaborately festooned with white and black. Similar drapery fell from the eves and columns; the pediments, both on the north and south entrances, were corrugated with evergreens, and the capitals draped with white and black muslin. All the windows were partially curtained with black-white trimmings at the top and black falling at the base; from the crown of the dome was a staff, on which was the national flag at half-mast with black streamers. The entrance to the Capitol and the rotunda was heavily draped, and festoons of evergreens hung from the dome.

In the Representatives Hall the general arrangement made the decorations correspond with the room, which is a semi-circular colonade of eleven Corinthian columns, supporting a half dome, the straight side being toward the west, at the centre of which was the Speaker's chair, which had been removed for the occasion. At the apex of the dome was a rising sun, radiant to the circumference. On the floor a dais was erected, ascended by three steps. On the dais a hexagon canopy, supported on columns twelve feet high, the shaft covered with black velvet; the capitals wrought in white velvet, with silver bands, filled the canopy, tent-shaped, rising seven feet in the centre, covered with heavy black broadcloth in radiating slack folds, surmounted at the apex and at each angle with black plumes having white centres. A draped eagle was perched on the middle of each crown-mould. The cornice was of Egyptian pattern, corresponding with the capitals covered with black velvet; the bands and mouldings were of silver; the lining of the canopy was white crape in radiating folds over blue, thickly set with stars of silver, and terminating at the cornice inside in a band of black velvet with silver fillets. Between the columns was a rich valance in folds, with heavy silver fringe, from under which depended velvet curtains extending from each column two-thirds of the distance from the capitals to the centre of the cornice, looped with silver bands—the whole so disposed as to exhibit both columns and capitals, inside and out. The effect of the canopy and its supports and the drapery was very imposing, the whole being unique and elegant, combining lightness with massiveness in harmony. Twelve brilliant jets of gas burning in ground glass globes springing from the columns, lighted the interior and reflected from the folds of double lining an opuline atmosphere to the whole.

The catafalque was covered with black velvet, trimmed with silver and satin, and adorned with thirty-six burnished silver stars, twelve at the head and twelve on each side. The floor of the dais was covered with evergreens and white flowers. The steps of the dais were covered with broadcloth drapery, banded with silver lace. The columns of the room were hung with black crape, and the capitals festooned and entwined with the same, so as to display the architecture to good advantage, without detriment to the effect. The cornice was appropriately draped, and, in large antique letters on a black ground, were the words of President Lincoln at Independence Hall, Philadelphia, Feb. 22, 1861:—"Sooner than surrender these principles, I would be assassinated on the spot." In front of the gallery were black panels nine feet by two and a half, having silver bands and centres of crossed olive branches; above the gallery looped curtains of black crape extended around the semi-circle; below the gallery white crape curtains overhung with black crape festoons. Each column was ornamented with a beautiful wreath of evergreens and white flowers, the gift of Mrs. Gehlman, of Springfield. On the top of the gallery, extending the entire length, was a festoon of evergreens. The Corinthian cornice was festooned on the west at each side, twenty-four feet forward of the centre, supported by pilasters of the same order, the space between being surmounted by an obtuse arch reaching within one foot of the apex, and projecting six inches, leaving, after the removal of the speaker's chair, a depression resembling a panel, thirty three feet wide by thirty-seven feet high. At the extreme height, in the upper portion of this was placed a blue semi-circular field, sixteen feet across, studded with thirty-six stars six inches in diameter, and from which radiated the thirteen stripes on the American flag in delicate crape, two feet wide at the circumference of the blue field, increasing to the extreme lower angle, breaking on the dais below and the pilasters on either side; the whole crowned with blue and black crape, and so disposed as to correspond with the blue field, the stars, and radiated panels of the ceiling; the central red stripe fell opposite the opening in the curtains at the head of the catafalque. On the cornice, each side of the flag work, were placed two mottoes, corresponding with that on the semi-circular freese, forming together these words: "*Washington the Father and Lincoln the Saviour.*" A life-sized portrait of Washington, the frame draped in blue crape, stood at the head of the dais. In the northwest and southwest corners living evergreen trees and flowers were arranged. The interior decorations were perfected under the direction of the Chairman of the committee, Mr. G. F. Wright, formerly from Hartford, Conn.

The catafalque was designed by Col. Schwarts. The exterior decorations and those of all other public buildings, were entirely under the superintendence of E. E. Myers, architect at Springfield.

Immediately after the body had been placed upon the catafalque, the waiting people were admitted to the State House. They were obliged to ascend a winding staircase into the Representatives' Hall, and return by the same route; and the passage was often obstructed, but the people were sad and patient, and rarely did confusion interrupt the stream of mourners, which continued in almost unbroken line from about ten o'clock on the morning of the 3d of May till ten o'clock on the morning of the 4th. It was estimated that at least seventy-five thousand persons visited the remains. All beholders were impressed with awe by the mournfulness of the surroundings, and by the solemn reminders of the grave which met their gaze, and moved through the Hall in silence. They approached at the left hand of the corpse, passed around the head, and out on the opposite side. At midnight a train of cars came in on the Great Western Railroad, and the whole body of passengers filed at once down to the Capitol, and passed through. Trains were continually arriving, bringing thousands more, and at three o'clock on the morning of the 3d, hundreds were walking the streets, unable to find any accommodation, although the citizens generally threw open their houses. A little before midnight the ladies of the Soldiers' Aid Society laid on the coffin a cross of evergreen and white flowers, and unknown persons placed on it three wreaths of the same. Some, as they passed the corpse, exhibited little emotion; but so soon as they were removed from the awe-inspiring scene, and fully realized that they had looked for the last time on earth, on the features of the great and good man, once their familiar neighbor, wept with a touching sorrow.

THE FINAL CEREMONIES.

The Committee of Arrangements decided upon the following order of funeral procession of Abraham Lincoln, late President of the United States, under the immediate direction of Maj. Gen. Joseph Hooker, Marshal-in-Chief, Brigadier General John Cook and Staff, Brevet Brigadier General James Oakes and Staff:

Military.
Funeral escort.

FIRST DIVISION.

Col. C. M. Prevost, 16th Regiment V. R. C., Marshal.
Aids—Lieut. Thomas B. Beach, A. A. A. General, Major Horace Holt, 1st Massachusetts Heavy Artillery, Capt. J. C. Reunison, 15th N. Y. Cavalry, Capt. E. C. Raymond, 124th Ill. Infantry, Capt. Eddy, 95th Ill. Infantry, Lieut. H. N. Schlick, 1st N. Y. Dragoons.
To consist of Cavalry, Artillery and Infantry.

SECOND DIVISION.

Major F. Bridgeman, Pay Department U. S. A., Marshal.
Aids—Major R. W. McClaughry, Major W. W. White.

Officers and Enlisted men of the Army and Navy, not otherwise assigned in the order stated; Officers in Uniform and Side Arms.

Major General John A. McClernand, Grand Marshal.

Aids—Lieut. Col. A. Schwartz, Capt. Henry Jayne, Capt. R. Rudolph, Capt. Benj. Ferguson, Thomas Owen, Hon. Charles Keys, J. L. Million, Wm. M. Springer, E. E. Myers, A. N. J. Crook, Ed. N. Merritt, and N. Higgins.

THIRD DIVISION.

Col. Dudley Wickersham, 1st Army Corps, Marshal.

Aids—Joshua Rogers, Isaac A. Hawley, W. F. Kimber, J. B. Perkins and Charles Canfield.

Marshals of Sections.—Col. William S. Barnum, Capt. A. J. Allen, Col. S. N. Hitt, C. L. Conkling, Robert P. Officer, Capt. T. G. Barnes, D. W. Smith.

Officiating Clergymen.

Surgeons and Physicians of the Deceased.

Guard of Honor.

Pall Bearers. HEARSE. Pall Bearers.

Horse of the late President, led by two grooms.

Mourners.

Family of the Deceased.

FOURTH DIVISION.

Col. Speed Butler, Marshal.

Aids—Major Robert Allen, Captain L. Rosette, and Captain Albert Williams.

Marshals of Sections—William E. Bennett, Hany W. Ives, Philip C. Latham, William V. Roll, K. H. Richardson, J. E. Williams, and J. D. Crabb.

Civil authorities of the United States according to their relative dignities.

Foreign Ministers.

Civil authorities of the States and Territories, and of the District of Columbia, in the order stated, and according to their dignity in said order.

FIFTH DIVISION.

Hon. George Huntington, Marshal.

Aids—Dr. S. Babcock, George Shepherd, Charles Ridgley, George Latham, Moses B. Condell.

Municipal authorities of the city of Springfield and other cities.

SIXTH DIVISION.

Hon. William H. Herndon, Marshal.

Aids—P. P. Enos, C. S. Zane, T. W. Dresser, M. D., John T. Jones, William G. Cochran, James Raybourne, Charles Vincent, Edward Beach, John Peters, C. W. Rearden, R. C. Huskey.

Marshals of Sections—Thomas Lyon, B. T. Hill, George Birge, Henry Yeakel, Jacob Halfen, —— Sweet, Dewitt C. Hartwell, Hamilton Hovey, Frederick B. Smith.

Members of the Christian, Sanitary, and other kindred Commissions.

Delegations from Bodies Politic, Universities and Colleges.

Clergy.

Members of the Legal Profession.

Members of the Medical Profession.

Representatives of the Press.

SEVENTH DIVISION.

Hon. Harmon G. Reynolds, Marshal.

Aids—George R. Teasdale, John A. Hughes, James Smith, P. Fitzpatrick, Henry Shuck, Thomas O'Conner.

Marshals of Sections.—Captain Charles Fisher, Frank W. Tracy, M. Connor, Frederick Smith, M. Armstrong, Richard Young.

Free Masons.

Odd Fellows and other Fraternities.

Firemen.

EIGHTH DIVISION.

Hon. John W. Smith, Marshal.

Aids—Capt. Isaac Keye, S. H. Jones, Hon. John W. Priest, O. H. Abel, Henry N. Alden, Wm. P. Crafton, G. A. Kimber, John W. Poorman, Henry Ridgely, J. H. Crow, John W. Davis, Presco Wright, N. V. Hunt, Geo. Dalby, Alfred A. North, John S. Bradford, Samuel P. Townsend.

Citizens at large.

Colored Persons.

On the 4th of May the crowds which filled the streets of Springfield were greatly augmented by each train which arrived on the several railways. According to the advertised arrangements, heavy guns were fired, solemn dirges were played, and bells were tolled. All places of business were closed. The weather was propitious. At eight o'clock a vast assemblage of people had collected about the State House grounds, and, while the funeral preparations were being completed, a choir of 250 singers, grouped on the Capitol steps, sang, with great sweetness and impressiveness, a hymn called "Peace, peace, troubled soul." The singers were under the direction of Mr. Messner, of Springfield, assisted by Mr. Palmer, of St. Louis. While the eight sergeants were carrying the coffin out on their shoulders, they sang, after a prelude by the band, Pleyl's beautiful hymn:

> "Children of the Heavenly King,
> As ye journey sweetly sing;
> Sing our Saviour's worthy praise,
> Glorious in His works and ways."

The military were drawn up on Washington street, north of the Capitol, and when the coffin was placed in the hearse they marched east along the street, allowing it to come in the rear. The procession was then formed in the order which had been announced. The pall-bearers were: Hon. Jesse K. Dubois, Hon. S. T. Logan, Hon. G. P. Kœrner, James L. Lamb, Esq., Hon. S. H. Treat, Col. John Williams, Erastus Wright, Esq., Hon. J. N. Brown, Jacob Bunn, Esq., C. W. Matheny, Esq., Elijah Iles, Esq., Hon. J. T. Stuart.

At half-past eleven the cortege began to move, a band playing at the moment of its departure "Lincoln's Funeral March." On the route to the cemetery the bands played the "Dead March in Saul," with solemn and mournful effect. The route led by the former house of Mr. Lincoln, on the corner of Eighth and Jefferson streets, and from thence west to Fourth, and thence on Fourth to Oak Ridge Cemetery, which is a mile and a half north of the city, near the line of the Chicago and St. Louis Railroad. But a small portion of the people who had assembled to witness the ceremonies took position in the procession, but hastened by shorter routes through its line to the cemetery, which very appropriately takes its name from two high ridges, running east and west, covered principally with large oak trees. Between these is a valley about seventy-five feet in depth, winding with pleasing irregularity, and watered by a little brook of clear water. The gate of the cemetery is at the head of this valley, and for several rods it descends quite rapidly, though near the tomb it is nearly level. The tomb stands on the south side in a little cove in the bank, where it is quite steep, so that the roof of it is but a few feet in length. It is built of Joliet limestone, the architecture of the main arch being rustic. The upper range of the arch projecting a few inches from the main wall, is of rubbed stone, and rests on Doric pilasters. The whole is about twelve feet high, and ten wide. The brick walls inside were covered with evergreen; and in the centre stood a foundation bearing a marble slab, on which the coffin was deposited. The remains of "Little Willie" were deposited in the same tomb.

The scene was most solemn, and, beyond the power of language to express, impressive, when in the presence of nearly all the citizens of the city which had so long been the home of Mr. Lincoln, and of a vast throng assembled from all the States of the Northwest, the imposing procession entered the cemetery under an evergreen arch, and filed toward the tomb to the music of dirges performed by many powerful bands.

Performing for the last time the melancholy service for which they had been detailed at Washington, the Veteran Reserve Guard stood round the hearse—and in the immediate presence of the Guard of Honor, the President's sons, Robert and Thaddeus Lincoln, and other relatives, and the family friends—bore the coffin into the tomb. The religious exercises were then opened with prayer by the Rev. A. Hale, after which the following dirge, the words by L. M. Dawn, the music by Geo. F. Root, was sung by the choir, assisted by the band:

All our land is draped in mourning,
Hearts are bowed and strong men weep;
For our loved, our noble leader,
Sleeps his last, his dreamless sleep—
Gone forever, fallen by a traitor's hand,
Though preserved his dearest treasure,
Our redeem'd, beloved land.
Rest in peace.

Thro' our night of bloody struggle,
Ever dauntless, firm and true,
Bravely, gently forth he led us,
Till the morn burst on our view—
Till he saw the day of triumph,
Saw the field our heroes won,
Then his honored life was ended,
Then his glorious work was done.
Rest in peace.

When from mountain, hill and valley,
To their homes our brave boys come,
When with welcome notes we greet them,
Song and cheer and pealing drum,
When we miss our loved ones fallen,
When to weep we turn aside,
Then for him our tears shall mingle—
He has suffered, he has died.
Rest in peace.

Honored leader, long and fondly
Shall thy memory cherished be,
Hearts shall bless thee for their freedom,
Hearts unborn shall sigh for thee.
He who gave thee might and wisdom
Gave thy spirit sweet repose,
Farewell, father, friend and guardian,
Rest forever, rest in peace.
Rest in peace.

Rev. N. W. Miner then read selections from the first chapter of John, and extracts from the writings of Paul. This was followed by the choral "To Thee, O Lord," St. Paul, as follows:

To Thee, O Lord, I yield my spirit,
Who break'st in love this mortal chain;
My life I but from thee inherit,
And death becomes my chiefest gain;
In Thee I live, in Thee I die,
Content, for Thou art ever nigh.

After this, Rev. N. C. Hubbard read the last inaugural of Mr. Lincoln, which was followed by a dirge. The music is from Otto, and familiar; the words were composed by the artist, Mr. G. F. Wright:

AS WHEN THY CROSS WAS BLEEDING.

As when Thy cross was bleeding,
The earth is draped in gloom!
Our brows are bound in ashes,
Our hearts are in the tomb!

O, God, our sovereign Savior!
Thy saving grace reveal;
O, stay Thy people's anguish,
And let Thy mercy heal!

Bishop Simpson then arose to deliver his address. In an instant every ear was strained to catch the accents of a man who had been deemed worthy to fill so great an honor.

BISHOP SIMPSON'S ORATION.

Fellow-citizens of Illinois, and of many parts of our entire Union:

Near the capital of this large and growing State, in the midst of this beautiful grove, and at the mouth of this vault which has just received the remains of our fallen chieftain, we gather to pay a tribute of respect and to drop the tear of sorrow around the ashes of the mighty dead.

A little more than four years ago, from his plain and quiet home in yonder city, he started, receiving the parting words of the concourse of friends who gathered around him, and in the midst of the dropping of the gentle shower, he told of the pangs of parting from the place where his children had been born and his home had been made pleasant by early recollections; and as he left, he made an earnest request in the hearing of some who are present at this hour, that as he was about to enter upon responsibilities which he believed to be greater than any which had fallen upon any man since the days of Washington, the people would offer up prayers that God would aid and sustain him in the work which they had given him to do.

His company left your quiet city, but as it went snares were in waiting for the Chief Magistrate. Scarcely did he escape the dangers of the way or the hands of the assassin, as he neared Washington; and I believe he escaped only through the vigilance of officers and the prayers of his people. So that the blow was suspended for more than four years, which was at last permitted through the providence of God to fall. How different the occasion which witnessed his departure from that which witnessed his return! Doubtless he expected to visit you all again; doubtless you expected to take him by the hand, and to feel the warm grasp which you had felt in other days, and to see the tall form walking among you, which you had delighted to honor in years past. But he was never permitted to return until he came with lips mute and silent, the frame encoffined, and a weeping nation following as his mourners. Such a scene as his return to you was never witnessed among the events of history. There have been great processions of mourners. There was one for the Patriarch Jacob, which came up from Egypt, and the Egyptians wondered at the evidences of reverence and filial affection which came up from the hearts of the Israelites.

There was mourning when Moses fell upon the heights of Pisgah, and was hid from human view. There have been mourning in the kingdoms of the earth, when kings and princes have fallen, but never was there in the history of man such mourning as that which has accompanied this funeral procession, and has gathered around the mortal remains of him who was our loved one, and who now sleepeth among us.

If we glance at the procession which followed him, we see how the nation stood aghast, tears filled the eyes of many sun-burnt faces—strong men, as they clasped the hands of their friends, were unable to find vent for their grief in words. Women and little children caught up the tidings as they ran through the land, and were melted into tears. The nation stood still. Men left their plows in the field and asked what the end should be. The hum of manufactories ceased, and the sound of the hammer was not heard—busy merchants closed their doors, and in the exchange gold passed no more from hand to hand. Though three weeks have passed, the nation has scarcely breathed easily yet. A mournful silence is abroad upon the land. Nor is this mourning confined to any one class or to any district of country. Men of all political parties and of all religious creeds have united in paying this mournful tribute. The Archbishop of the Roman Catholic Church in New York and a Protestant minister walked side by side in the sad procession, and a Jewish Rabbi performed a part of the solemn services. Here are gathered around his tomb the representatives of the Army and

Navy, Senators, Judges, Governors, and officers of all the branches of the Government.

But the great cause of this mourning is to be found in the man himself. Mr. Lincoln was no ordinary man. And I believe the conviction has been growing on the nation's mind, as it certainly has been on mine, especially in the last years of his administration, that by the hand of God he was especially singled out to guide our Government in these troubled times; and it seems to me that the hand of God may be traced in many of the events connected with his history.

Here, too, are members of civic processions, with men and women, from the humblest as well as the highest occupations. Here and there, too, are tears as sincere and warm as any that drop, which come from the eyes of those whose kindred and whose race have been freed from their chains by him whom they mourn as their deliverer.

Far more eyes have gazed upon the face of the departed than ever looked upon the face of any other departed man. More eyes have looked upon the procession for sixteen hundred miles or more, by night and by day, by sunlight, dawn, twilight and by torchlight, than ever before watched the progress of a procession.

We ask, why this wonderful mourning—this great procession? I answer, first: A part of the interest has arisen from the times in which we live and in which he that has fallen was a principal actor. It is a principle of our nature that feelings once excited pass readily from the object by which they are excited to some other object which may for the time being take possession of the mind. Another principle is, that the deepest affections of our hearts gather around some human form, in which are incarnated the living thoughts and ideas of the passing age. If we look, then, at the times we see an age of excitement.

For four years the popular heart has been stirred to its utmost depths. War had come upon us, dividing families, separating nearest and dearest friends. A war, the extent and magnitude of which no one could estimate; a war in which the blood of brethren was shed by a brother's hands. A call was made by this voice, now hushed, and all over this land, from hill and mountain, from plain and prairie, there sprang up hundreds of thousands of bold hearts, ready to go forth and save our National Union. This feeling of excitement was transferred next into a feeling of deep grief, because of the danger in which our country was placed. Many said, is it possible to save the nation? Some in our own country, and nearly all the leading men in other countries, declared it to be impossible to maintain the Union, and many an honest and patriotic heart was deeply pained with apprehensions of common ruin; and many in grief and almost in despair anxiously inquired, what shall the end of these things be? In addition to this, wives had given their husbands, mothers their sons—the pride and joy of their hearts. They saw them put on the uniform. They saw them take the martial step, and they tried to hide their deep feeling of sadness. Many of these dear ones sleep upon the battle-field never to return again, and there was mourning in every mansion and every cabin in our broad land. Then came a feeling of deeper sadness as the story came of prisoners tortured to death, or starved through the mandates of those who are called the representatives of the chivalry, or who claim to be the honorable ones of the earth, and as we read the stories of frames attenuated and reduced to mere skeletons, our grief turned partly into horror, and partly into a cry for vengeance.

Then this feeling was changed to one of joy. There came signs of the end of this rebellion. We followed the career of our glorious Generals; we saw our armies, under the command of the brave officer who is guiding this procession, climb up the heights of Lookout Mountain and drive the rebels from their strongholds. Another brave General swept through Georgia, South and North Carolina, and drove the combine armies of the rebels before him, while the honored Lieutenant General held Lee and his hosts in a death grasp. Then the tidings came that Richmond was evacuated and that Lee had surrendered. The bells rang merrily all over the land; booming of cannon was heard; illuminations and torch-light processions manifested the general joy, and families were looking for the speedy return of their loved ones from the fields of battle. Just in the midst of this wildest joy, in one hour, nay, in one moment, the tidings thrilled through our land that Abraham Lincoln, the best of Presidents, had perished by the hand of an assassin! and then all that feeling which had been gathering for four years in forms of grief, horror and joy, turned in an instant into one wail of woe—a sadness inexpressible, an anguish unutterable.

But it is not the times merely which cause this mourning. The mode of his death must be taken into account. Had he died on a bed of illness, with kind friends around him; had the sweat of death been wiped from his brow by gentle hands while he was yet conscious; could he have lived to speak words of affection to his stricken widow, or words of counsel to us, like those we heard in his parting address—that inaugural which shall now be immortal—how it would have softened or assuaged something of the grief. There might at least have been preparation for the event. But no moment of warning was given to him or to us. He was stricken down, too, when his hopes for the end of the rebellion were bright, and the prospects of a joyous life were before him. There was a Cabinet meeting that day, said to have been the most cheerful and happy of any held since the beginning of the rebellion.

After this meeting he talked with his wife—spoke of the four years of tempest—of the storm being over, and of the four years of pleasure and joy now awaiting him, as the weight of care and anguish would be taken from his mind, and he could have happy days with his family again. In the midst of these anticipations he left his home never to return alive. The evening was Good Friday—the saddest day in the whole calendar for the Christian church—henceforth in this country to be made sadder, if possible, by the memory of our nation's loss. And so filled with grief was every Christian heart that even all the joyous thoughts of Easter Sunday failed to remove the crushing sorrow under which the true worshippers bowed in the house of God.

But the great cause of this mourning is to be found in the man himself. Mr. Lincoln was no ordinary man; and I believe the conviction has been growing on the nation's mind, as it certainly has been on my own, especially in the last years of his administration. By the hand of God he was especially singled out to guide our Government in these troublous times, and it seems to me that the hand of God may be traced in many of the events connected with his history.

First, then, I recognize this in his physical education, which he received, and which prepared him for enduring herculean labors. In the toils of his boyhood and the labors of his manhood, God was giving him an iron frame. Next to this was his identification with the heart of the great people, understanding their feelings because he was one of them, and connected with them in their movements and life. His education was simple. A few months spent in the school house gave him the elements of education. He read but few books, but mastered all. He read Bunyon's Pilgrim's Progress, Æsop's Fables, and the life of Washington, which were his favorites. In these we recognize the works which gave the bias to his character, and which partly moulded his style.

His early life, with its varied struggles, joined him indissolubly to the working masses, and no elevation in society diminished his respect for the sons of toil. He knew what it was to fell the tall trees of the forest, and to stem the current of the broad Mississippi. His home was in the growing West—the heart of the Republic—and invigorated by the winds that swept over its prairies, he learned lessons of self-reliance that sustained him in scenes of adversity.

His genius was soon recognized, as true genius always will be, and he was placed in the Legislature of his State. Already acquainted with the principles of law, he devoted his thoughts to matters of public interest, and began to be looked upon as the "coming statesman." As early as 1839 he presented resolutions in the Legislature, asking for emancipation in the District of Columbia, while, with but rare exceptions, the whole popular mind of his State was opposed to the measure. From that hour he was a steady and uniform friend of humanity, and was preparing for the conflict of later years.

If you ask me on what mental characteristics his greatness rested, I answer, on a quick and ready perception of facts—on a memory unusually tenacious and retentive, and on a logical turn of mind which followed sternly and unwaveringly every link in the chain of thought on any subject which he was called upon to investigate. I think there have been minds more broad in their character, more comprehensive in their sweep; but I doubt whether there has been a mind which could follow step by step with logical power the points which he desired to illustrate. He gained this power by the close study of geometry, and by a determination to perceive the truth in all its relations and simplicity, and when perceived to utter it. It is said of him, that in childhood when he had any difficulty in listening to a conversation to ascertain what people meant, he retired to rest, he could not sleep till he tried to understand the precise point intended, and when understood, to convey it in a clearer manner to others. Who that has read his messages fails to perceive the directness and the simplicity of his style; and this very trait, which was scoffed at and derided by opponents, is now recognized as one of the strong points of that mighty mind, which has so powerfully influenced the destiny of this nation, and which shall, for ages to come, influence the destiny of humanity.

It was not, however, chiefly by his mental faculties that he gained such control over mankind. His moral power gave him pre-eminence. The convictions of men that Abraham Lincoln was an honest man, led them to yield to his guidance. As has been said of Cobden, whom he greatly resembled, he made all men feel a kind of sense of himself—a recognized individuality, a self-relying power. They saw in him a man whom they believed would do what was right, regardless of all consequences. It was this moral feeling which gave him the greatest hold upon the people, and made his utterances almost oracular.

When the nation was angered by the perfidy of foreign nations in allowing privateers to be fitted out, he uttered the significant expression, "one war at a time," and it stilled the national heart. When his own friends were divided as to what steps should be taken as to slavery, that simple utterance, "I will save the Union if I can with slavery, but if not, slavery must perish, for the Union must be saved,"—that became the rallying word. Men felt the struggle was for the Union, and all other questions must be subsidiary.

But after all, by the acts of a man shall his fame be perpetuated. Where are his acts? Much praise is due to the men who aided him. He called able counsellors around him, and able generals into the field, men who have borne the sword as bravely as ever any human arm has borne it. He had the aid of prayerful and thoughtful men everywhere, but under his own guiding hands the movements of our land have been conducted.

Turn towards the different departments. We had an unorganized militia, a mere skeleton army, yet under his care that army has been enlarged into a force, which for skill, intelligence, efficiency and bravery, surpasses any which the world had ever seen. Before its veterans the fame of even the renowned veterans of Napoleon shall pale; and the mothers and sisters on these hillsides, and all over the land, shall take to their arms again braver men than ever fought in European wars.

The reason is obvious. Money or a desire for fame collected those armies—or they were rallied to sustain favorite thrones or dynasties. But the armies he called into being fought for liberty, for the Union, and for the right of self-government; and many of them feel that the battles they won were for humanity everywhere, and for all time—for I believe that God has not suffered this terrible rebellion to come upon our land merely for a chastisement to us or a lesson to our age.

There are moments which involve in themselves eternities. There are instants which seem to contain germs which shall develop and bloom forever. Such a moment came in the tide of time to our land when a question must be settled, affecting all the powers of the earth. The contest was for human freedom. Not for this republic merely. Not for the Union simply, but to decide whether the people, as a people, in their entire majesty, were destined to be the government, or whether they were to be subject to tyrants or aristocrats, or to class-rule of any kind.

This is the great question for which we have been fighting, and its decision is at hand, and the result of this contest will affect the ages to come. If successful, republics will spread in spite of monarchs all over this earth. [Exclamations of Amen! Thank God!] I turn from the army to the navy. What was it before the war commenced? Now we have our ships of war at home and abroad, to guard privateers in foreign sympathizing ports, and to care for every port of our own coast. They have taken ports that military men said could not be taken, and a brave admiral for the first time in the world's history, lashed himself to the mast, there to remain as long as he had a particle of skill or strength to watch over his ship while it engaged in the perilous contest of taking the strong forts of the enemy.

Then again I turn to the Treasury Department. Where should the money come from? Wise men predicted ruin, but our national credit has been maintained, and our currency is safer to-day than it ever was before. Not only so, but through our national bonds, if properly used, we shall have a permanent basis for currency, and an investment so desirable for capitalists of other nations, that under the law of trade, I believe the center of exchange will be transferred from England to the United States.

But the great act of the Mighty Chieftain, on which his power shall rest long after his frame shall moulder away, is that of giving freedom to a race. We have all been taught to revere the sacred characters. We have thought of Moses, of his power, and the prominence he gave to the moral law, how it lasts and how his name towers high among the names in Heaven, and how he delivered those millions of his kindred out of bondage. And yet we may assert that Abraham Lincoln, by his proclamation, liberated more enslaved people than ever Moses set free—and those not of his kindred. God has seldom given such a power or such an opportunity to man. When other events shall have been forgotten; when this world shall have become a network of republics; when every throne shall be swept from the face of the earth; when literature shall enlighten all minds; when the claims of humanity shall be recognized everywhere, this act shall still be conspicuous on the pages of history. And we are thankful that God gave to Abraham Lincoln the decision and wisdom and grace to issue that proclamation, which stands high above all other papers which have been penned by uninspired men.

Abraham Lincoln was a good man. He was known as an honest, temperate, forgiving man; a just man, a man of noble heart in every way. As to his religious experience I cannot speak definitely, because I was not privileged to know much of his private sentiments. My acquaintance with him did not give me the opportunity to hear him speak on those topics. This I know, however: he read the Bible frequently—loved it for its great truths and profound teachings, and he tried to be guided by its precepts. He believed in Christ the Saviour of sinners, and, I think, he was sincerely trying to bring his life into harmony with the great principles of revealed religion.

Certainly if there ever was a man who illustrated some of the principles of pure religion, that man was our departed President. Look over all his speeches, listen to his utterances; he never spoke unkindly of any man. Even the rebels received no words of anger from him, and the last days of his life illustrated, in a remarkable manner, his forgiving disposition. A dispatch was received that afternoon that Thompson and Tucker were trying to escape through Maine, and it was proposed to arrest them. Mr. Lincoln, however, preferred to let them quietly escape. He was seeking to save the very men who had been plotting his destruction, and this morning we read a proclamation offering $25,000 for the arrest of these men, as aiders and abettors of his assassination. So that in his expiring acts he was saying, Father forgive them, they know not what they do. As a ruler, I doubt if any President has ever showed such trust in God, or in public documents so frequently referred to Divine aid. Often did he remark to friends and delegations that his hope for our success rested in his conviction that God would bless our efforts, because we were trying to do right. To the address of a large religious body, he replied, "Thanks be unto God, who in our national trials, giveth us the Churches." To a minister who said "he hoped the Lord was on our side," he replied, "that it gave him no concern whether the Lord was on our side or not," for he added, "I know the Lord is always on the side of right," and with deep feeling added, "But God is my witness that it is my constant anxiety and prayer that both myself and this nation should be on the Lord's side."

In his domestic life he was exceedingly kind and affectionate. He was a devoted husband and father. During his Presidential term he lost his second son, Willie. To an officer of the army he said, not long since, "Do you ever find yourself talking with the dead?" and added: "Since Willie's death I catch myself every day involuntarily talking with him, as if he were with me." For his widow, who is unable to be here, I need only invoke the blessing of Almighty God that she be comforted and sustained. For his son, who has witnessed the exercises of this hour, all that I can desire is that the mantle of his father may fall upon him. [Exclamations of "Amen."]

Let us pause a moment on the lesson of the hour before we part. This man, though felled by an assassin, still fell underthe permissive hand of God. He had some wise purpose in allowing him to fall. What more could he have desired of life for himself? Were not his honors full? There was no office to which he could aspire; the popular heart clung around him as around no other man. The nations of the world had learned to honor our Chief Magistrate. If rumors of a desired alliance with England be true, Napoleon trembled when he heard of the fall of Richmond, and asked what nation would join him to protect him against our government. This had the guidance of such a man. His fame was full—his work was done—and he sealed his glory by being the nation's just martyr for liberty.

He had a strange presentiment, in early political life, that some day he would be President. You see it indicated in 1859, when of the slave power he said: "Broken by it, I, too, may be; bow to it, I never will. The *probability* that we may fail in the struggle *ought not* to deter us from the support of a cause which I deem to be just; it *shall not* deter me. If ever I feel the soul within me elevate and expand to those dimensions not wholly unworthy of its Almighty Architect, it is when I contemplate the cause of my country, deserted by all the world besides, and I standing up boldly and alone, and hurling defiance at her victorious oppressors. Here, without contemplating consequences, before high Heaven, and in the face of the world, I swear eternal fidelity to the just cause, as I deem it, of the land of my life, my liberty, and my love."

And yet he recently said to more than one, "I never shall live out the four years of my term. When the rebellion is crushed my work is done." So it was. He lived to see the last battle fought and to dictate a dispatch from the home of Jefferson Davis—lived till the power of the rebellion was broken, and then, having done the work for which God sent him, angels, I trust, were sent to shield him from one moment of pain or suffering, and to bear him from this world to that high and glorious realm were the patriot and good shall live forever. His example teaches young men that every position of eminence is open before the diligent and worthy. To the active men of the country his example urges to trust in God and do right.

To the ambitious there is this fearful lesson: Of the four candidates for Presidential honors in 1860, two of them—Douglas and Lincoln, once competitors, but now sleeping patriots—rest from their labors; Bell perished in poverty and misery, as a traitor might perish; and Breckinridge is a frighted fugitive, with the brand of traitor on his brow.

Standing, as we do to-day, by his coffin and his sepulcher, let us resolve to carry forward the work which he so nobly begun. Let us do right to all men. Let us vow in the sight of Heaven to eradicate every vestige of human slavery, to give every human being his true position before God and man, to crush every form of rebellion, and to stand by the flag which God has given us. How joyful, that it floated over parts of every State before Mr. Lincoln's career was ended! How singular, that to the fact of the assassin's heel being caught in the folds of the flag we are probably indebted for his capture! The flag and the traitor must ever be enemies.

Traitors will probably suffer by the change of rulers, for one of sterner mould, and one who himself has deeply suffered from the rebellion now wields the sword of justice.

Our country, too, is stronger for the trial. A republic was declared, by monarchists, too weak to endure a civil war; yet we have crushed the most gigantic rebellion in history, and have grown in strength and population every year of the struggle. We have passed through the ordeal of a popular election while swords and bayonets were in the field, and have come out unharmed. And now in our hour of excitement, with a large minority, having proffered another man for President, the bullet of the assassin has laid our President prostrate. Has there been a mutiny? Has any rival proposed his claim? Out of our army of near a million, no officer or soldier uttered one note of dissent, and in an hour or two after Mr. Lincoln's death, another, by constitutional power, occupied his chair. If the government moved forward, without one single jar, the world will learn that republics are the strongest governments on earth.

And now, my friends, in the words of the departed, "with malice towards none," free from all feeling of personal vengeance, yet believing the sword must not be borne in vain, let us go forward in our painful duty. Let every man who was a Senator and Representative in Congress, and who aided in beginning this rebellion, and thus led to the slaughter of our sons and daughters, be brought to speedy and to certain punishment. Let every officer, educated at public expense, and who, having been advanced to position has perjured himself, and has turned his sword against the vitals of his country, be doomed to a felon's death. This, I believe, is the will of the American people. Men may attempt to compromise and to restore these traitors and murderers to society again, but the American people will rise in their majesty and sweep all such compromises and compromisers away, and shall declare that there shall be no peace to rebels.

But to the deluded masses we shall extend arms of forgiveness. We will take them to our hearts. We will walk with them side by side, as we go forward to work out a glorious destiny. The time will come when in the beautiful words of him whose lips are now forever sealed, "the mystic cords of memory which stretch from every battle-field and from every patriot's grave, shall yield a sweeter music when touched by the angels of our better nature."

At the conclusion of this oration, which had been heard with devout attention and marked approval by the large and most remarkable audience, the choir chanted another dirge, composed for the occasion, by Mr. Wright, and set to the music of Storch:

OVER THE VALLEY THE ANGELS SMIL

Over the valley the angels smile,
Glory awaits him, they welcome so kindly;
Finished his labor, tho' ne'er so blindly,
Perfidy vaunts the deed of his guile.

Over the valley the angels smile,
Tho' we must grieve thee,
Our God will receive thee,
Blessing thy labor,
Our friend and our neighbor;
Crowning thee bright as the babe of the Nile.

The closing prayer was offered up by Dr. Harkey. Next in continuation was the requiem, "Peace, troubled soul," the benediction, by Dr. P. D. Gurley, the President's former pastor, and last of all, a funeral hymn, composed by Dr. Gurley, for the occasion, and the doxology:

Rest, noble martyr! rest in peace;
  Rest with the true and brave,
Who, like thee, fell in Freedom's cause,
  The Nation's life to save.

Thy name shall live while time endures,
  And men shall say of thee,
"He saved his country from its foes,
  And bade the slave be free."

These deeds shall be thy monument,
  Better than brass or stone;
They leave thy fame in glory's light,
  Unrival'd and alone.

This consecrated spot shall be
  To Freedom ever dear;
And Freedom's sons of every race
  Shall weep and worship here.

O God! before whom we, in tears,
  Our fallen Chief deplore,
Grant that the cause, for which he died,
  May live forevermore.

DOXOLOGY.

To Father, Son, and Holy Ghost,
  The God whom we adore,
Be glory as it was, is now,
  And shall be evermore.

With this the exercises ended, the doors of the tomb were closed, and slowly and thoughtfully the vast assemblage wended their way homeward from off the hill-sides and out of the valley where they had collected, and the dead was left alone.

During the hours in which the funeral ceremonies were conducted, by order of the President, all public buildings at Washington were closed. The Courts also adjourned, and all the municipal offices were closed. Citizens closed their stores, and half-hour guns were fired all the latter part of the day, closing with a national salute at sunset.

At all the Capitals of the loyal States and in many of

the cities of the Union, official business was also suspended, and minute guns and salutes were fired.

The correspondent of the *Cincinnati Commercial* very appropriately concluded his report of the ceremonies of the day with the following touching words:

"There in that little grass-grown valley, away from the busy haunts of men, where the timid hare shall gambol, the birds build their nests unscared, and the purling brook shall sing an eternal requiem—there let Abraham Lincoln rest. What more fitting place would himself have chosen wherein to sleep his dreamless sleep? Is that common impulse of those whom the world calls not great a mere superstition, which prompts them to bury their loved ones in the quiet places of the earth? It * * *

"There let him sleep in that lowly valley by the brook. Not the garish light of cities nor the noise of trade is fitting dweller in presence of his tomb; let the oaks of the forest and the ever-returning flowers be watchers by his grave. And there through the future years the grateful freedman shall come to pay the offering of his broken shackles, and there the humble and the toiling poor shall perform his rites of homage undisturbed, and shall hear the kindly voice of Nature saying to him

'So shalt thou rest. And what if thou shalt fall
Unnoticed by the living, and no friend
Take note of thy departure? All that breathe
Will share thy destiny; the gay will laugh
When thou art gone, the solemn brood of care
Plod on, and each one as before will chase
His favorite phantom. Yet all these shall leave
Their mirth and their employments, and shall come
And make their bed with thee.'

"Thus has the nation buried Abraham Lincoln with a burial more illustrious than that of kings. When was it ever permitted to crowned rulers to receive such lavish tributes of their people's love, as were paid to this citizen? For 1,500 miles through mourning States has his sacred dust been borne in more than a triumphal chariot, visited by a million of citizens, who wept as they beheld him And, yet not many months, are gone by since a time when many even of his fellow-citizens would have destroyed his life, and many more, who do him reverence to-day; would have spurned his person and teachings with contempt,

'For humanity sweeps onward; where to-day the martyr stands,
On the morrow crouches Judas with the silver in his hands—
Far in front the cross stands ready, and the crackling fagots burn—
And the hooting mob of yesterday in silent awe return
To glean up the scattered ashes nto history's golden urn.'"

THURSDAY, MAY 4th, 1865.

Memorable day—Thursday, May Fourth, Eighteen Hundred and Sixty-Five: at his home, where the major part of an active life, singularly pure, had been spent, Abraham Lincoln was buried; Abraham Lincoln, the assassinated President, without a personal enemy—remarkably kind-hearted—of genial disposition, but brave and solemn-minded—forbearing, because far-seeing—uneducated in the management of public affairs, but successful because patient and honest, possessing native tact and practical shrewdness.

Alone in history stand the journey of Abraham Lincoln, President elect, from Springfield to Washington, 1861; and that of Abraham Lincoln, President assassinated, from Washington to Springfield, 1865.

What events crowd each other for review in those intervening four years! How the incidents of the two journeys—their objects and their associations—contrast!

Twenty days after the terrible night on which the assassin's bullet destroyed the most precious life in the American nation, the body which that great and good life animated, is deposited in the humble cemetery where lie the remains of neighbors, relatives, and personal friends in private life; and friends, neighbors, and relatives in public life, join the surviving of private life in ceremonies which are the saddest that may ever be performed on the American soil.

What do those twenty days suggest! twenty days of National mourning; twenty days with flags at half-mast; twenty days with emblems of sorrow on the peoples' dwellings, with sable drapery and solemn mottoes on all public buildings; twenty days of such tokens of love, such tributes of respect as never before were paid to mortal man?

Do not those twenty days suggest something more solemn, more searching than tribute to personal worth, or acknowledgment of public service, however dear that worth—however valuable that service?

Those twenty days embody and will develop clear purpose—earnest determination—purpose and determination born in sorrow—vowed in affliction, before which oppression may tremble, and by which justice shall rule.

Wherever cannon announced to day that Abraham Lincoln's grave was open at Springfield — wherever church bells tolled in harmony with the historic services at that grave—in thousands of homes—in places of business, heads were bowed and hearts were sad as if it were the grave of one by whose death an intimate family circle had been broken. Indeed it is scarcely a figure of speech to say, that by the open grave of Abraham Lincoln stood this day the American people.

What a tribute! How solemn! A nation in habiliments of mourning looking into the open grave of a President—assassinated in the hour of jubilation over a great victory for justice, because he was true to the whole country—because he directed the crushing of an atrocious rebellion which the sum of villainies had instigated.

Oh, People of the United States—Friends of Freedom —Defenders of Right—Protectors of Intelligence—Promoters of Morals and Religion—do not forget that open grave, nor the unparalleled crime which caused it to be dug.

Never did any people possess holier ground on which to register solemn pledges than that which surrounds the grave of the martyr, Abraham Lincoln. Placing him among the men whose lives have been sacrificed that the

Nation might live, may not every true American citizen repeat, and for himself adopt, and, to this memorable day, adapt those pregnant words spoken by Abraham Lincoln in the Soldiers' Cemetery at Gettysburg:

"We cannot consecrate, we cannot hallow this ground. "The brave men, living and dead, who struggled here "have consecrated it far above our power to add or de- "tract.

"The world will little note nor long remember what "we say here; but it can never forget what they did here. "It is for us, the living, rather to be dedicated here to "the finished work that they have thus so far nobly car- "ried on.

"It is rather for us to be here dedicated to the great "task remaining before us, that from these honored dead "we take increased devotion to that cause for which they "here gave the last full measure of devotion; that we "here highly resolve that the dead shall not have died in "vain; that the nation shall under God have a new birth "of freedom, and that governments of the people, by the "people and for the people, shall not perish from the "earth."

LINCOLN MEMORIAL.

THE

JOURNEYS

OF

ABRAHAM LINCOLN:

FROM SPRINGFIELD TO WASHINGTON, 1861,

AS PRESIDENT ELECT;

AND

FROM WASHINGTON TO SPRINGFIELD, 1865,

AS PRESIDENT MARTYRED;

COMPRISING AN ACCOUNT OF PUBLIC CEREMONIES ON THE ENTIRE ROUTE, AND FULL DETAILS OF BOTH JOURNEYS.

BY WILLIAM T. COGGESHALL.

PUBLISHED FOR THE BENEFIT OF THE OHIO SOLDIERS' MONUMENT FUND,

BY THE OHIO STATE JOURNAL, COLUMBUS.

1865.

Mourn for the man of long-enduring blood,
The patriot, statesman, moderate, resolute,
Whole in himself, a common good.
Mourn for the man of amplest influence,
Yet clearest of ambitious crime,
Our greatest, yet with least pretence,
Rich in saving common sense,
And, as the greatest only are,
In his simplicity sublime.
O voice from which good omens all men drew,
O trusting faith to true occasion true,
O fall'n at length that tower of strength.

* * * * * * *

His voice is silent in your council hall
Forever; and whatever tempests lower,
Forever silent; even if they broke
In thunder, silent; yet remember all
He spoke among you, and the man who spoke;
Who never sold the truth to serve the hour,
Whose life was work, whose language rife
With rugged maxims hewn from life;
Who never spoke against a foe.
Such was he: his work is done;
But while the races of mankind endure,
Let his great example stand
Colossal, seen of every land,
Till in all lands and thro' all human story,
The path of duty be the way to glory.

He is gone who seemed so great—
Gone; but nothing can bereave him
Of the force he made his own
Being here; and we believe him
Something far advanced in state,
And that he wears a truer crown
Than any wreath that man can weave him.

Statue to Abraham Lincoln,

AND

Monument to Deceased Ohio Soldiers.

At a meeting held in the City Hall, Columbus, Ohio, on the evening of April 25th, for the purpose of devising means to erect a statue to Abraham Lincoln, Col. James A. Godman was appointed Chairman, and J. J. Janney Secretary.

The following Executive Committee was appointed:

CENTRAL EXECUTIVE COMMITTEE.

Gov. JOHN BROUGH, Chairman.
CHARLES ANDERSON, Lieut.-Governor.
Col. J. H. GODMAN, Auditor of State.
G. VOLNEY DORSEY, Treas. of State.
WM. HENRY SMITH, Sec. of State.
CHAUNCEY N. OLDS, Attorney-General.
B. R. COWEN, Adjutant-General.
MERRILL BARLOW, Q. M. General.

J. J. JANNEY, B. GILMORE,
W. G. DESHLER, JOSEPH SULLIVANT,
S. N. FIELD, GEO. M. PARSONS,
S. M. SMITH, SAMUEL GALLOWAY,
WILLIAM T. COGGESHALL,
Citizens of Columbus.

After remarks by Hon. Samuel Galloway, Gen. George B. Wright, Dr. G. V. Dorsey, W. T. Coggeshall, Esq., Major R. P. L. Baber, and J. E. St. Clair, on motion of L. J. Critchfield, Esq., the Executive Committee was authorized to fill vacancies in its own body, and to appoint County Committees.

On motion of Hon. Samuel Galloway, the Executive Committee was instructed to receive contributions for a fund to be applied to the erection of suitable memorials in Capitol Square to the late lamented President Lincoln, and to the Soldiers of Ohio fallen in defense of the country during the rebellion; and that the manner and kind of memorials to be erected shall be left to the future action of the people as may be expressed by their representatives of the General Committee, and that the said General Committee shall consist of the committee appointed this evening, and an additional member from each Congressional District, to be appointed by the local committees of the counties in the respective districts. JAMES H. GODMAN, *President.*

J. J. JANNEY, *Secretary.*

April 25, 1865.

Statue to Abraham Lincoln,

AND

Monument to Deceased Ohio Soldiers.

At a meeting held in the City Hall, Columbus, Ohio, on the evening of April 25th, for the purpose of devising means to erect a statue to Abraham Lincoln, Col. James A. Godman was appointed Chairman, and J. J. Janney Secretary.

The following Executive Committee was appointed:

CENTRAL EXECUTIVE COMMITTEE.

Gov. JOHN BROUGH, Chairman.
CHARLES ANDERSON, Lieut.-Governor.
Col. J. H. GODMAN, Auditor of State.
G. VOLNEY DORSEY, Treas. of State.
WM. HENRY SMITH, Sec. of State.
CHAUNCEY N. OLDS, Attorney-General.
B. R. COWEN, Adjutant-General
MERRILL BARLOW, Q. M. General.

J. J. JANNEY,
W. G. DESHLER,
S. N. FIELD,
S. M. SMITH,
B. GILMORE,
JOSEPH SULLIVANT,
GEO. M. PARSONS,
SAMUEL GALLOWAY,
WILLIAM T. COGGESHALL,

Citizens of Columbus.

After remarks by Hon. Samuel Galloway, Gen. George B. Wright, Dr. G. V. Dorsey, W. T. Coggeshall, Esq., Major R. P. L. Baber, and J. E. St. Clair, on motion of L. J. Critchfield, Esq., the Executive Committee was authorized to fill vacancies in its own body, and to appoint County Committees.

On motion of Hon. Samuel Galloway, the Executive Committee was instructed to receive contributions for a fund to be applied to the erection of suitable memorials in Capitol Square to the late lamented President Lincoln, and to the Soldiers of Ohio fallen in defense of the country during the rebellion; and that the manner and kind of memorials to be erected shall be left to the future action of the people as may be expressed by their representatives of the General Committee, and that the said General Committee shall consist of the committee appointed this evening, and an additional member from each Congressional District, to be appointed by the local committees of the counties in the respective districts. JAMES H. GODMAN, *President.*

J. J. JANNEY, *Secretary.*

April 25, 1865.

www.ingramcontent.com/pod-product-compliance
Lightning Source LLC
LaVergne TN
LVHW020215110826
845151LV00003B/719

* 9 7 8 1 4 2 5 5 3 3 2 0 5 *